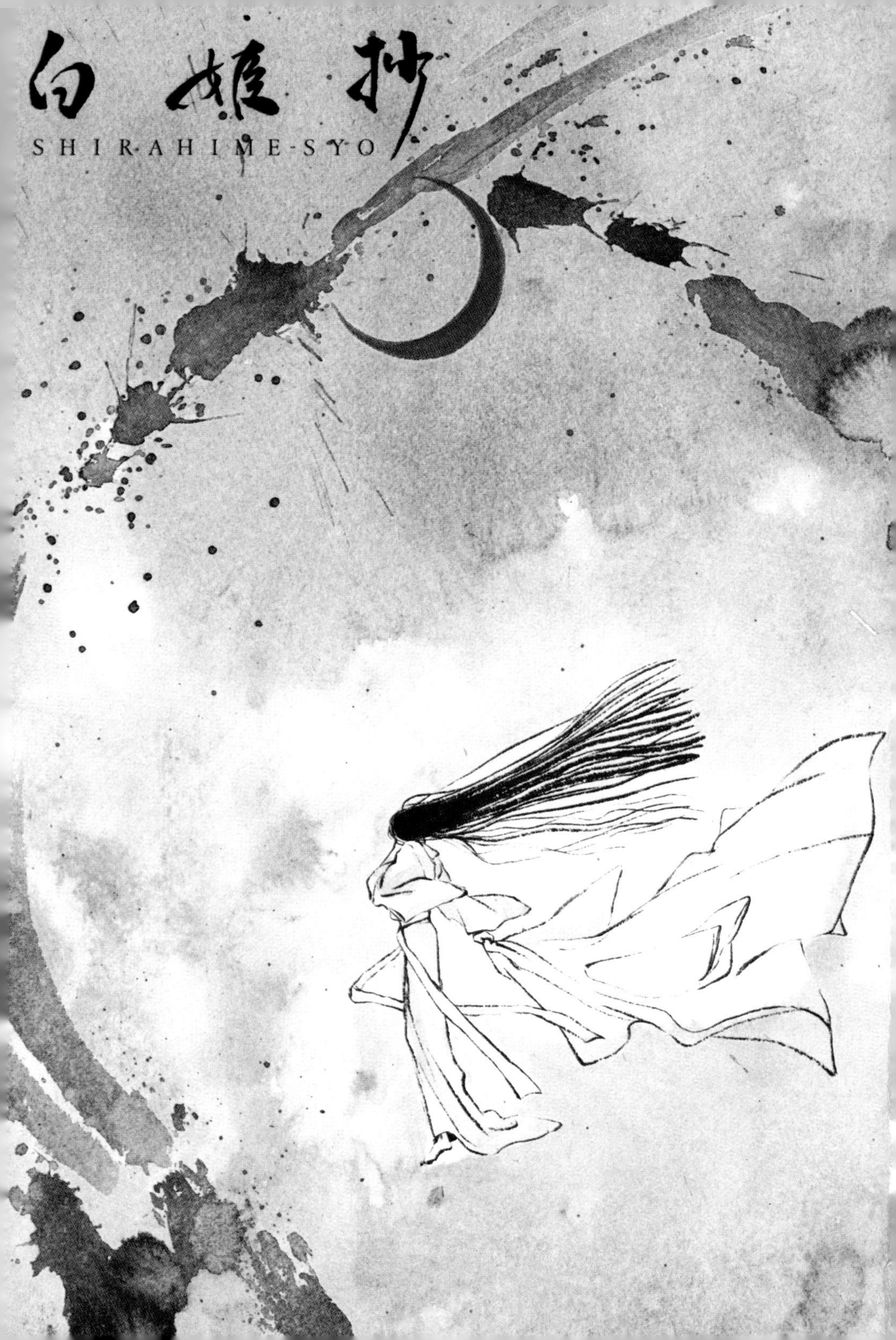
白姫抄
SHIRAHIME-SYO

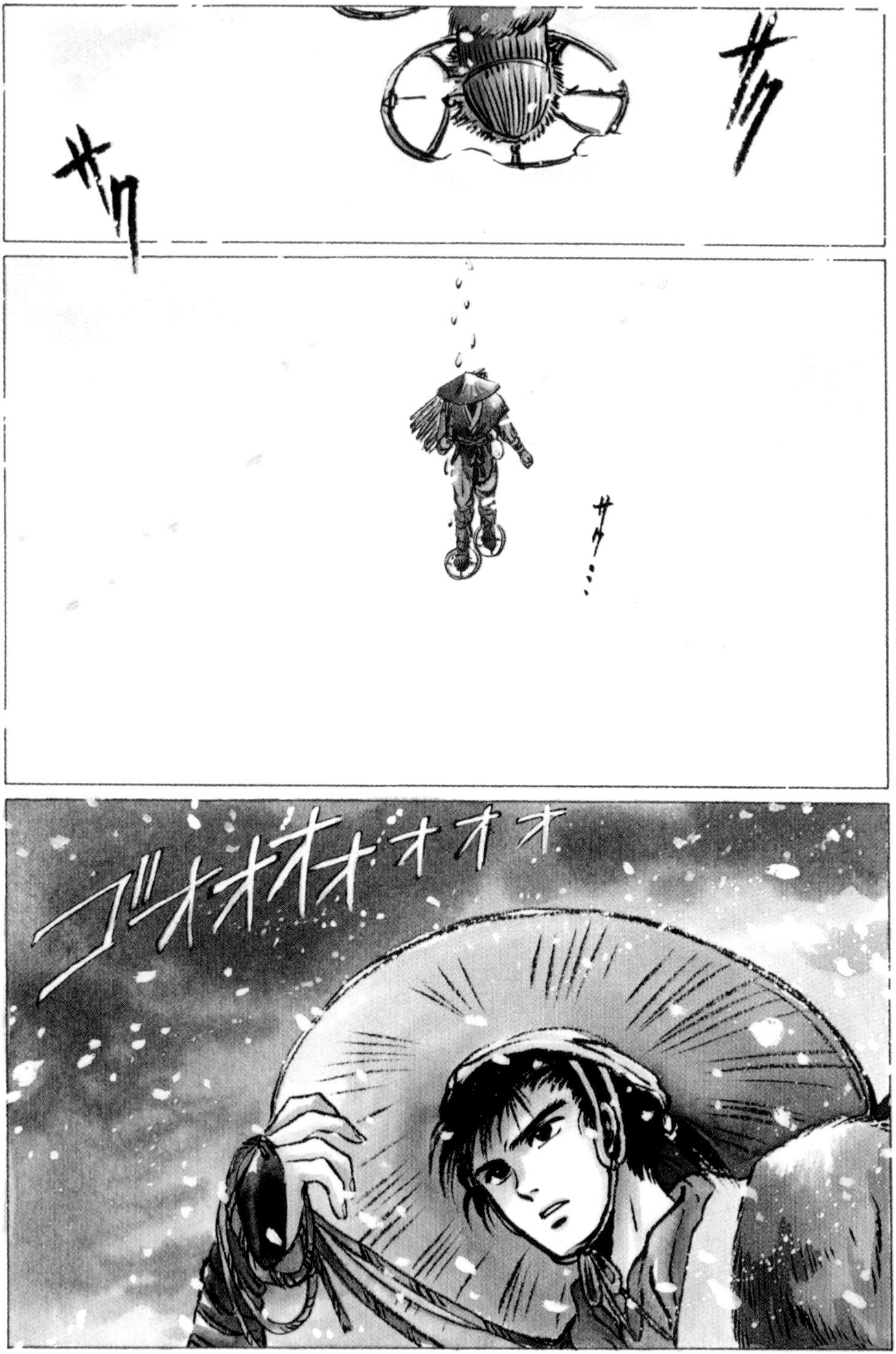
ザク
ザク
ザク…
ゴオオオオオオオオ

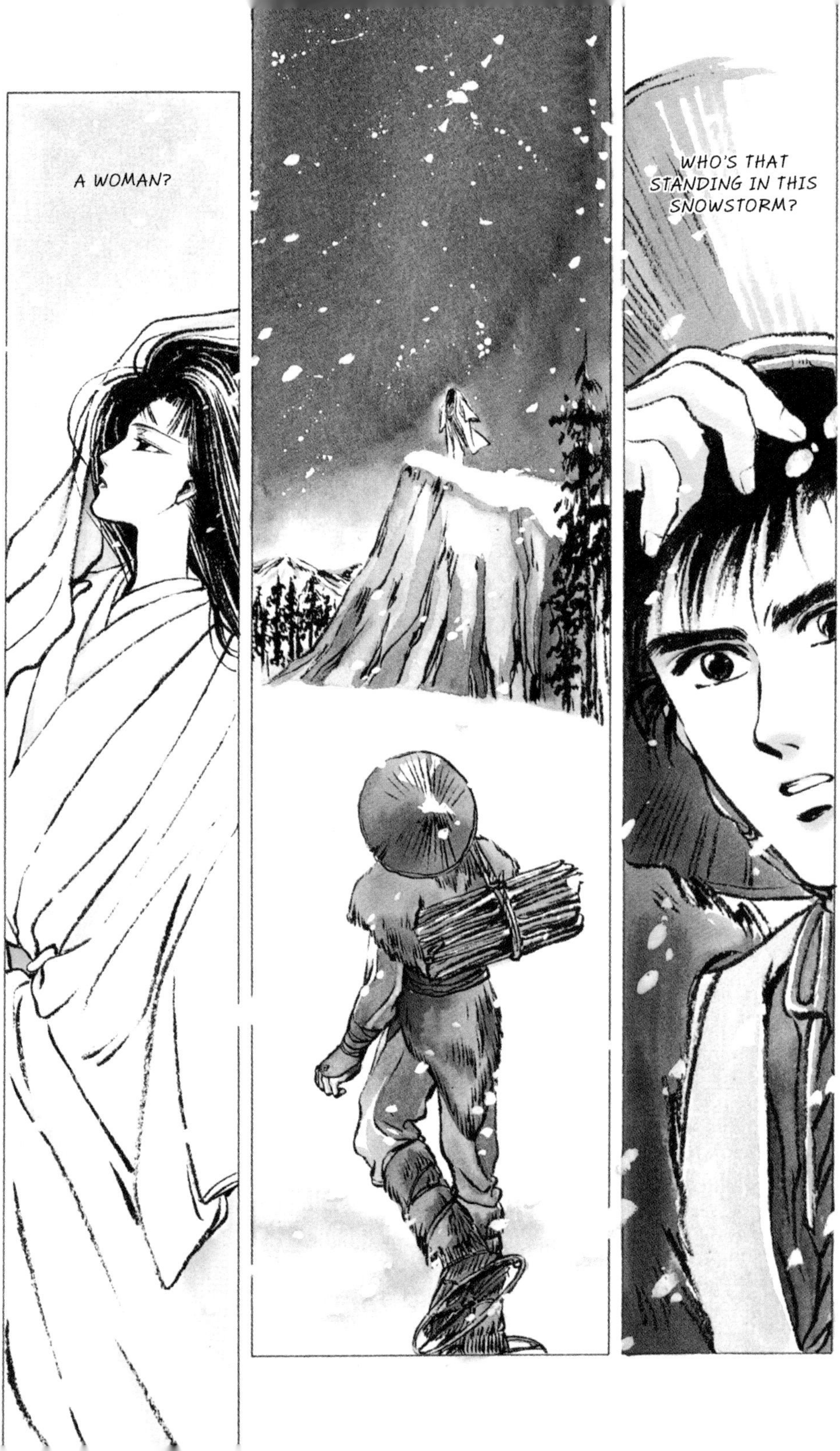
WHO'S THAT STANDING IN THIS SNOWSTORM?
A WOMAN?

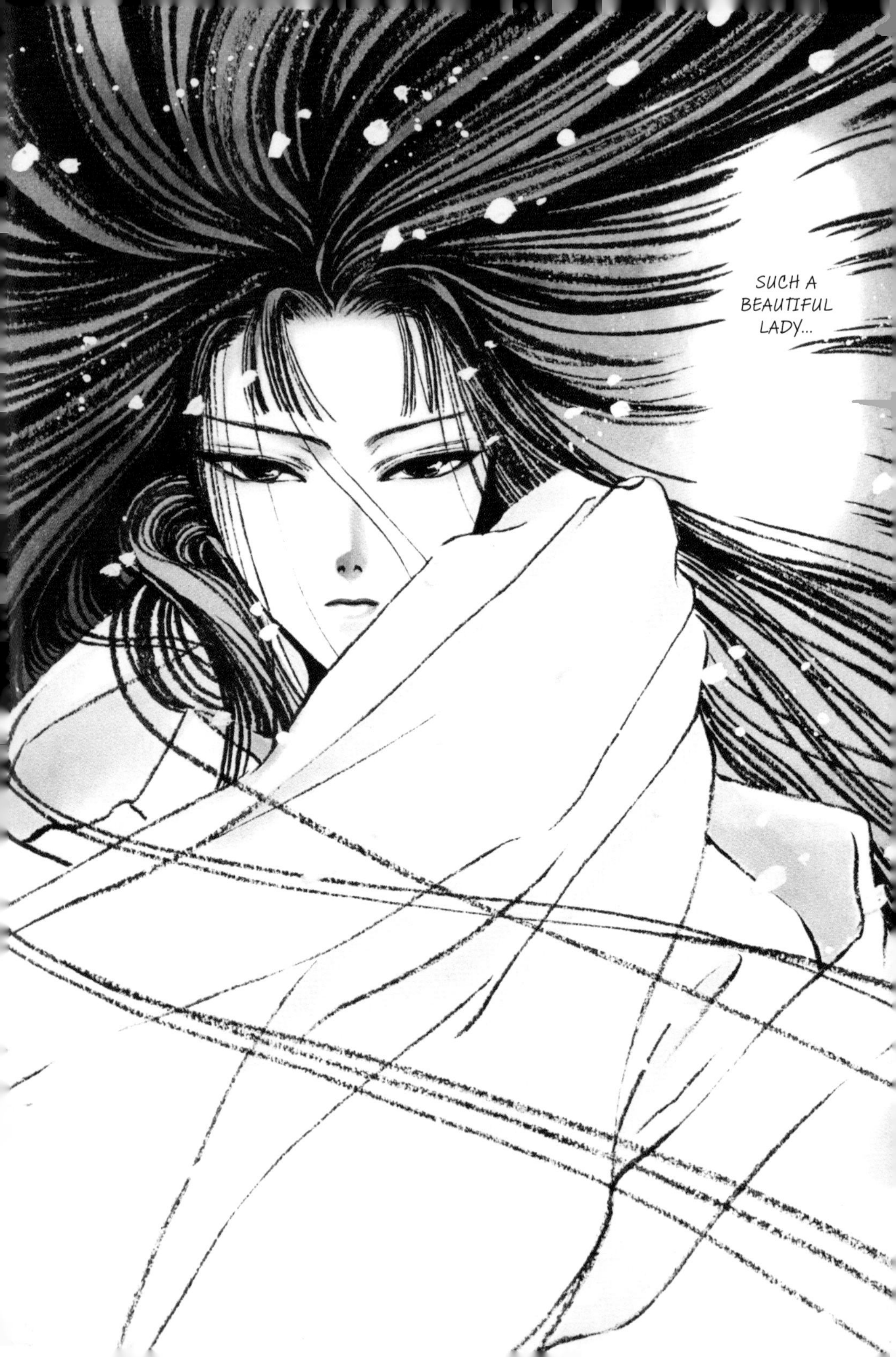
SUCH A BEAUTIFUL LADY...

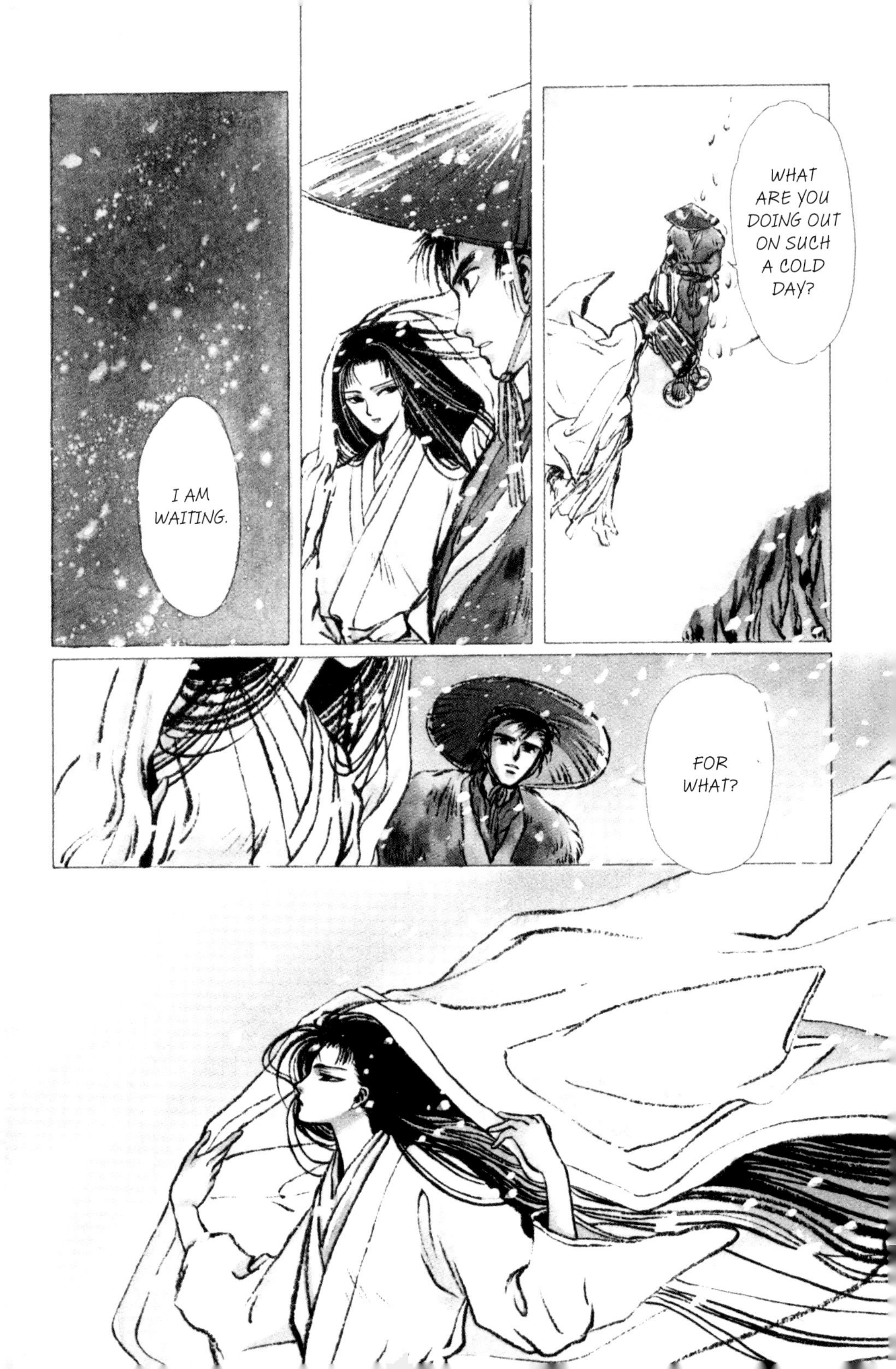
WHAT ARE YOU DOING OUT ON SUCH A COLD DAY?
I AM WAITING.
FOR WHAT?

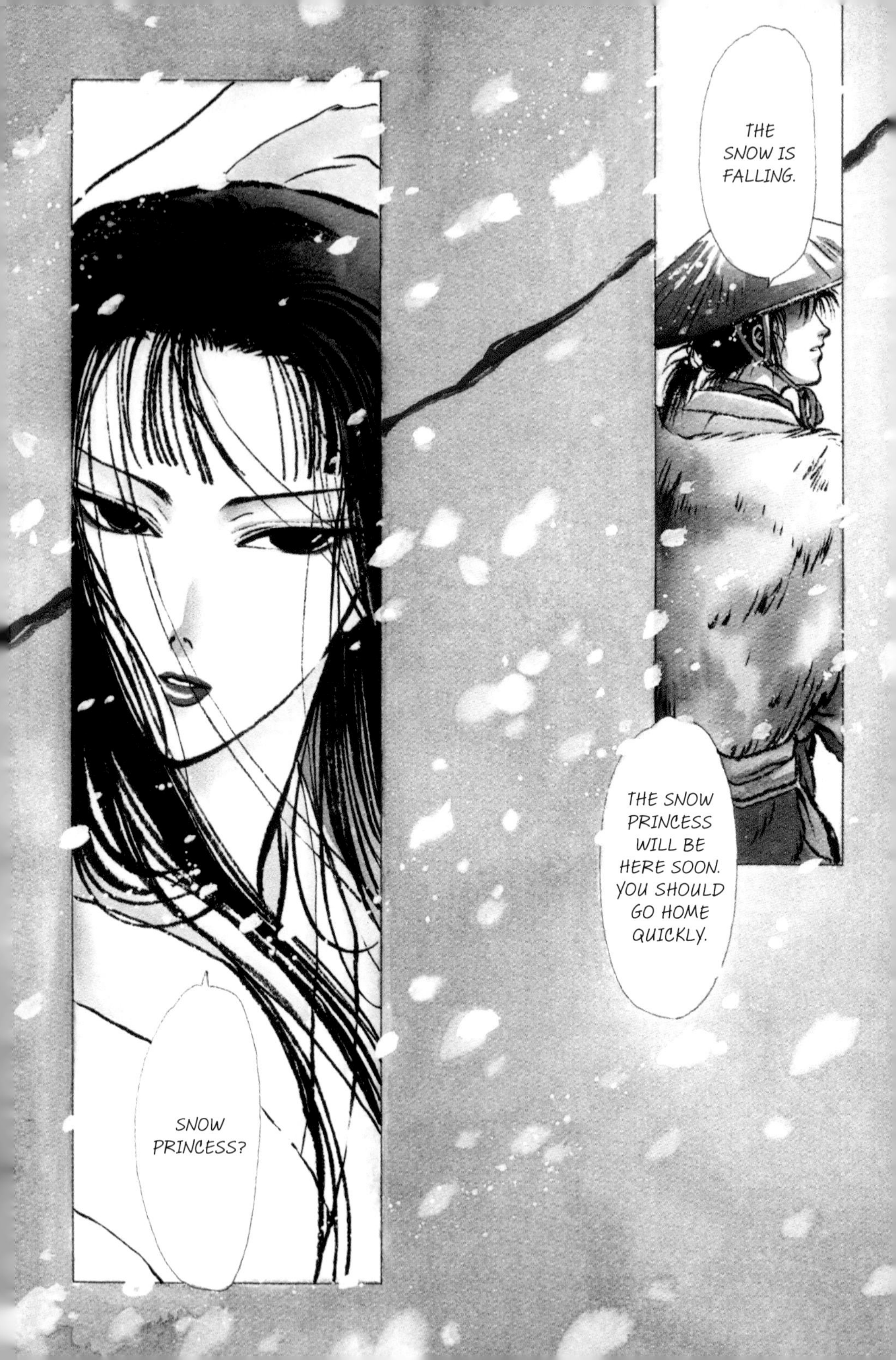
THE SNOW IS FALLING.
THE SNOW PRINCESS WILL BE HERE SOON. YOU SHOULD GO HOME QUICKLY.
SNOW PRINCESS?

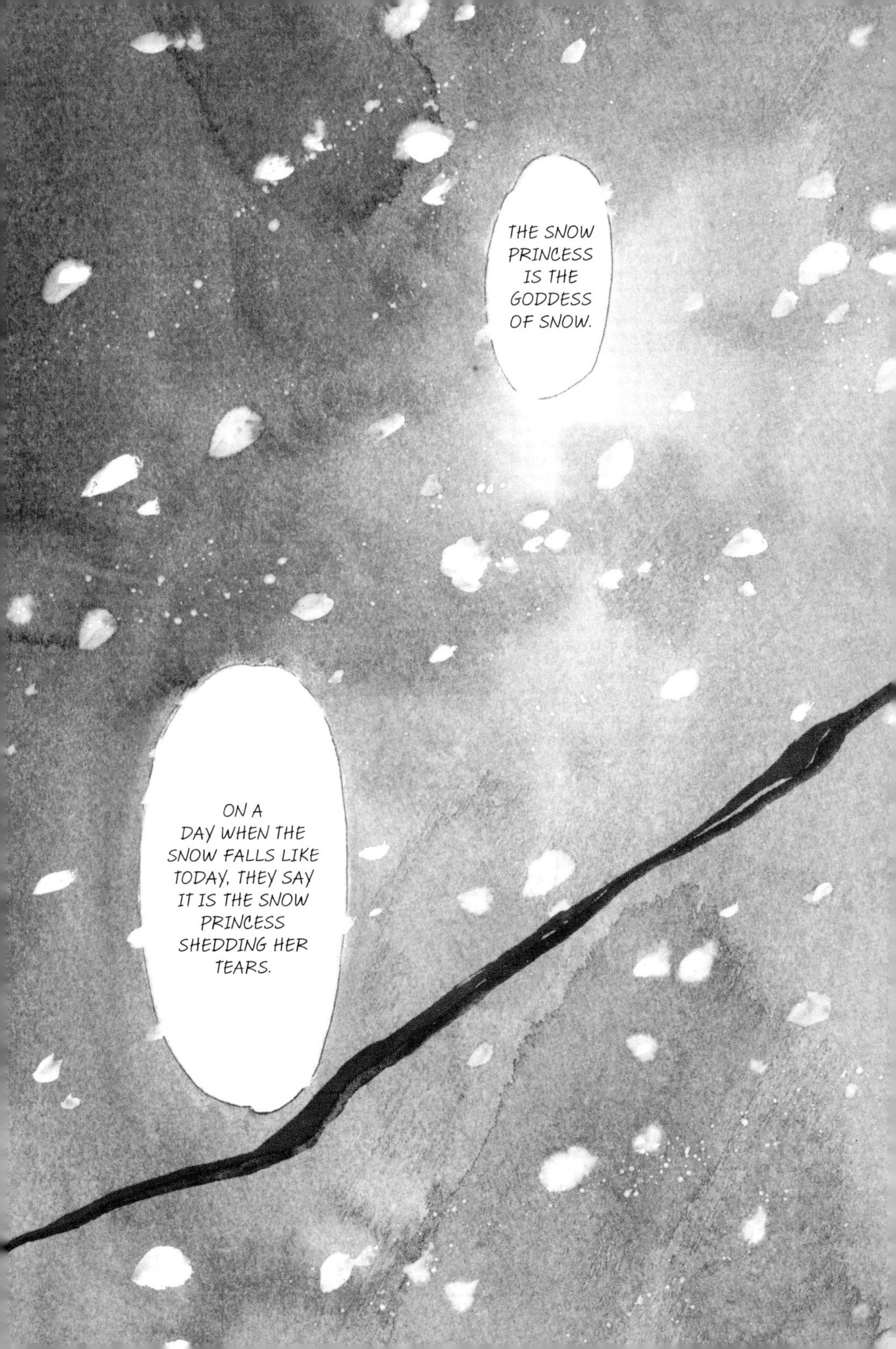
THE SNOW PRINCESS IS THE GODDESS OF SNOW.
ON A DAY WHEN THE SNOW FALLS LIKE TODAY, THEY SAY IT IS THE SNOW PRINCESS SHEDDING HER TEARS.

白姫抄

SHIRAHIME

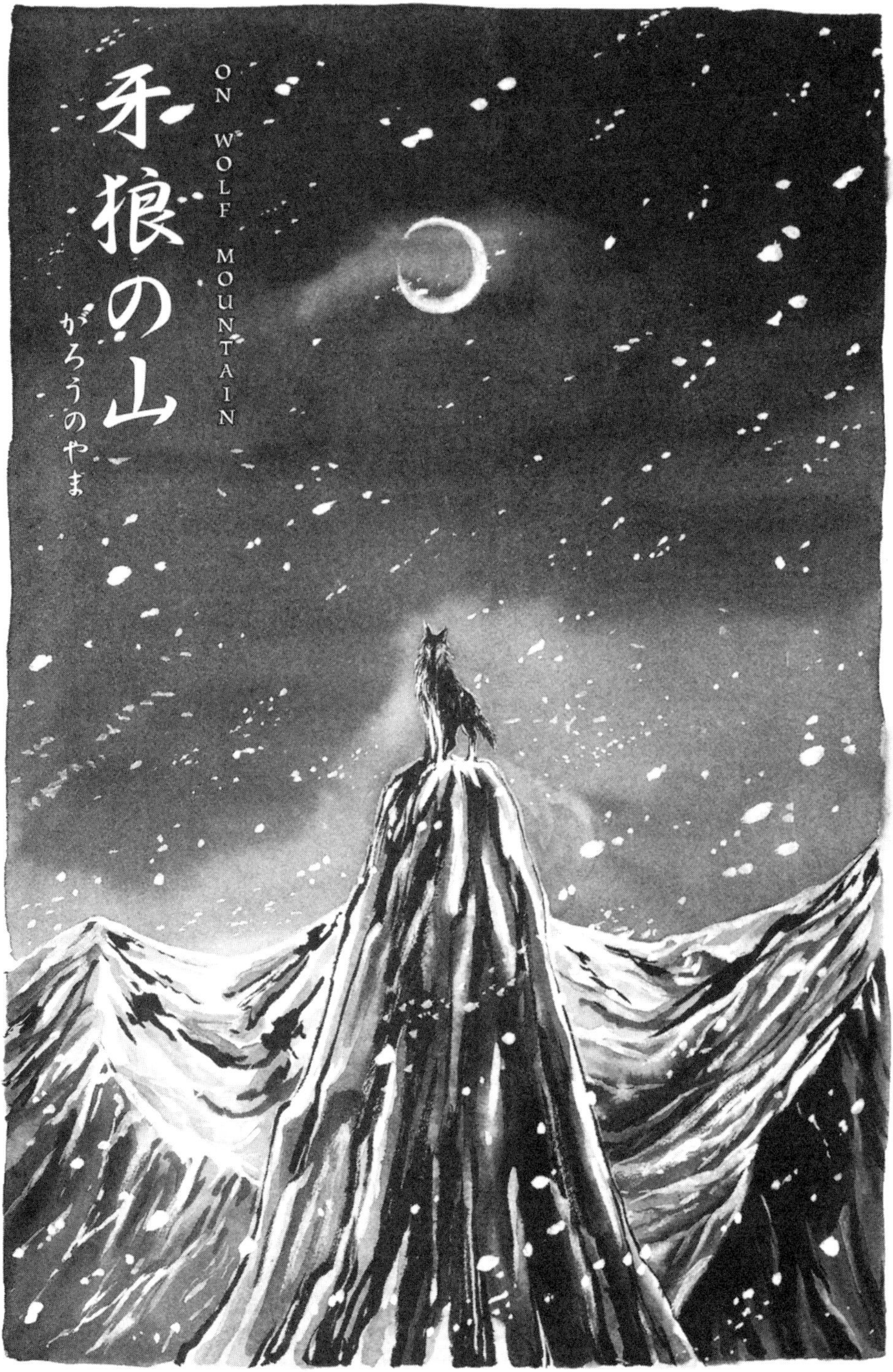
牙狼の山
がろうのやま
ON WOLF MOUNTAIN

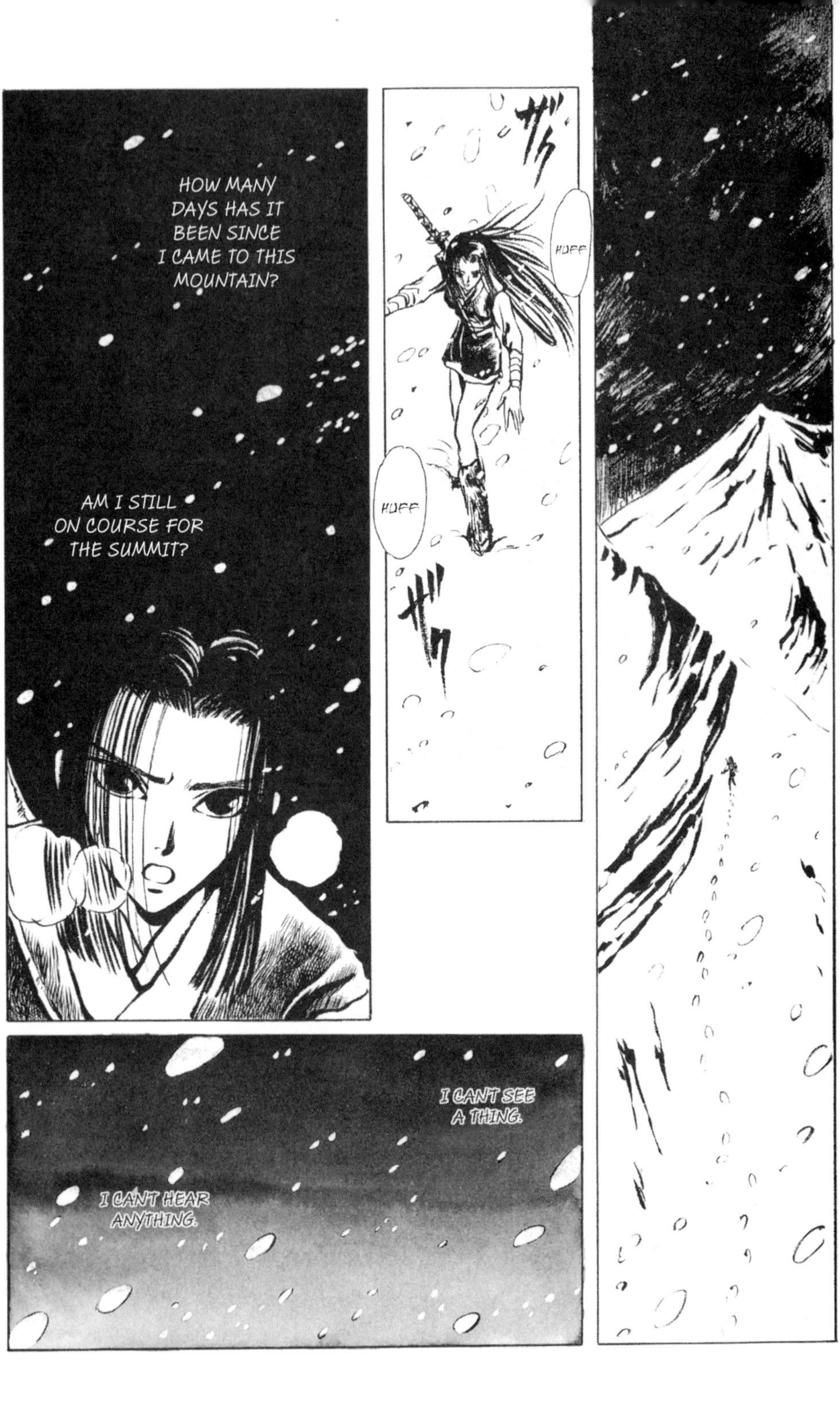
HUFF
HUFF
HOW MANY DAYS HAS IT BEEN SINCE I CAME TO THIS MOUNTAIN?
AM I STILL ON COURSE FOR THE SUMMIT?
I CAN'T SEE A THING.
I CAN'T HEAR ANYTHING.

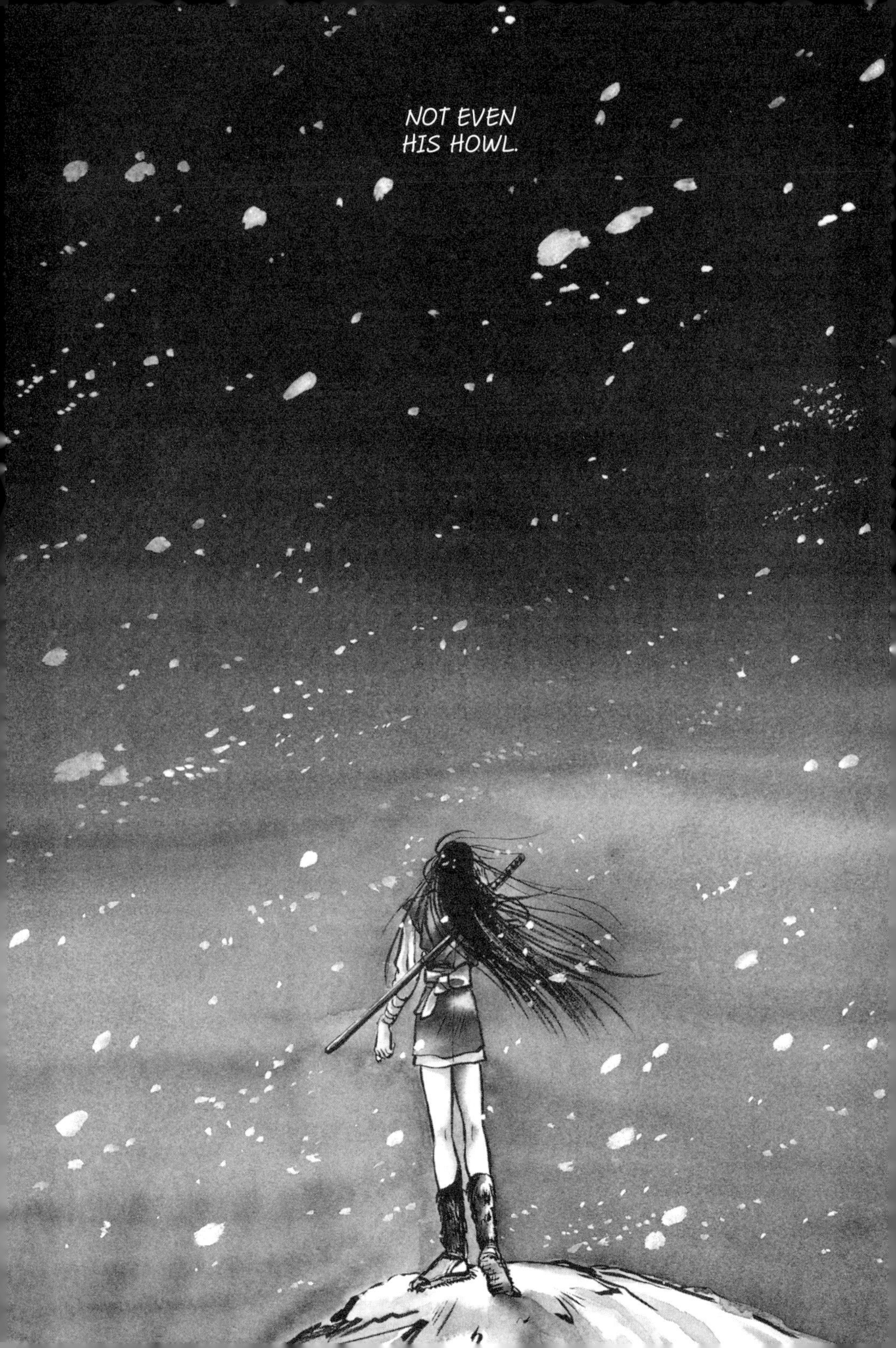
NOT EVEN
HIS HOWL.

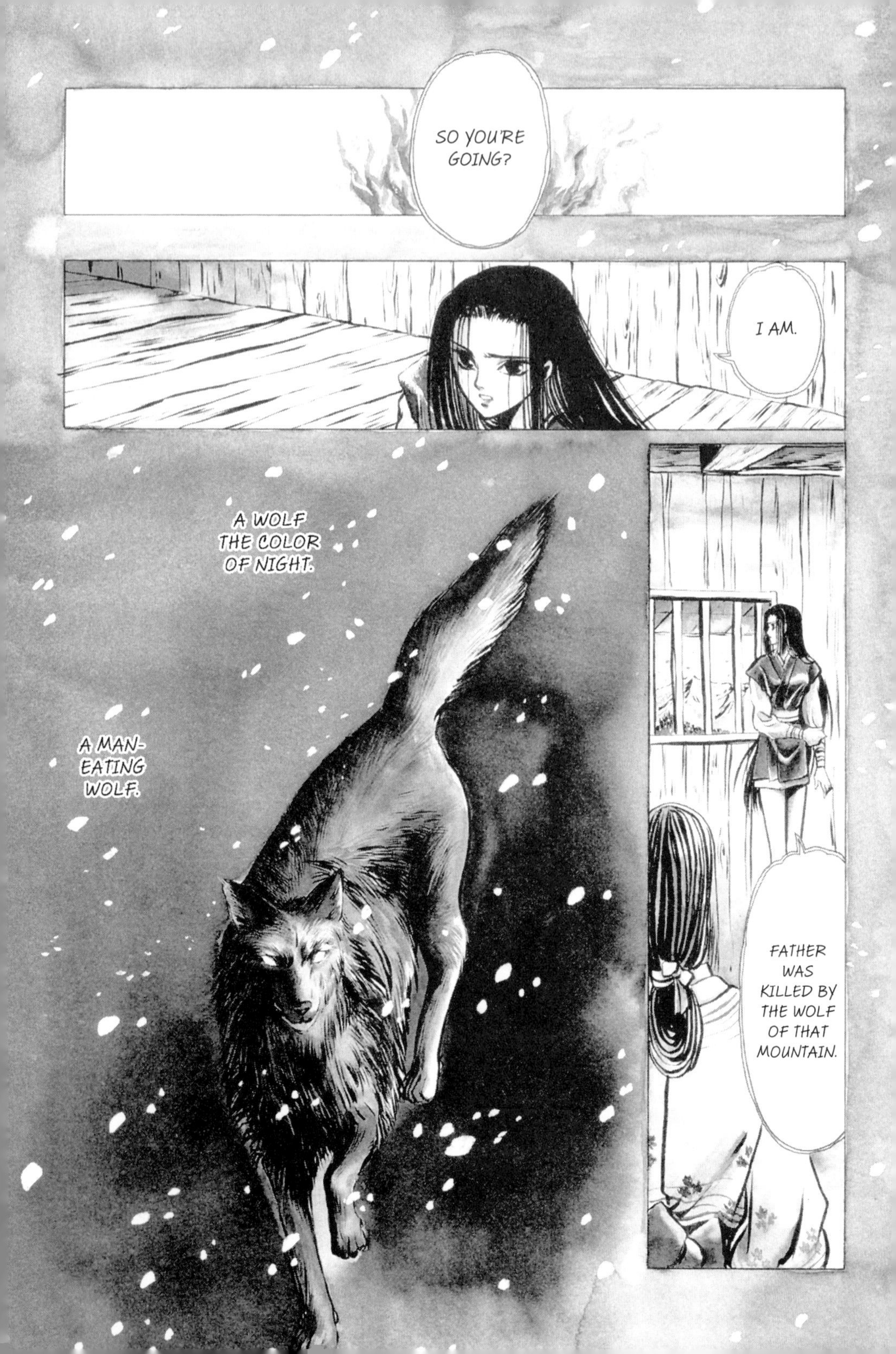
SO YOU'RE GOING?
I AM.
FATHER WAS KILLED BY THE WOLF OF THAT MOUNTAIN.
A WOLF THE COLOR OF NIGHT.
A MAN-EATING WOLF.

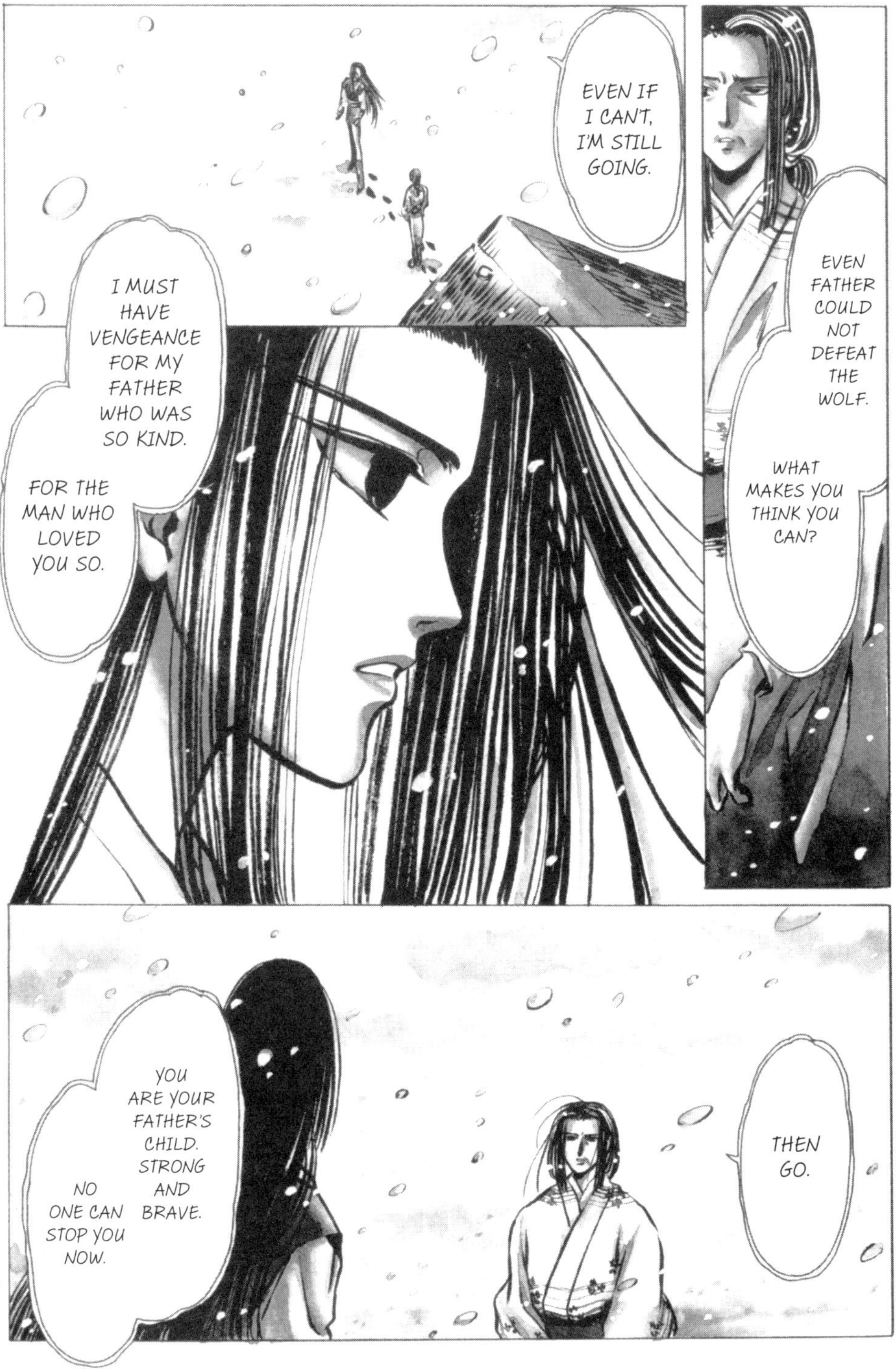
EVEN FATHER COULD NOT DEFEAT THE WOLF.
WHAT MAKES YOU THINK YOU CAN?
EVEN IF I CAN'T, I'M STILL GOING.
I MUST HAVE VENGEANCE FOR MY FATHER WHO WAS SO KIND.
FOR THE MAN WHO LOVED YOU SO.
THEN GO.
YOU ARE YOUR FATHER'S CHILD. STRONG AND BRAVE.
NO ONE CAN STOP YOU NOW.

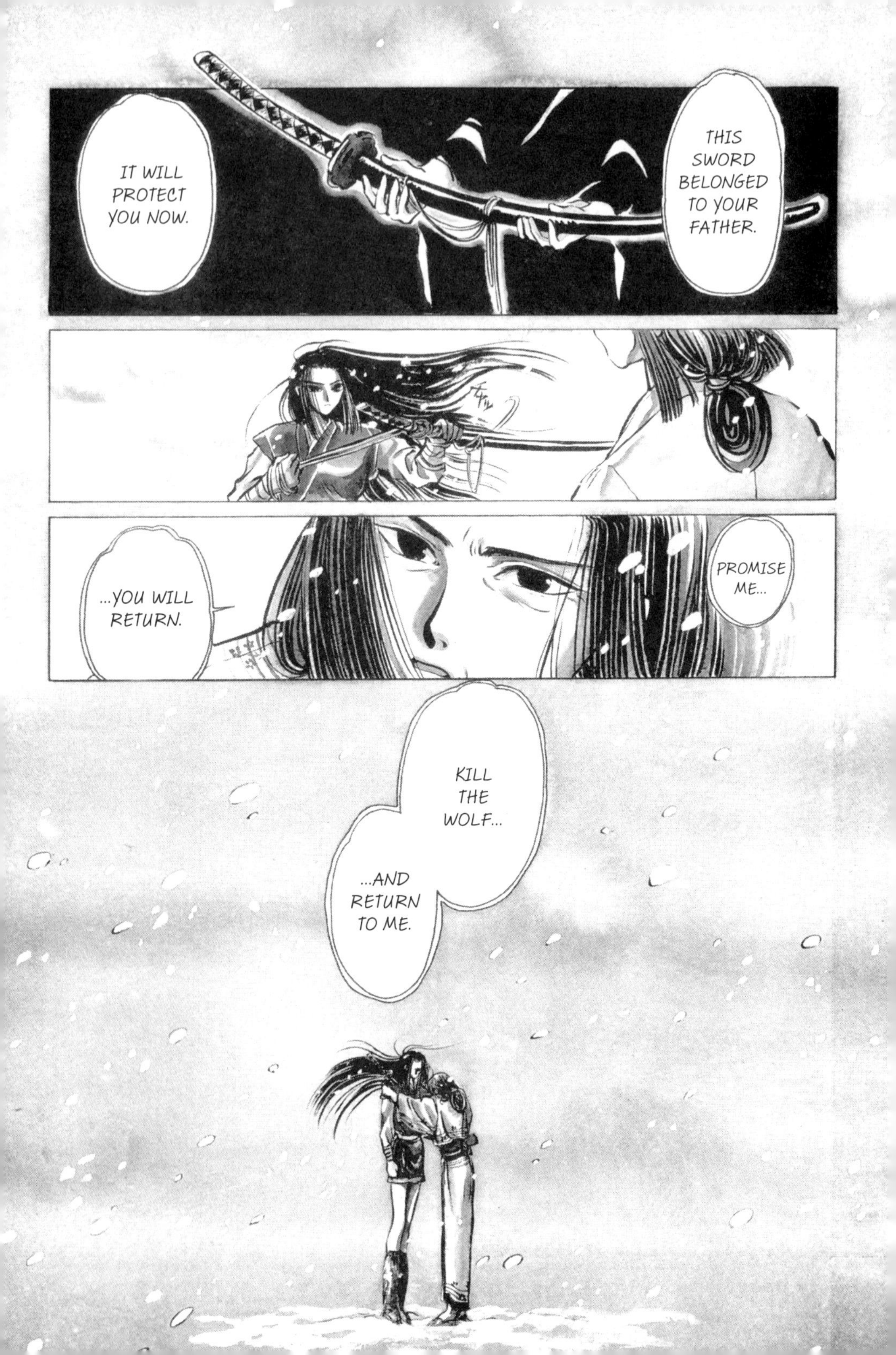
THIS SWORD BELONGED TO YOUR FATHER.
IT WILL PROTECT YOU NOW.
PROMISE ME...
...YOU WILL RETURN.
KILL THE WOLF...
...AND RETURN TO ME.

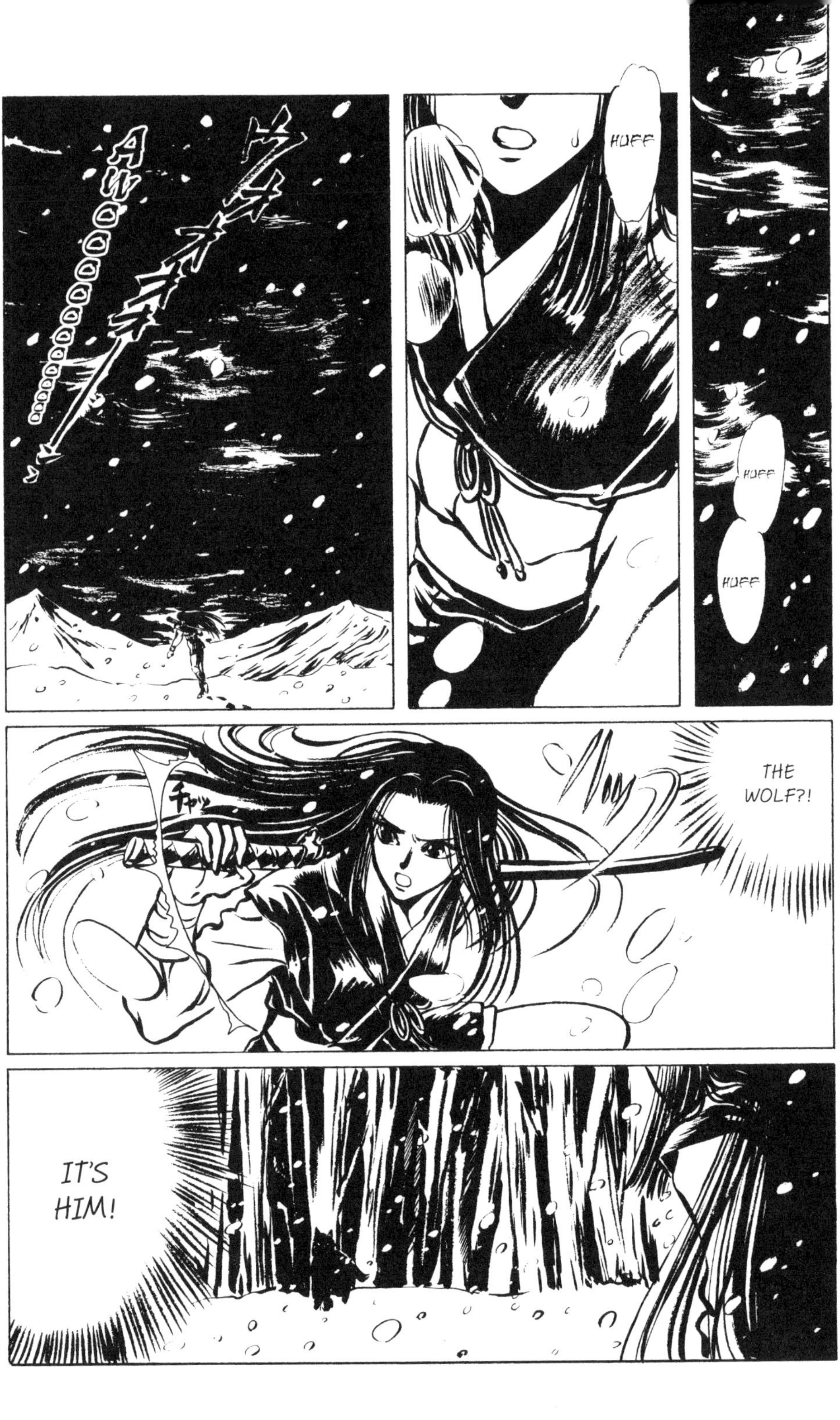
HUFF
HUFF
HUFF
AWOOOOOOOOOOOOOO
THE WOLF?!
IT'S HIM!

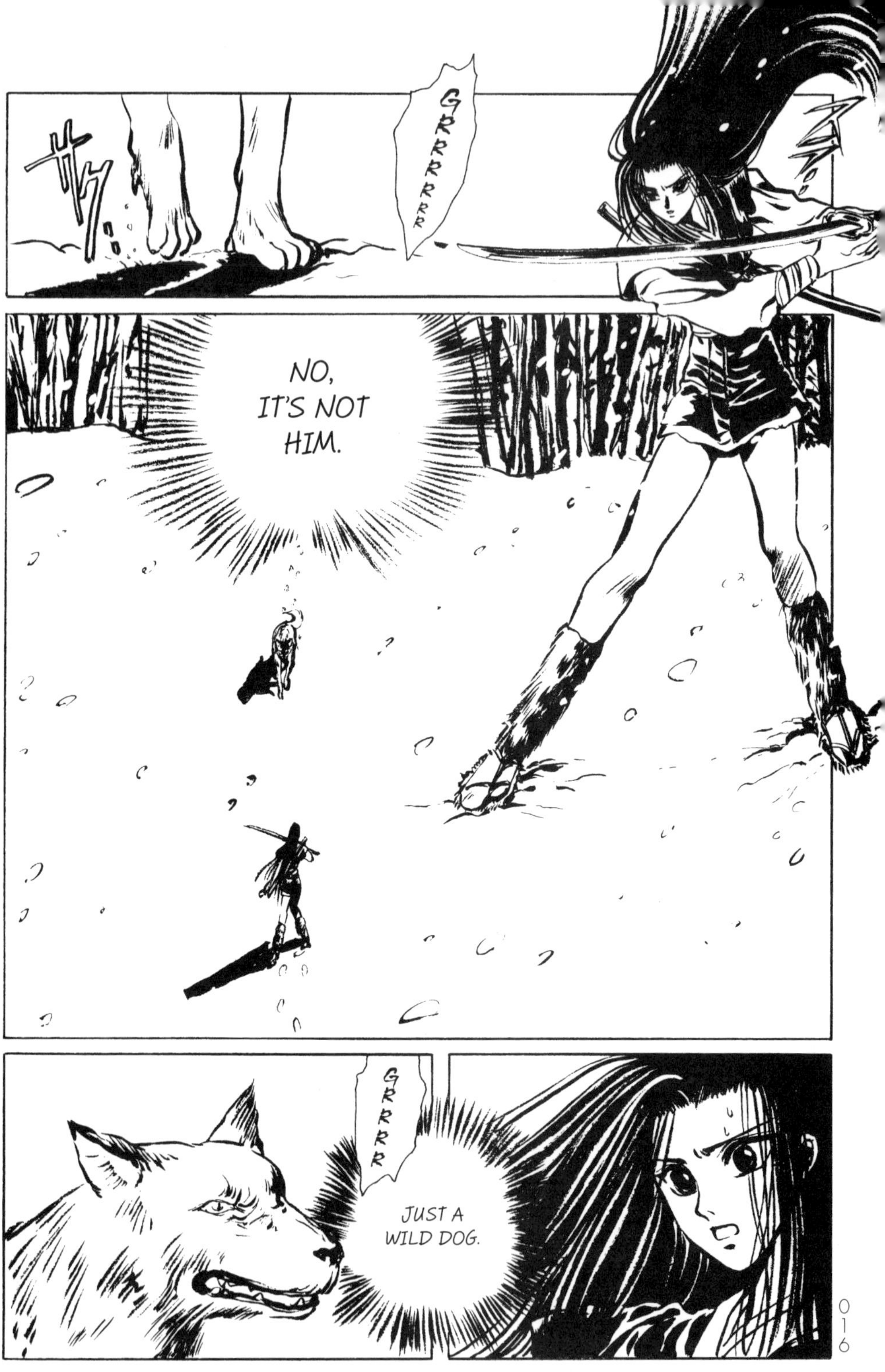
GRRRRRRR
NO, IT'S NOT HIM.
JUST A WILD DOG.
GRRRRR

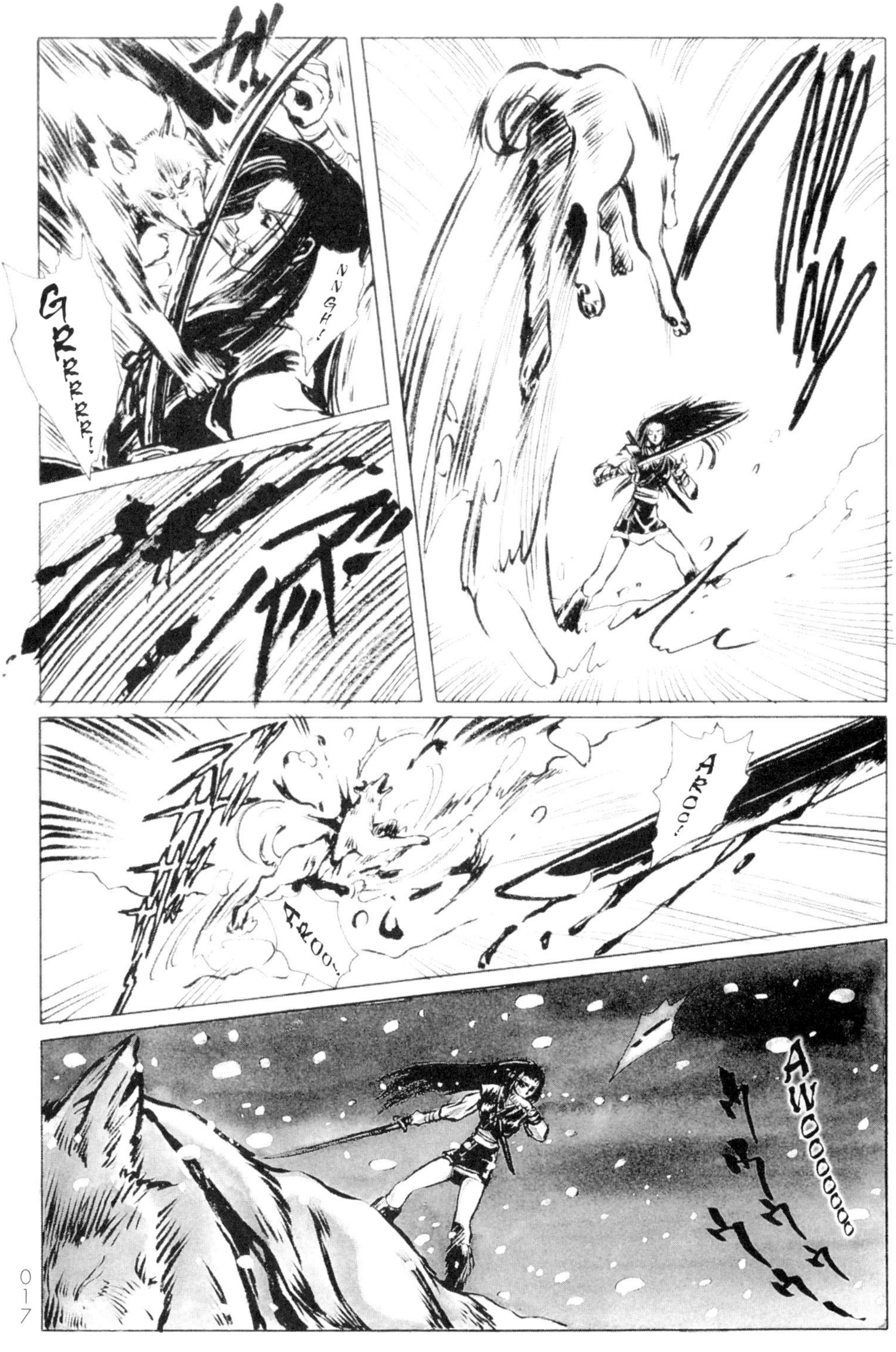
NNGH!
GRRRRRR!
AROO!
TROO!
AWOOOOOOO

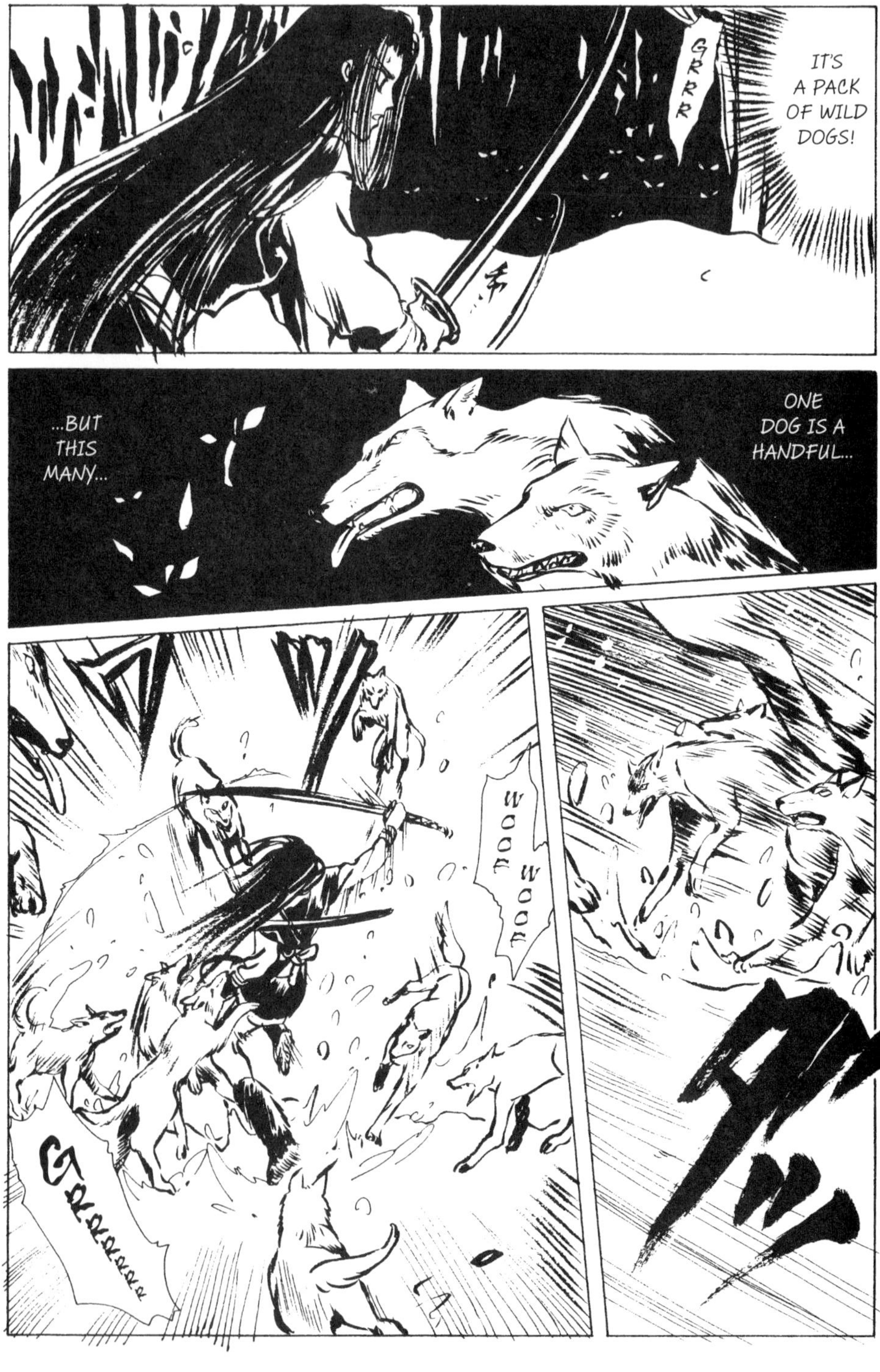
IT'S A PACK OF WILD DOGS!
GRRR
ONE DOG IS A HANDFUL...
...BUT THIS MANY...
WOOF WOOF
GRRRRRRR

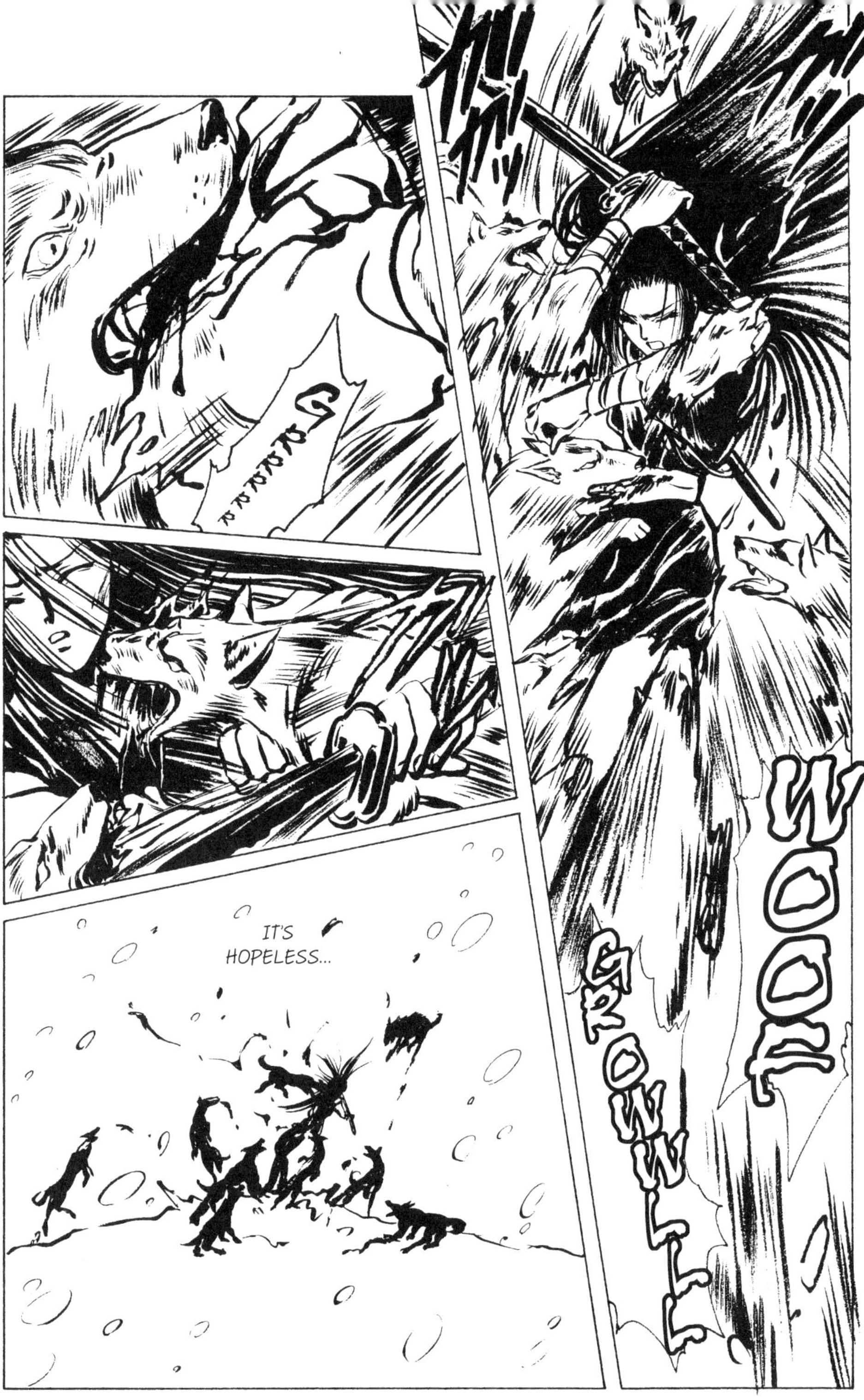
WOOO!
GROWLLL
GRRRRRRR
IT'S HOPELESS...

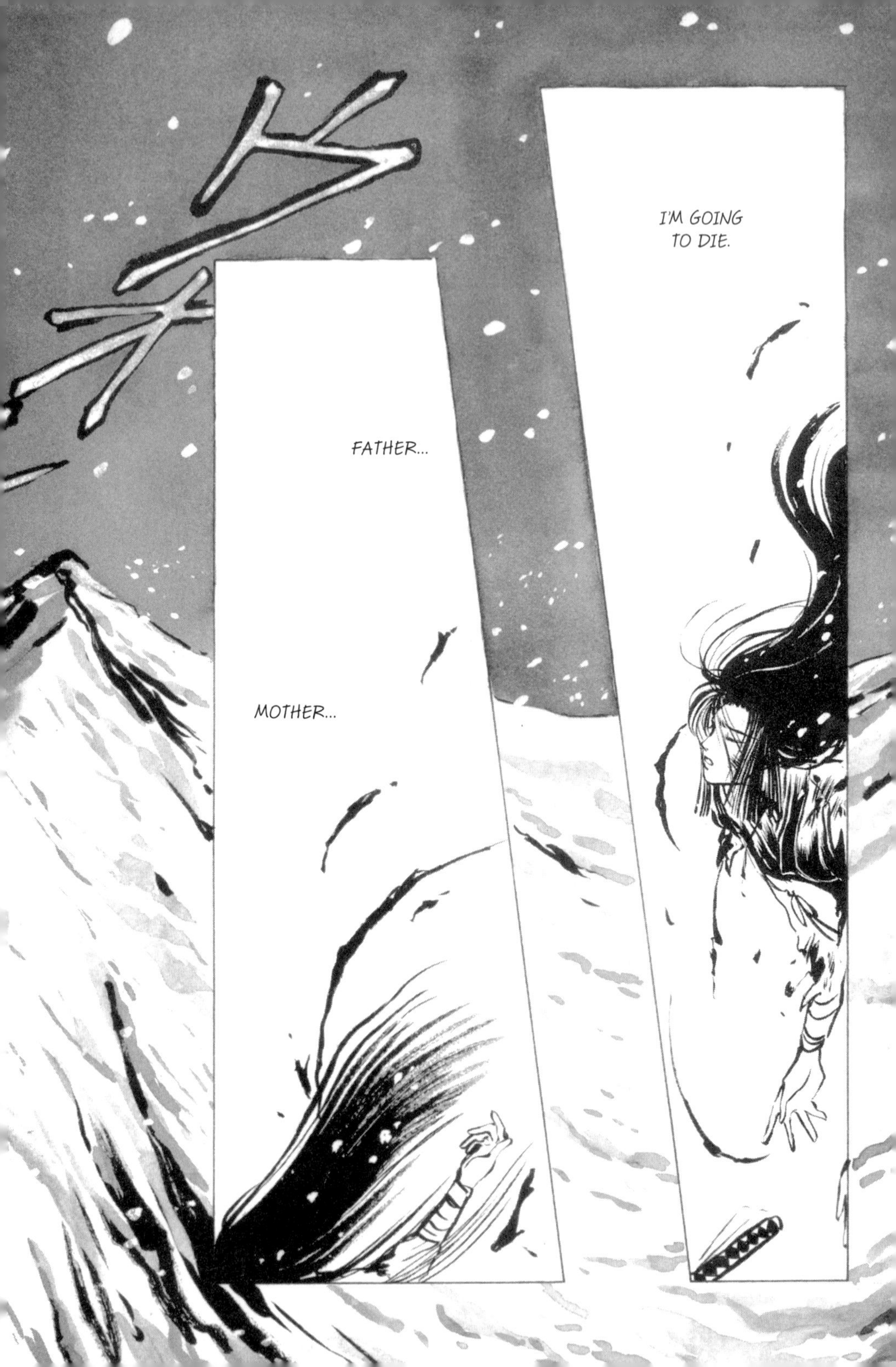
I'M GOING
TO DIE.
FATHER...
MOTHER...

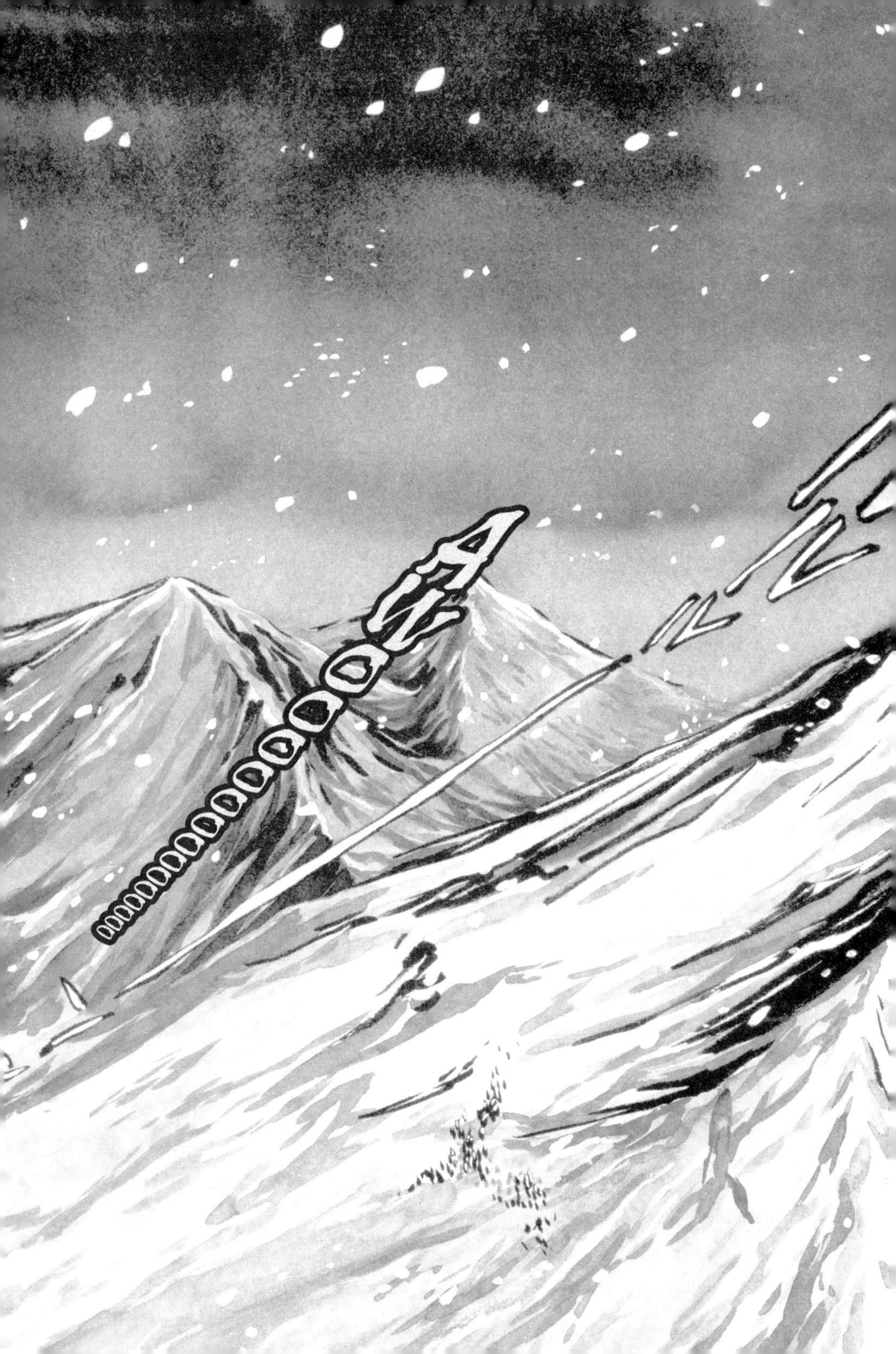
AWOOOOOOOOOOOOOOOOO

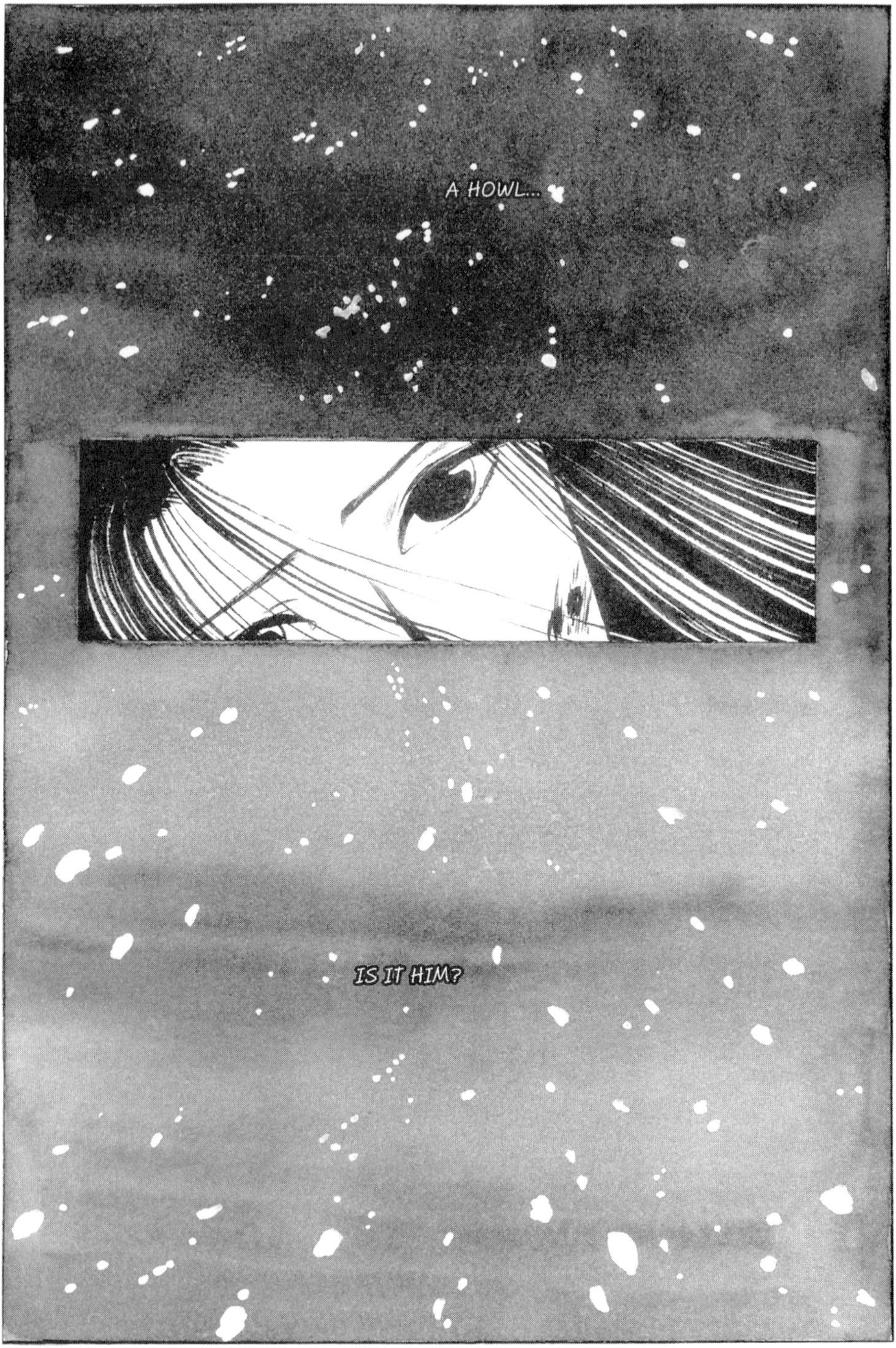
A HOWL...
IS IT HIM?

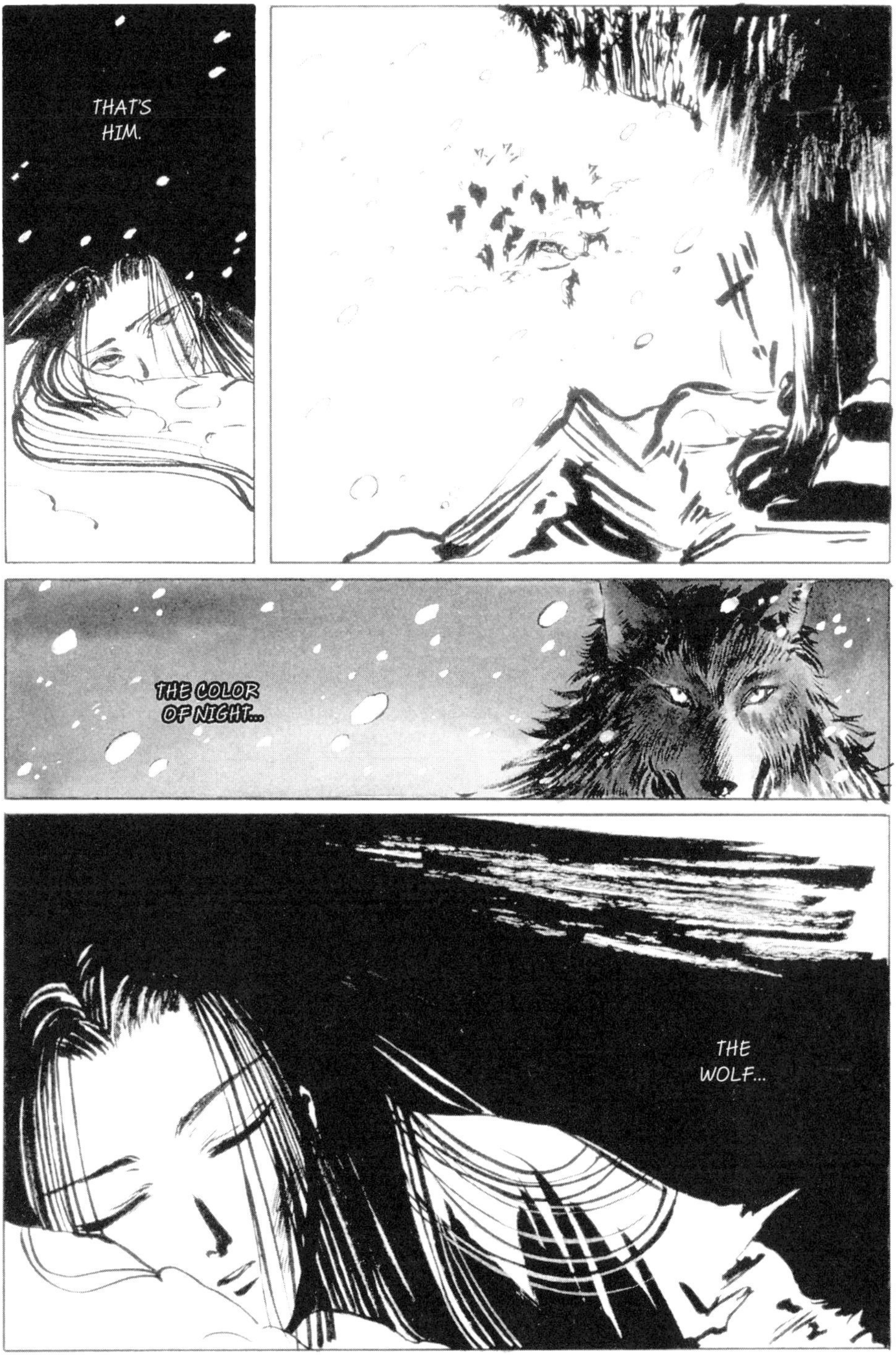
THAT'S HIM.
THE COLOR OF NIGHT...
THE WOLF...

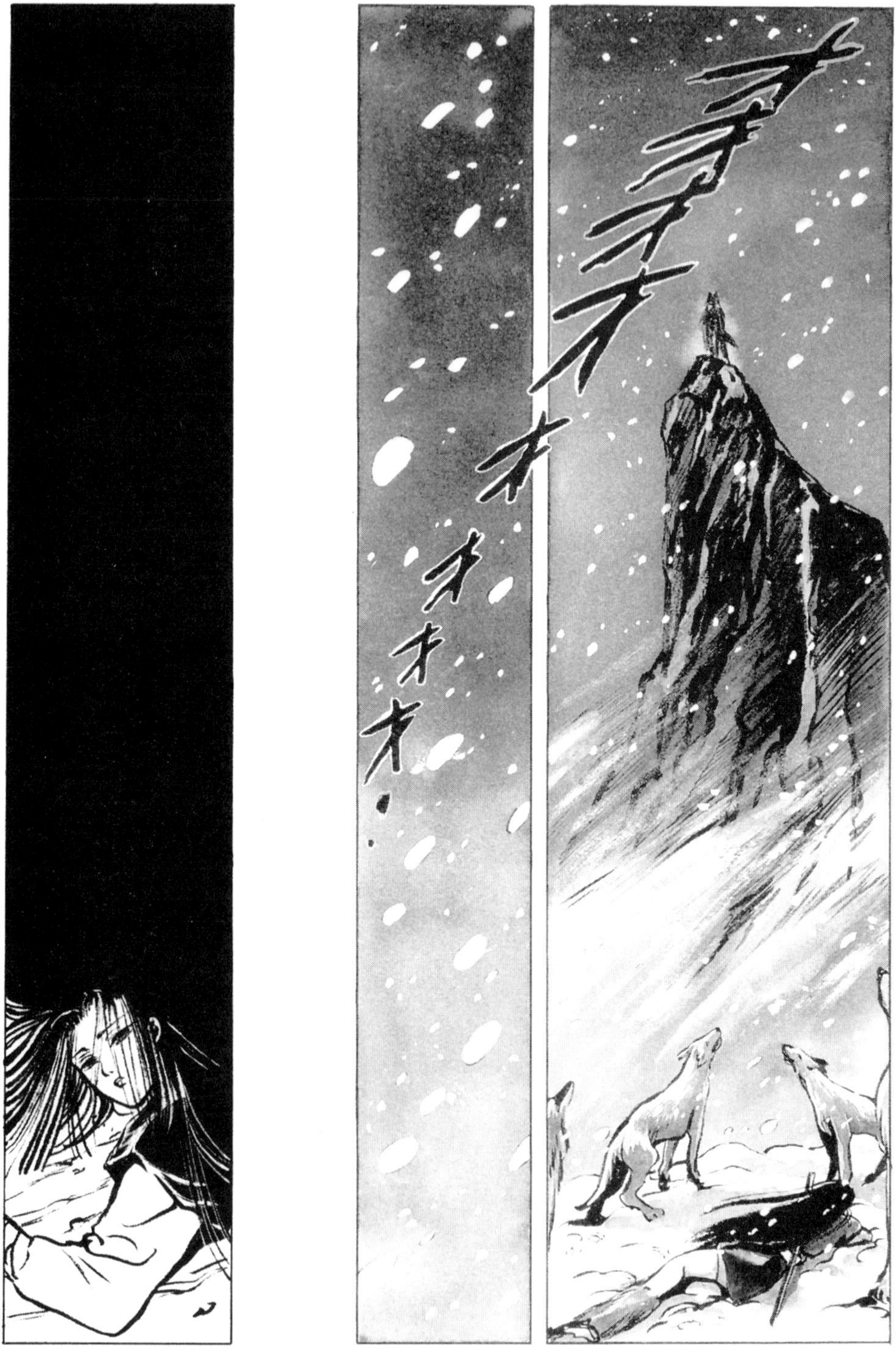
オオオオオオオオオ…

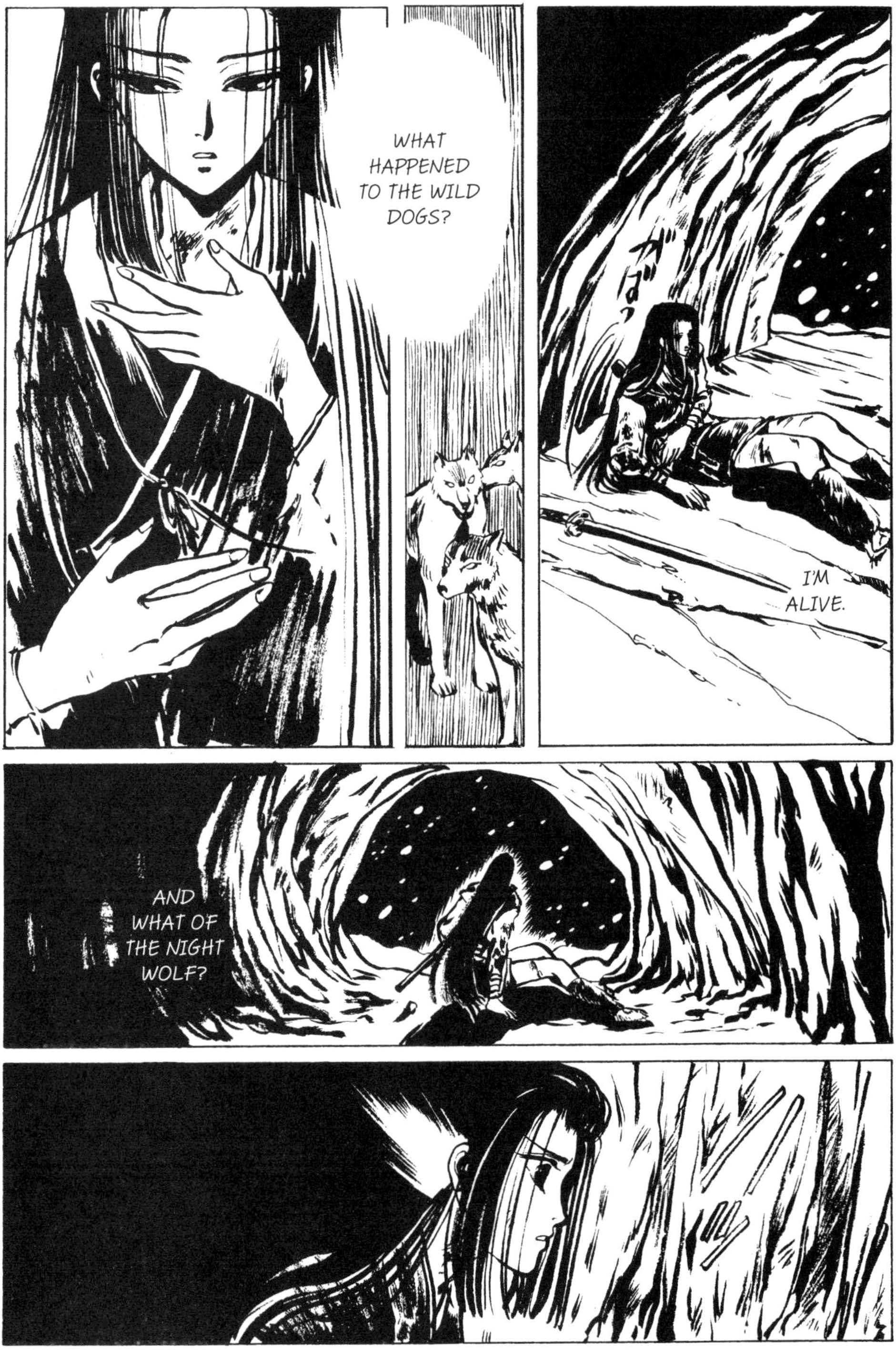
I'M ALIVE.
WHAT HAPPENED TO THE WILD DOGS?
AND WHAT OF THE NIGHT WOLF?

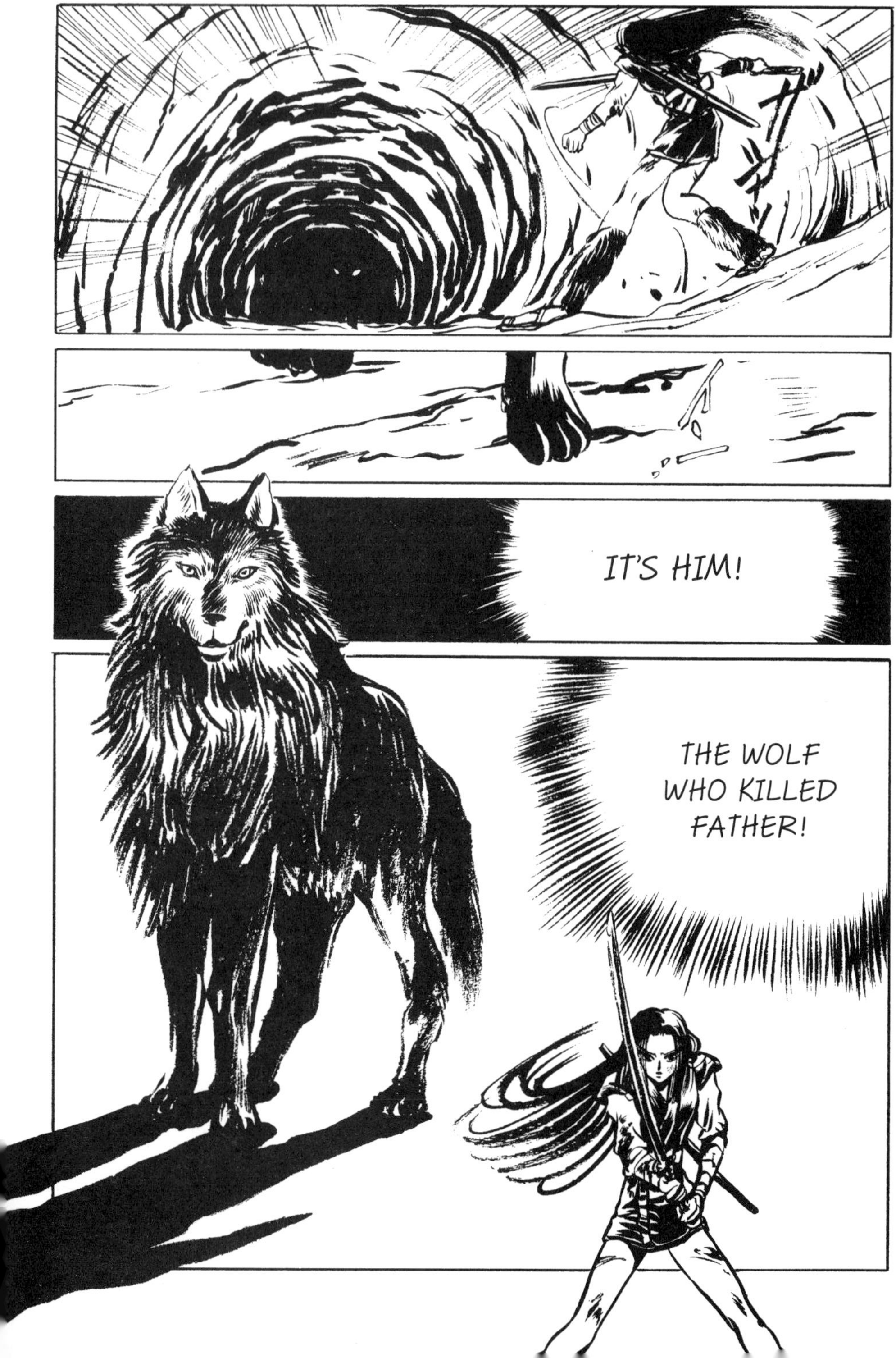
IT'S HIM!
THE WOLF WHO KILLED FATHER!

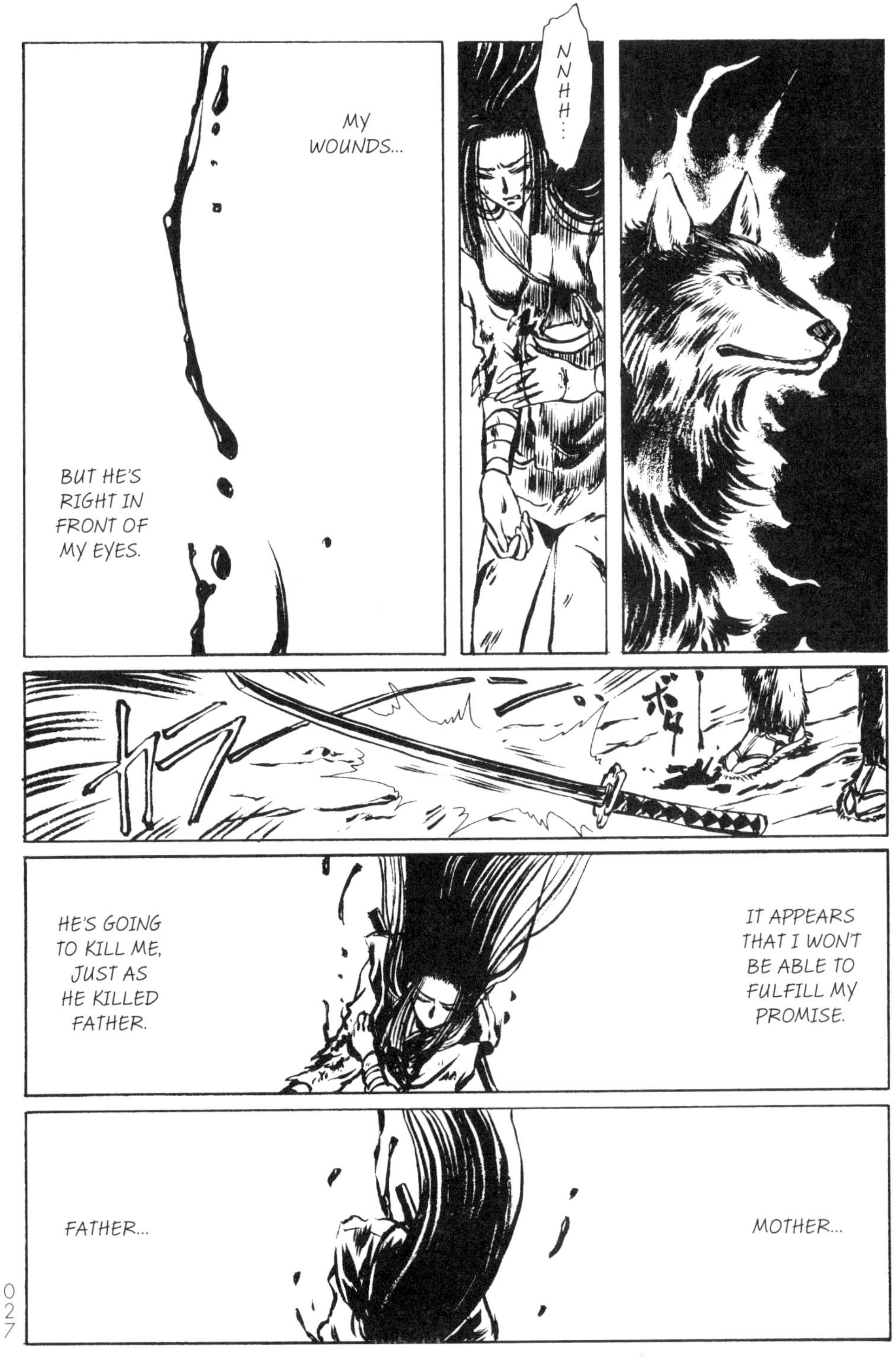
NNHH...
MY WOUNDS...
BUT HE'S RIGHT IN FRONT OF MY EYES.
IT APPEARS THAT I WON'T BE ABLE TO FULFILL MY PROMISE.
HE'S GOING TO KILL ME, JUST AS HE KILLED FATHER.
MOTHER...
FATHER...

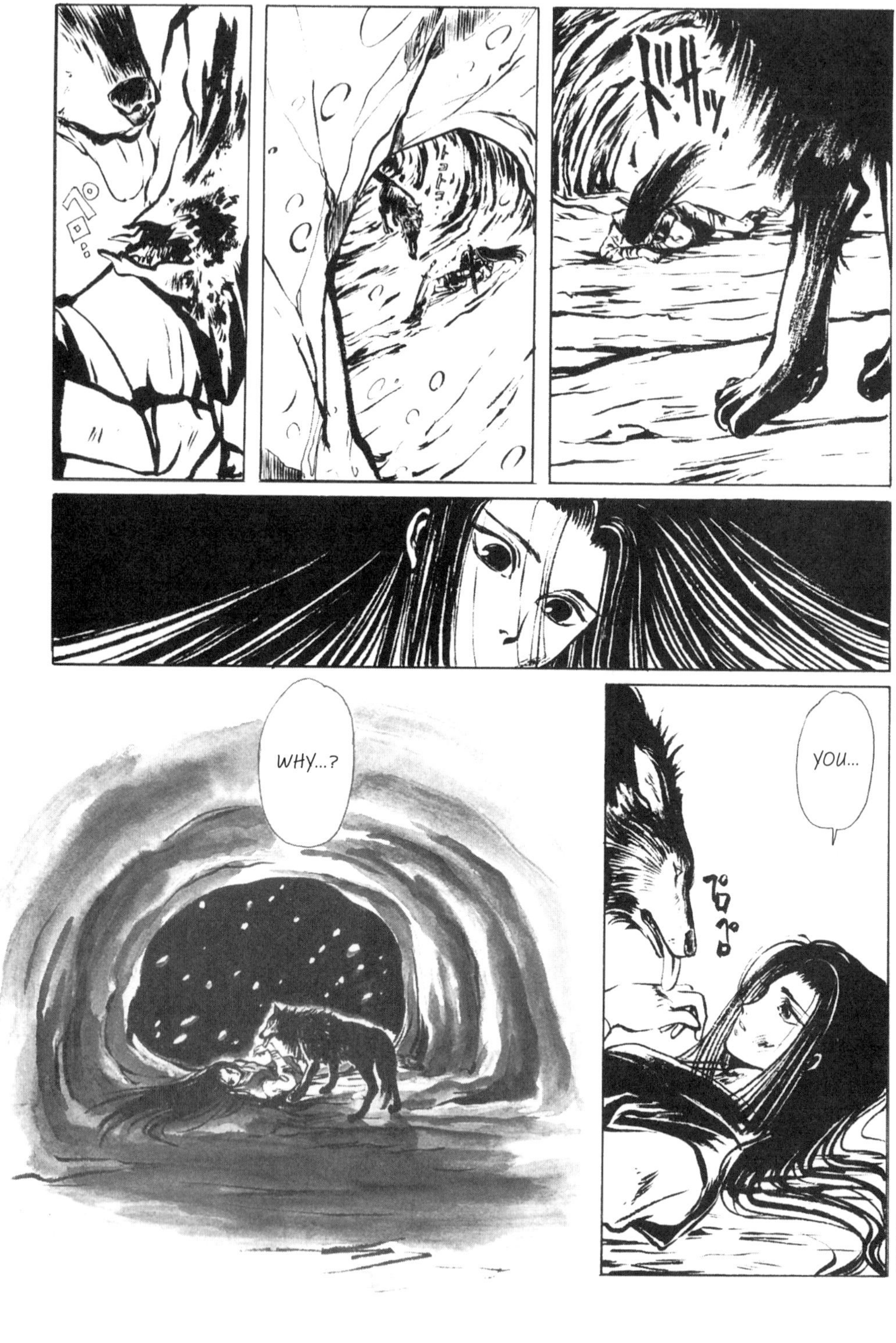
YOU...
WHY...?

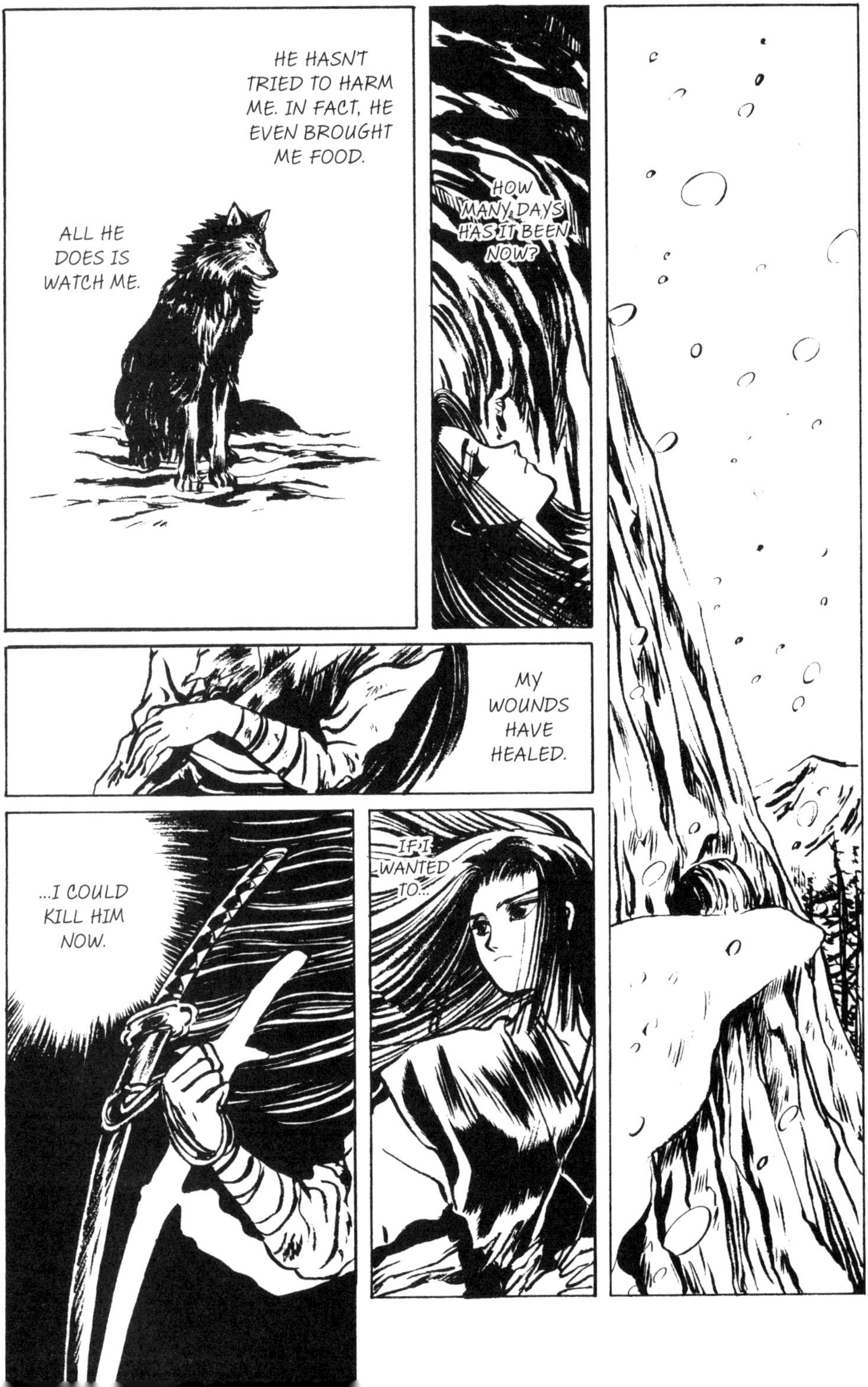
HOW MANY DAYS HAS IT BEEN NOW?
HE HASN'T TRIED TO HARM ME. IN FACT, HE EVEN BROUGHT ME FOOD.
ALL HE DOES IS WATCH ME.
MY WOUNDS HAVE HEALED.
IF I WANTED TO...
...I COULD KILL HIM NOW.

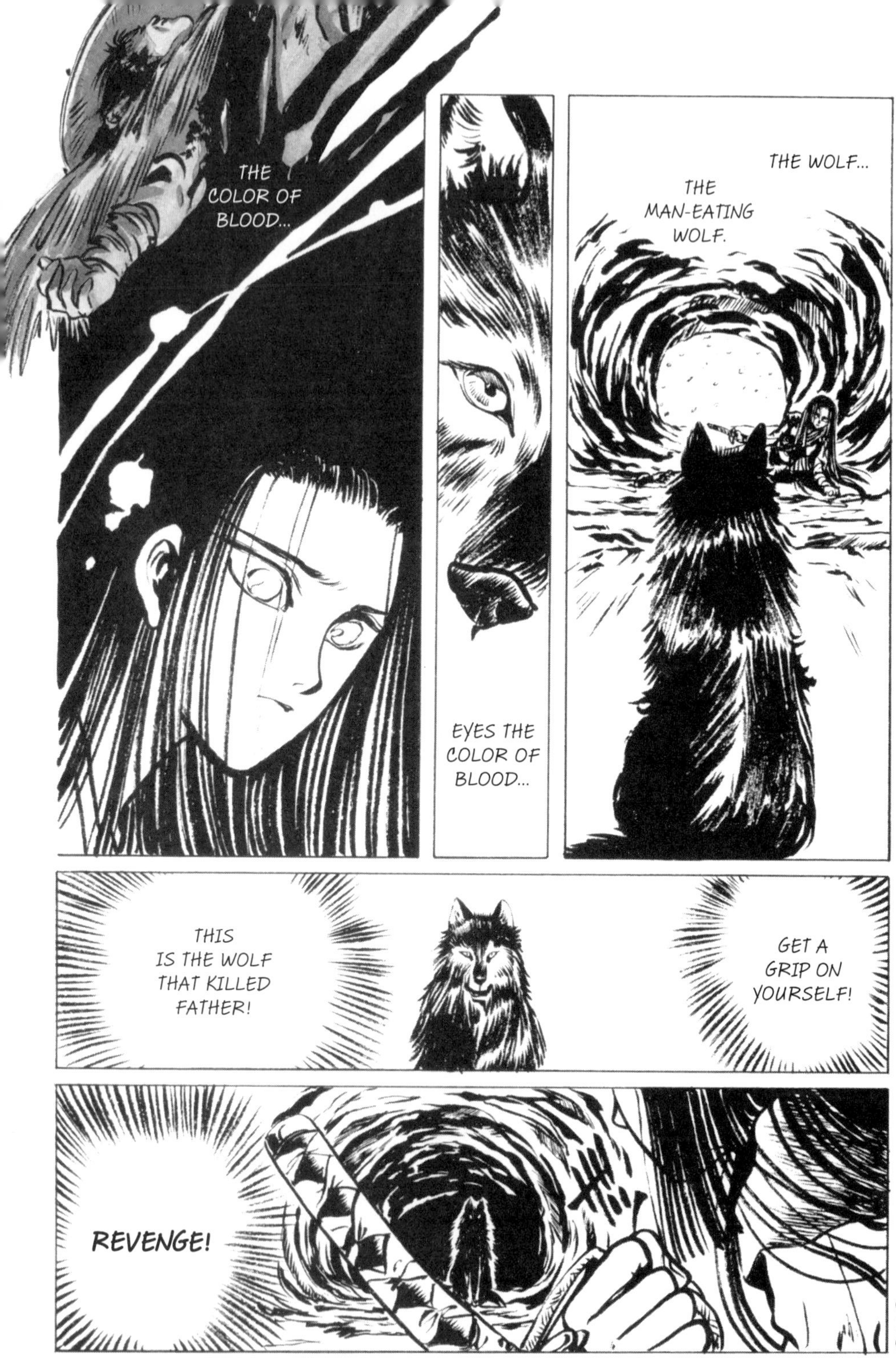
THE WOLF...
THE MAN-EATING WOLF.
EYES THE COLOR OF BLOOD...
THE COLOR OF BLOOD...
GET A GRIP ON YOURSELF!
THIS IS THE WOLF THAT KILLED FATHER!
REVENGE!

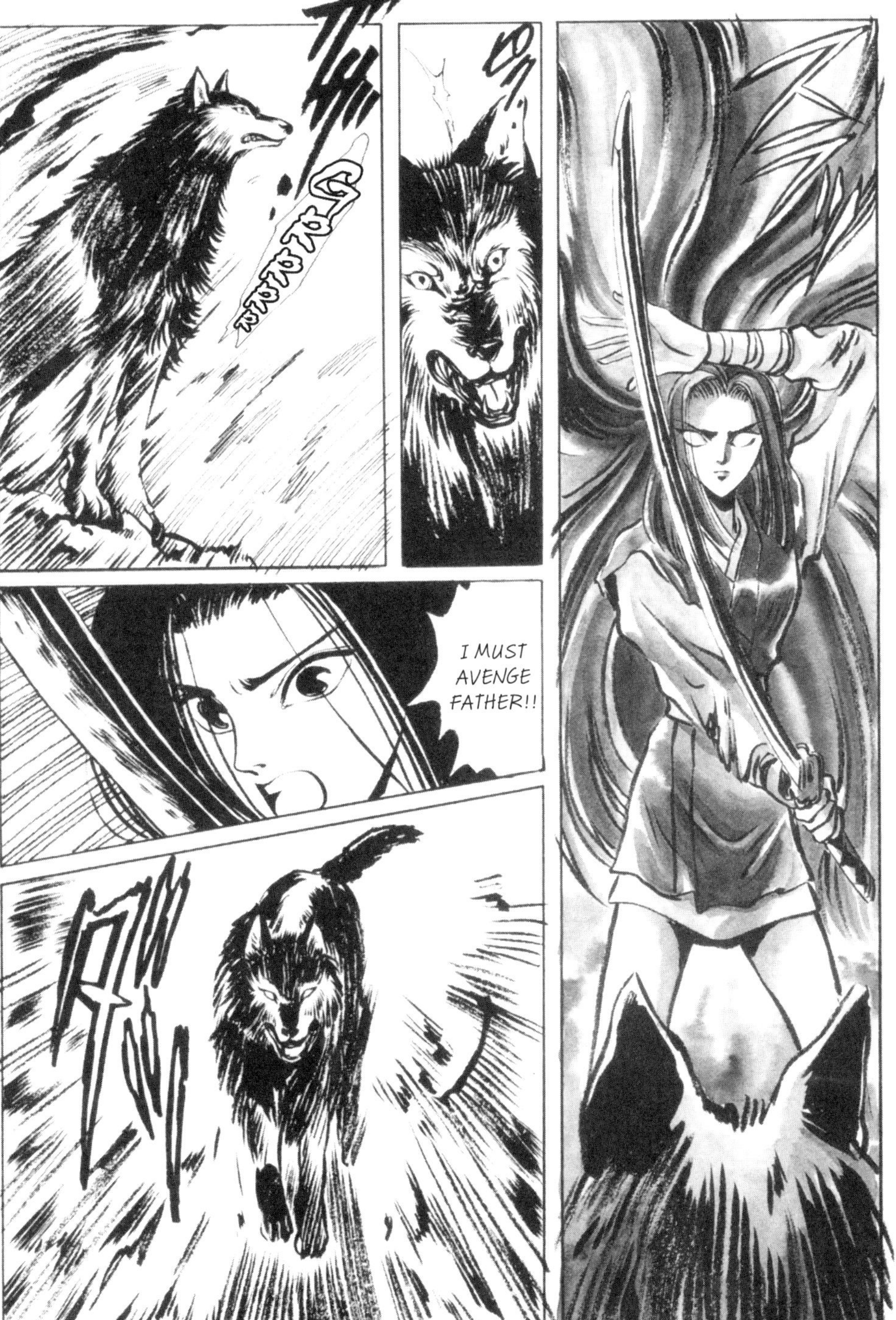
I MUST AVENGE FATHER!!

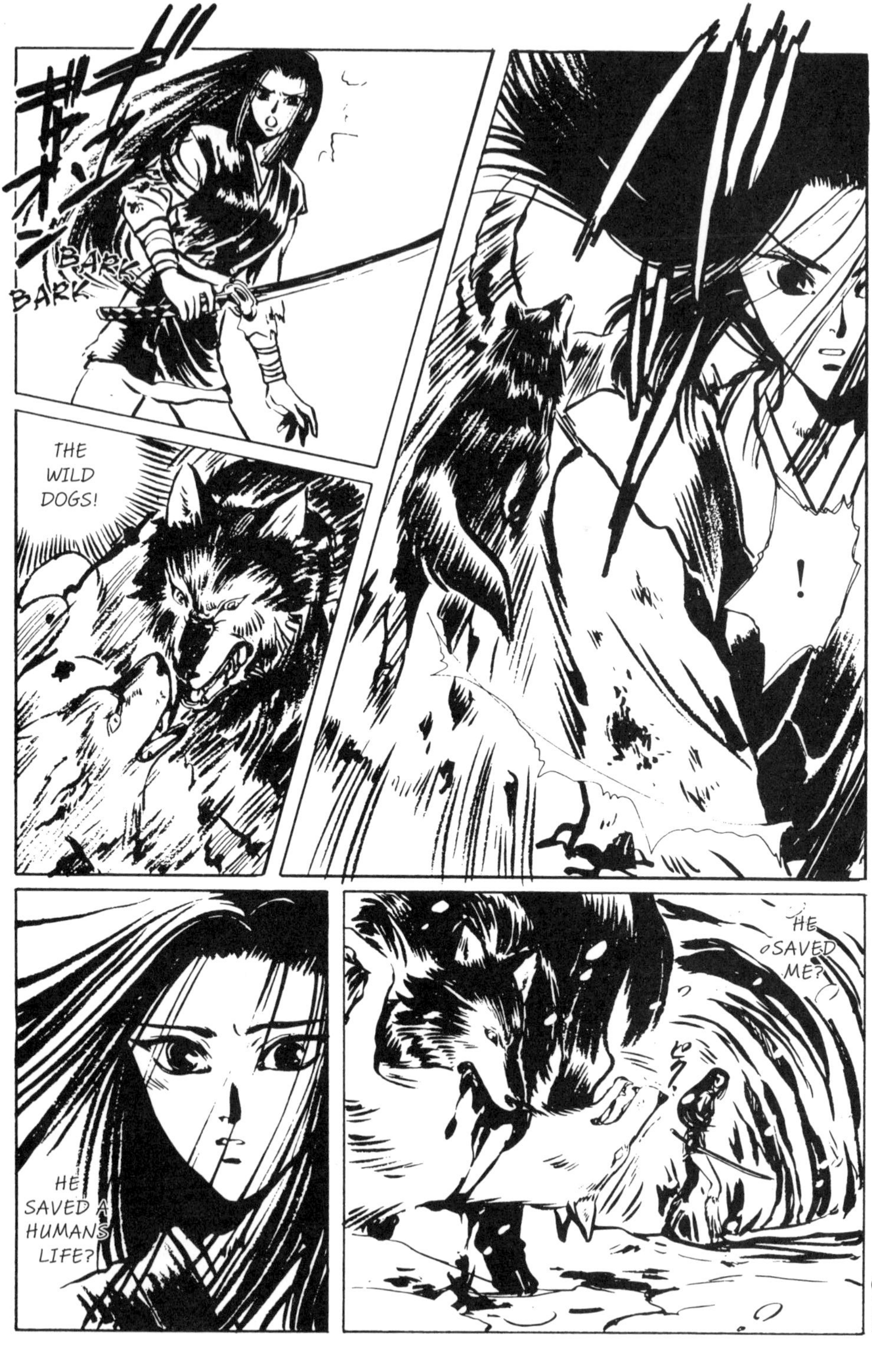
!
BARK
BARK
THE WILD DOGS!
HE SAVED ME?
HE SAVED A HUMANS LIFE?

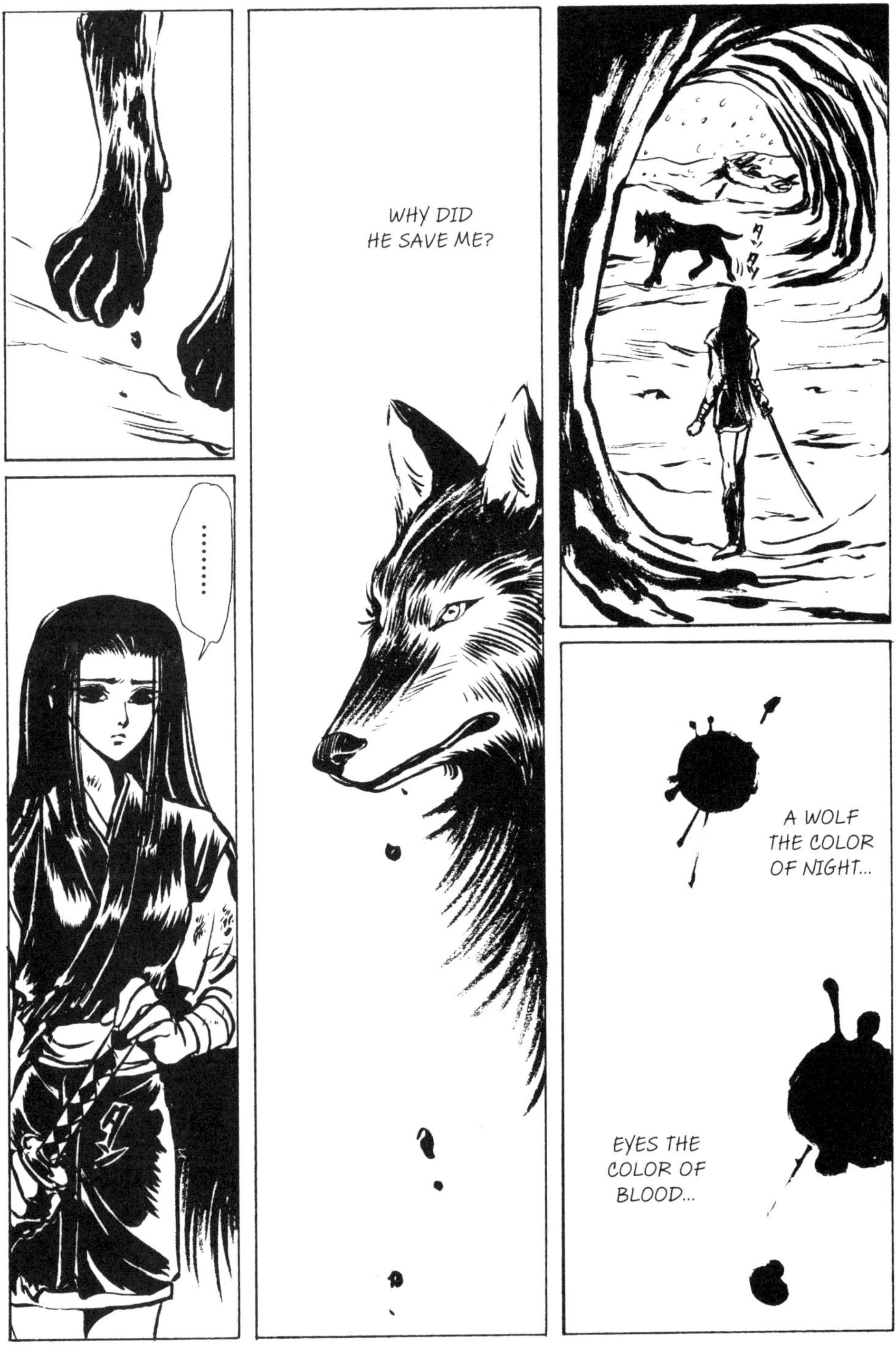
A WOLF THE COLOR OF NIGHT...
EYES THE COLOR OF BLOOD...
WHY DID HE SAVE ME?
....

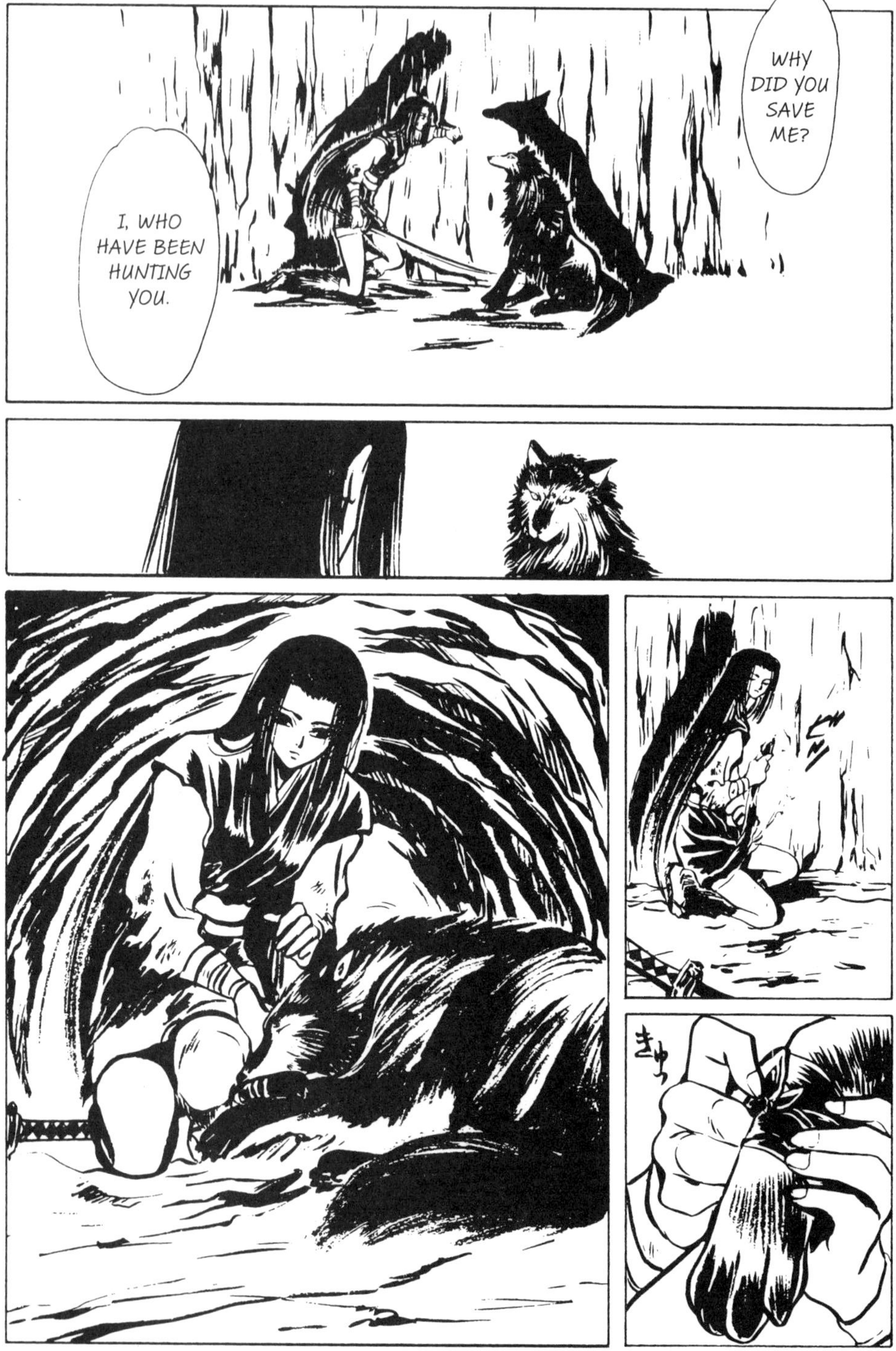
WHY DID YOU SAVE ME?
I, WHO HAVE BEEN HUNTING YOU.

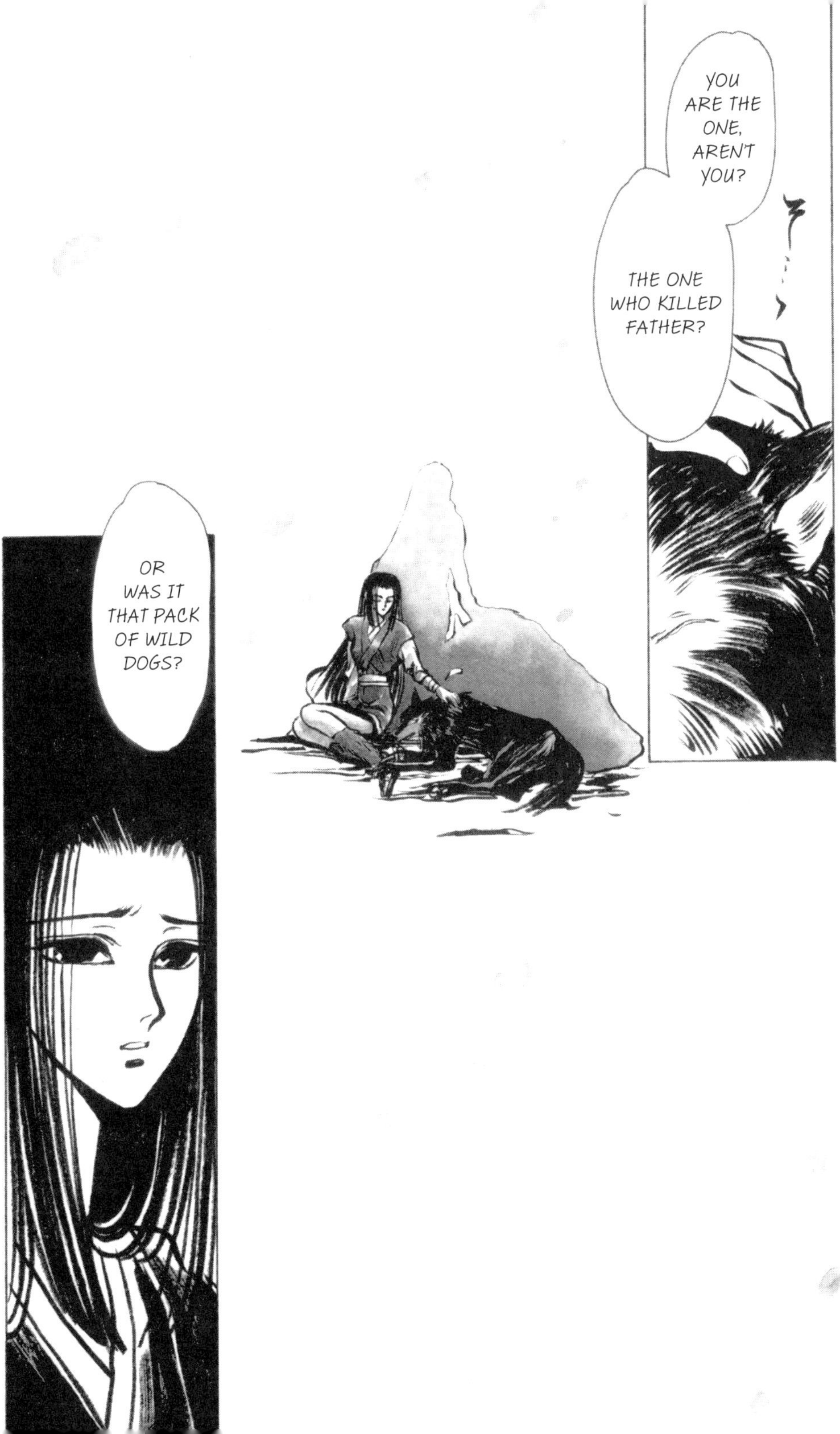
YOU ARE THE ONE, AREN'T YOU?
THE ONE WHO KILLED FATHER?
OR WAS IT THAT PACK OF WILD DOGS?

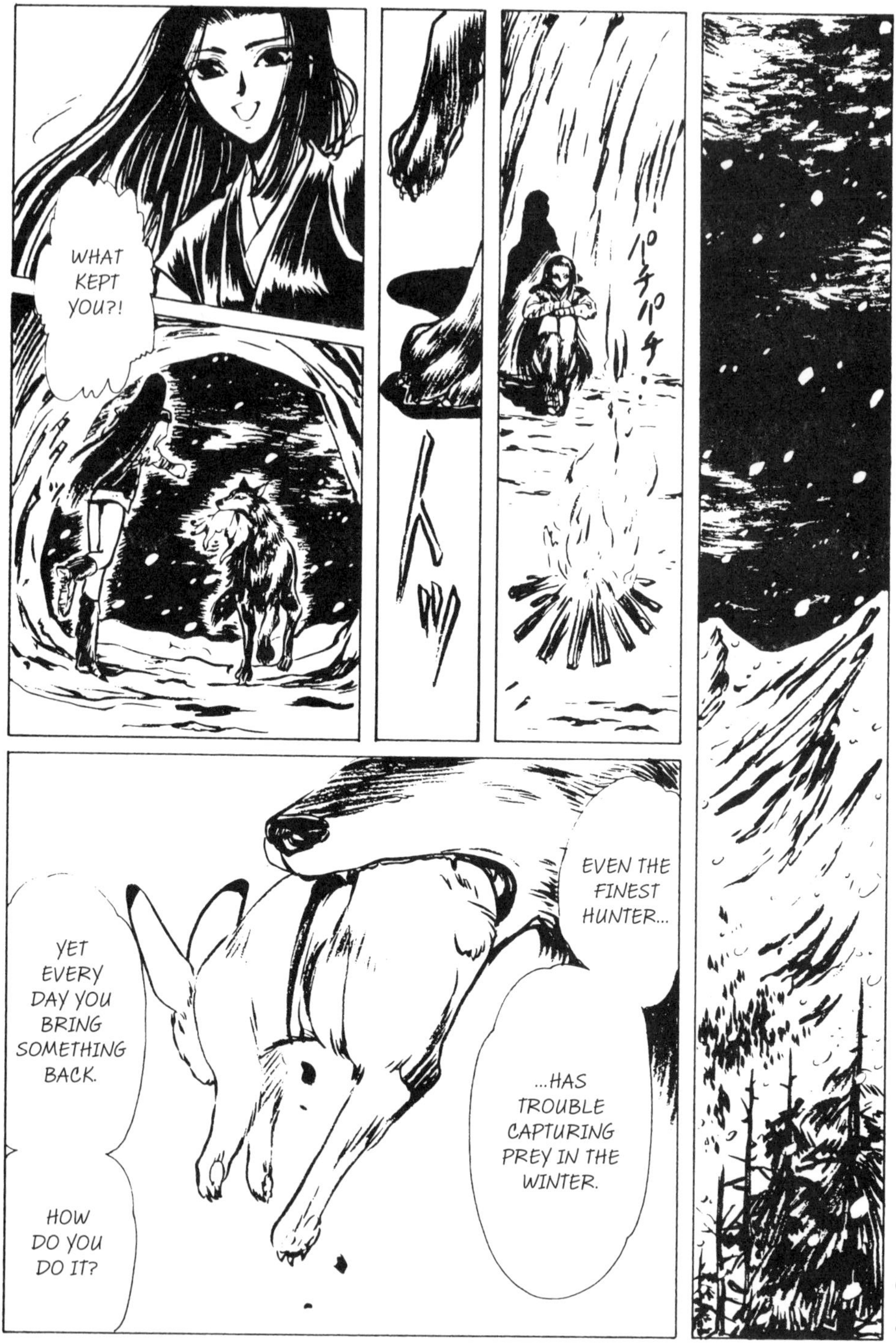
パチパチ
WHAT KEPT YOU?!
EVEN THE FINEST HUNTER...
...HAS TROUBLE CAPTURING PREY IN THE WINTER.
YET EVERY DAY YOU BRING SOMETHING BACK.
HOW DO YOU DO IT?

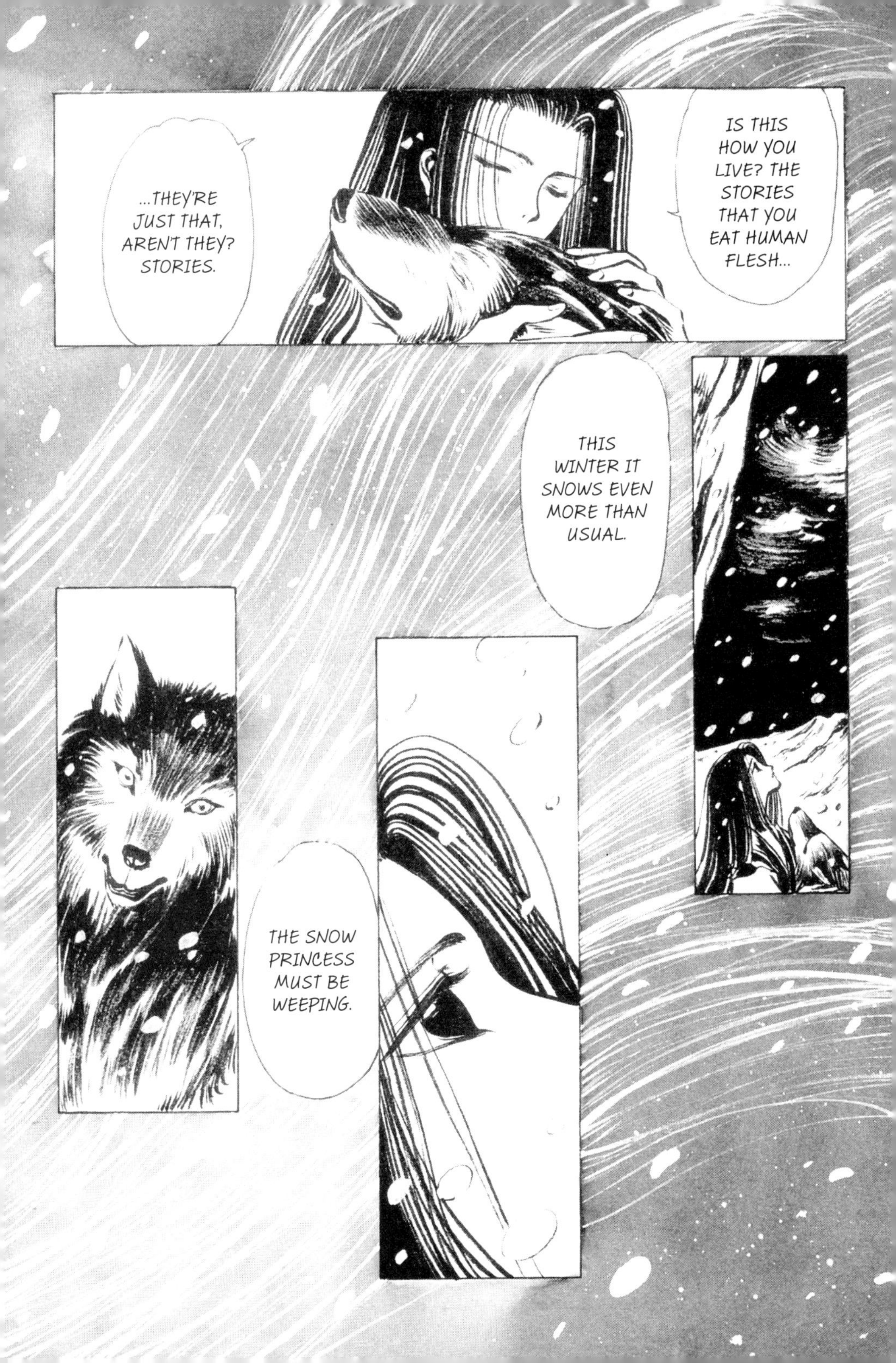
IS THIS HOW YOU LIVE? THE STORIES THAT YOU EAT HUMAN FLESH...
...THEY'RE JUST THAT, AREN'T THEY? STORIES.
THIS WINTER IT SNOWS EVEN MORE THAN USUAL.
THE SNOW PRINCESS MUST BE WEEPING.

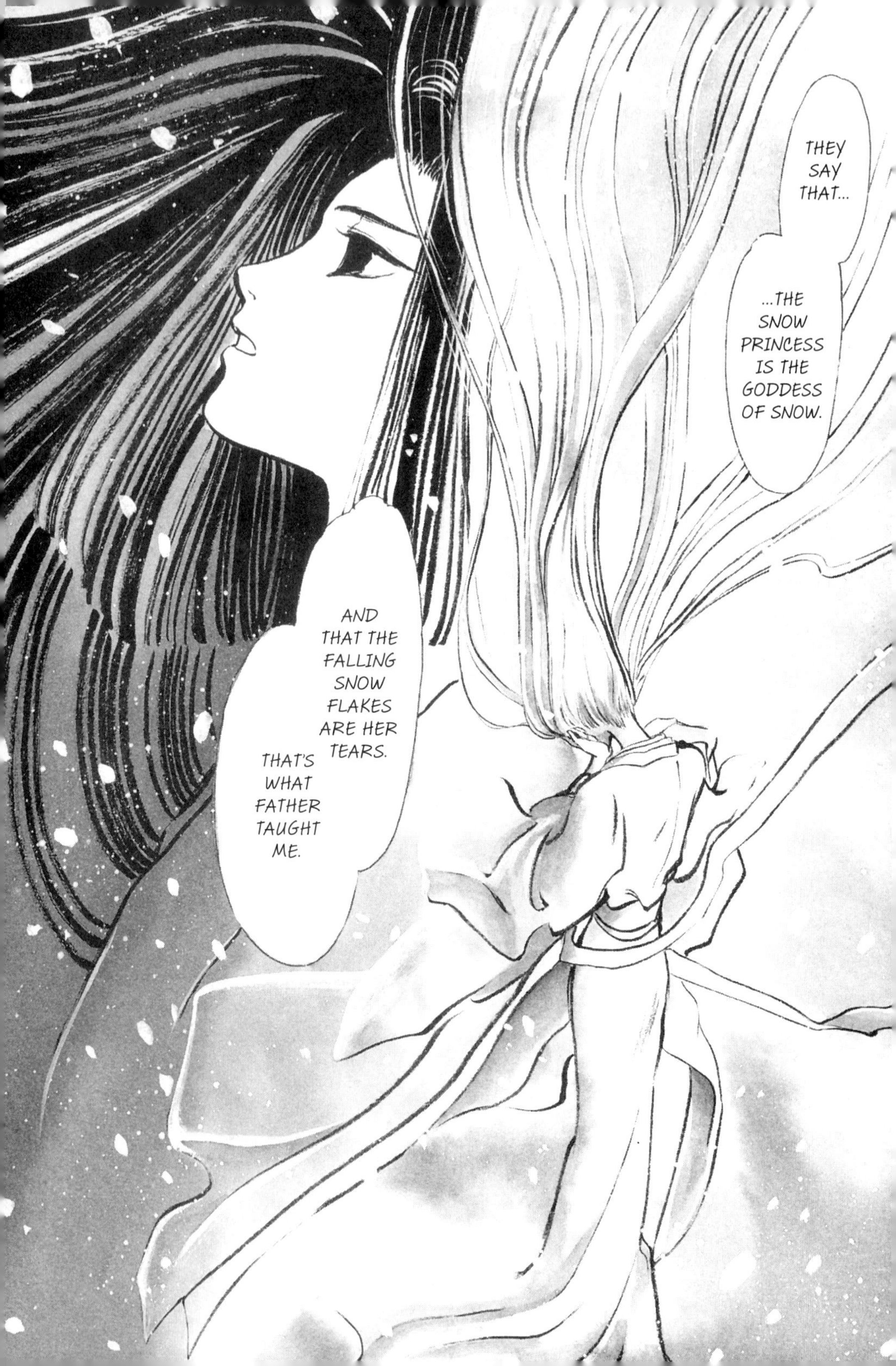
THEY SAY THAT...
...THE SNOW PRINCESS IS THE GODDESS OF SNOW.
AND THAT THE FALLING SNOW FLAKES ARE HER TEARS.
THAT'S WHAT FATHER TAUGHT ME.

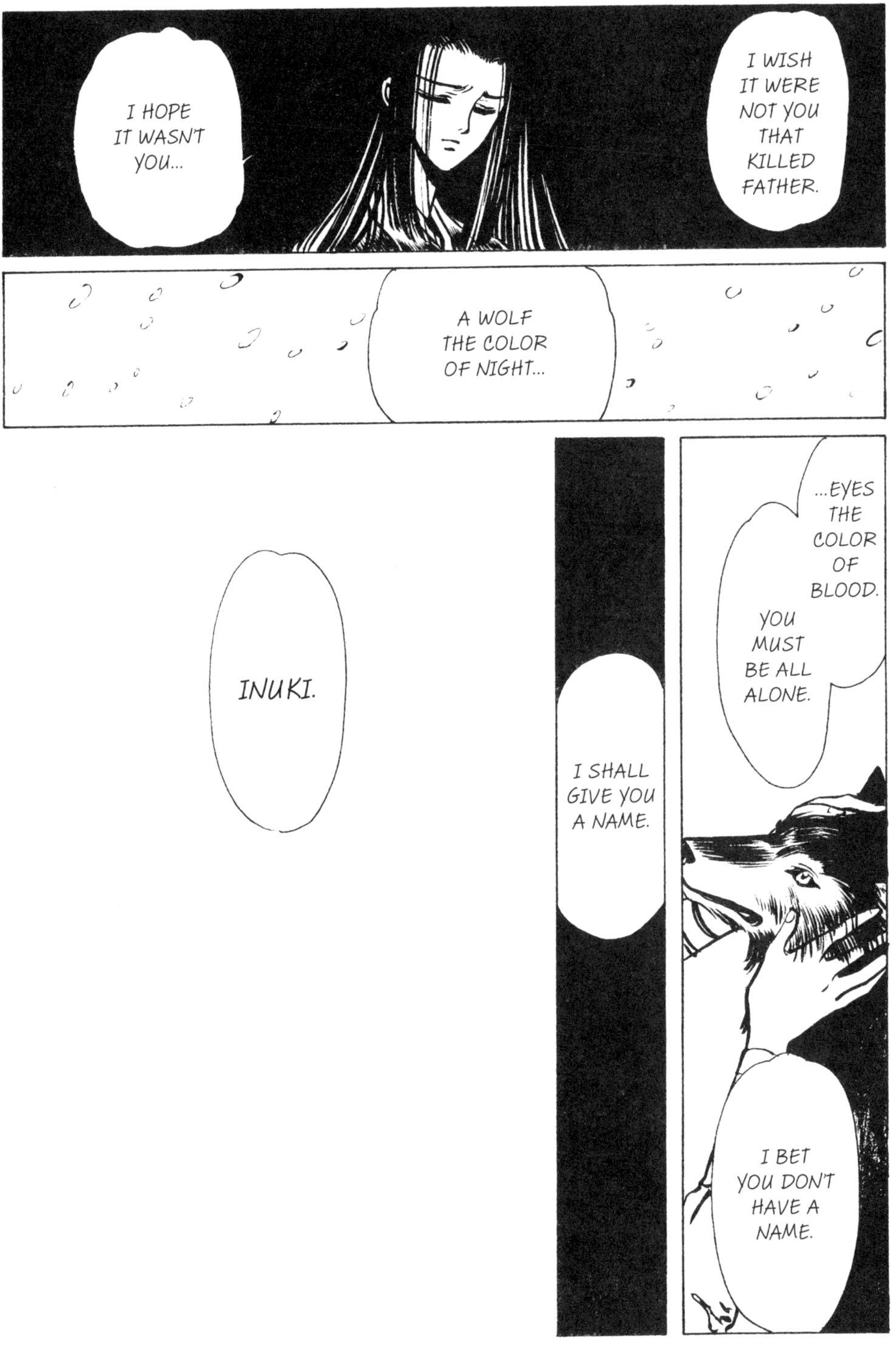
I WISH IT WERE NOT YOU THAT KILLED FATHER.
I HOPE IT WASN'T YOU...
A WOLF THE COLOR OF NIGHT...
...EYES THE COLOR OF BLOOD.
YOU MUST BE ALL ALONE.
I BET YOU DON'T HAVE A NAME.
I SHALL GIVE YOU A NAME.
INUKI.

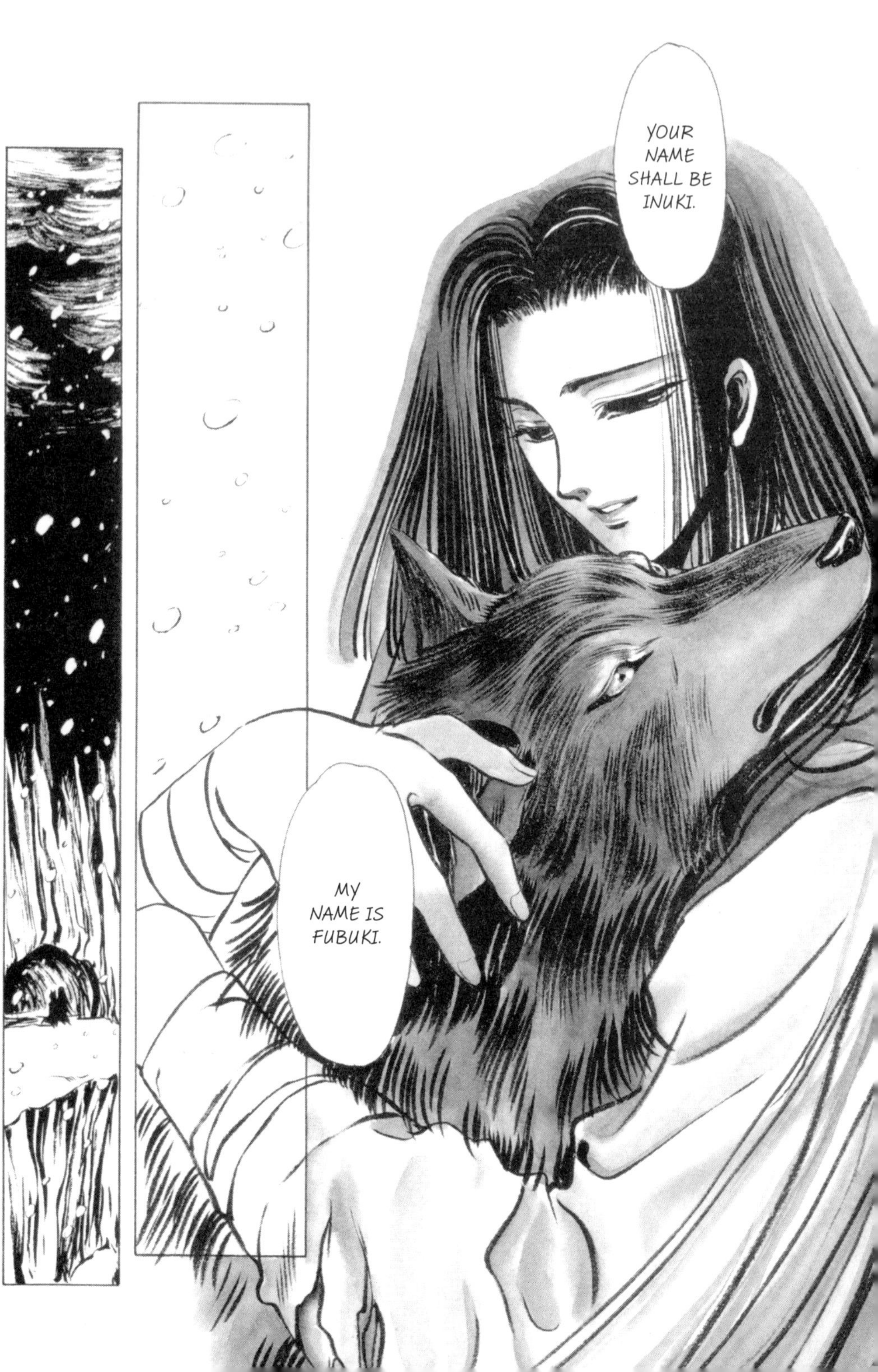
YOUR NAME SHALL BE INUKI.
MY NAME IS FUBUKI.

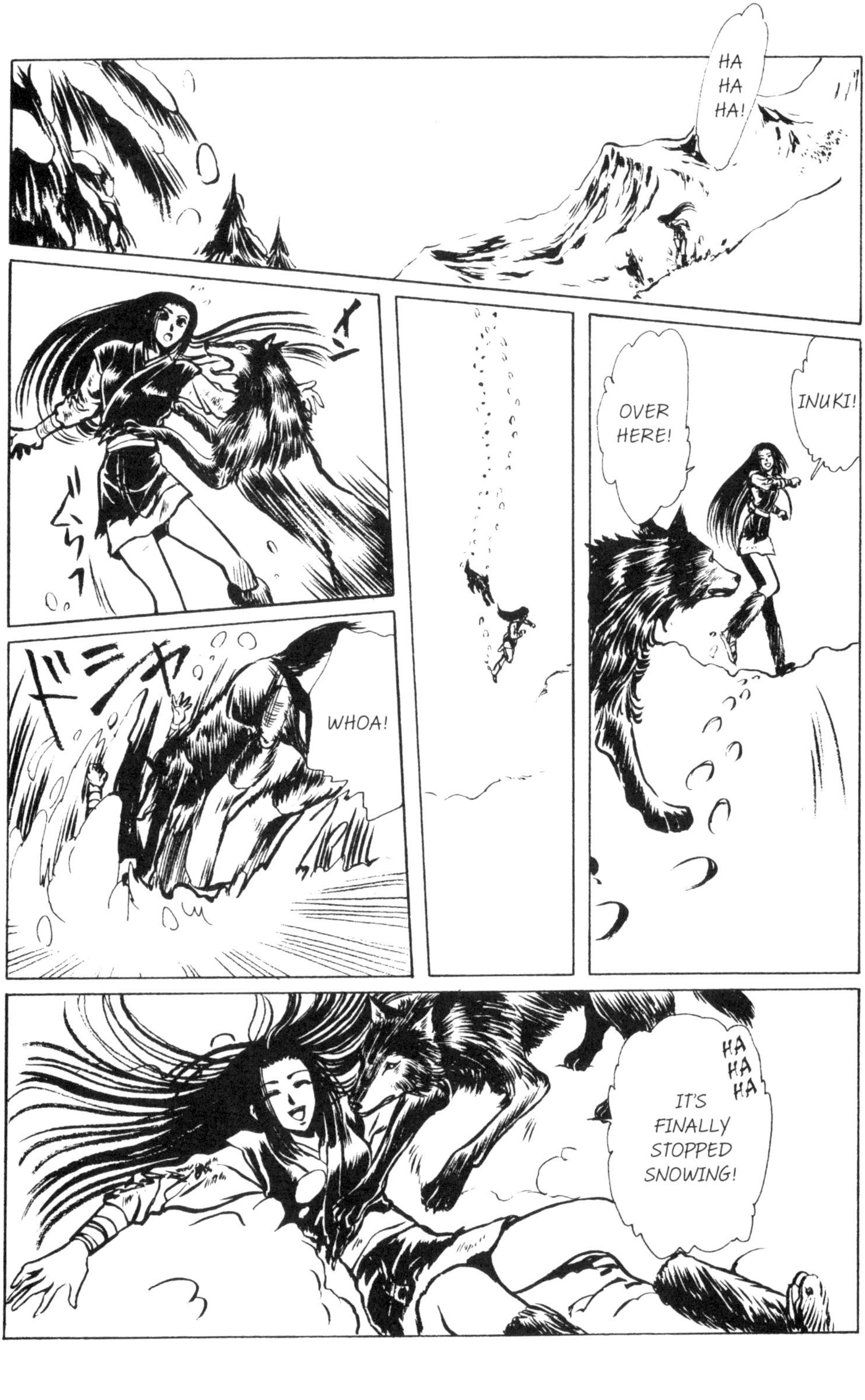
HA HA HA!
INUKI!
OVER HERE!
WHOA!
HA HA HA
IT'S FINALLY STOPPED SNOWING!

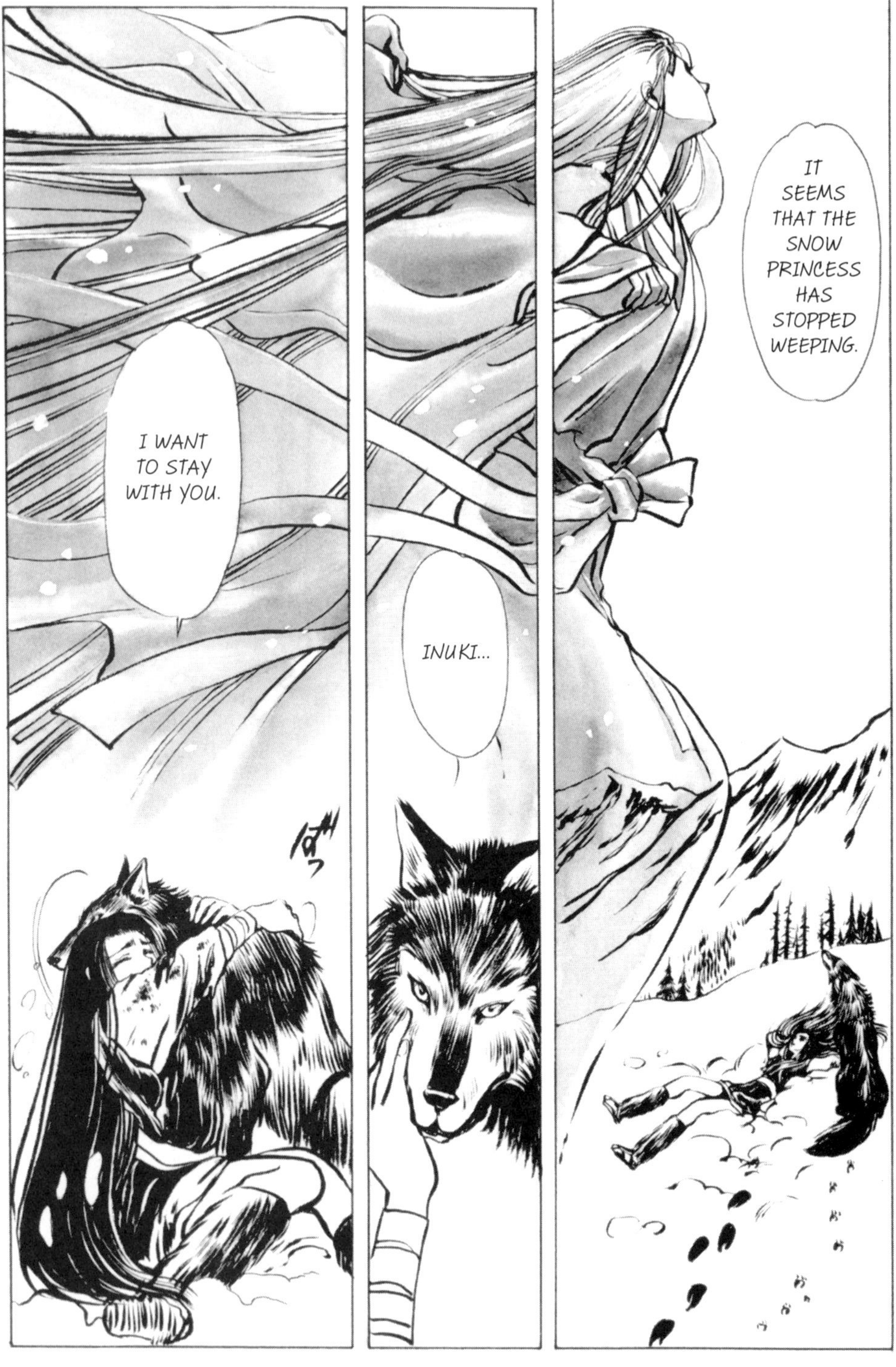
IT SEEMS THAT THE SNOW PRINCESS HAS STOPPED WEEPING.
INUKI...
I WANT TO STAY WITH YOU.

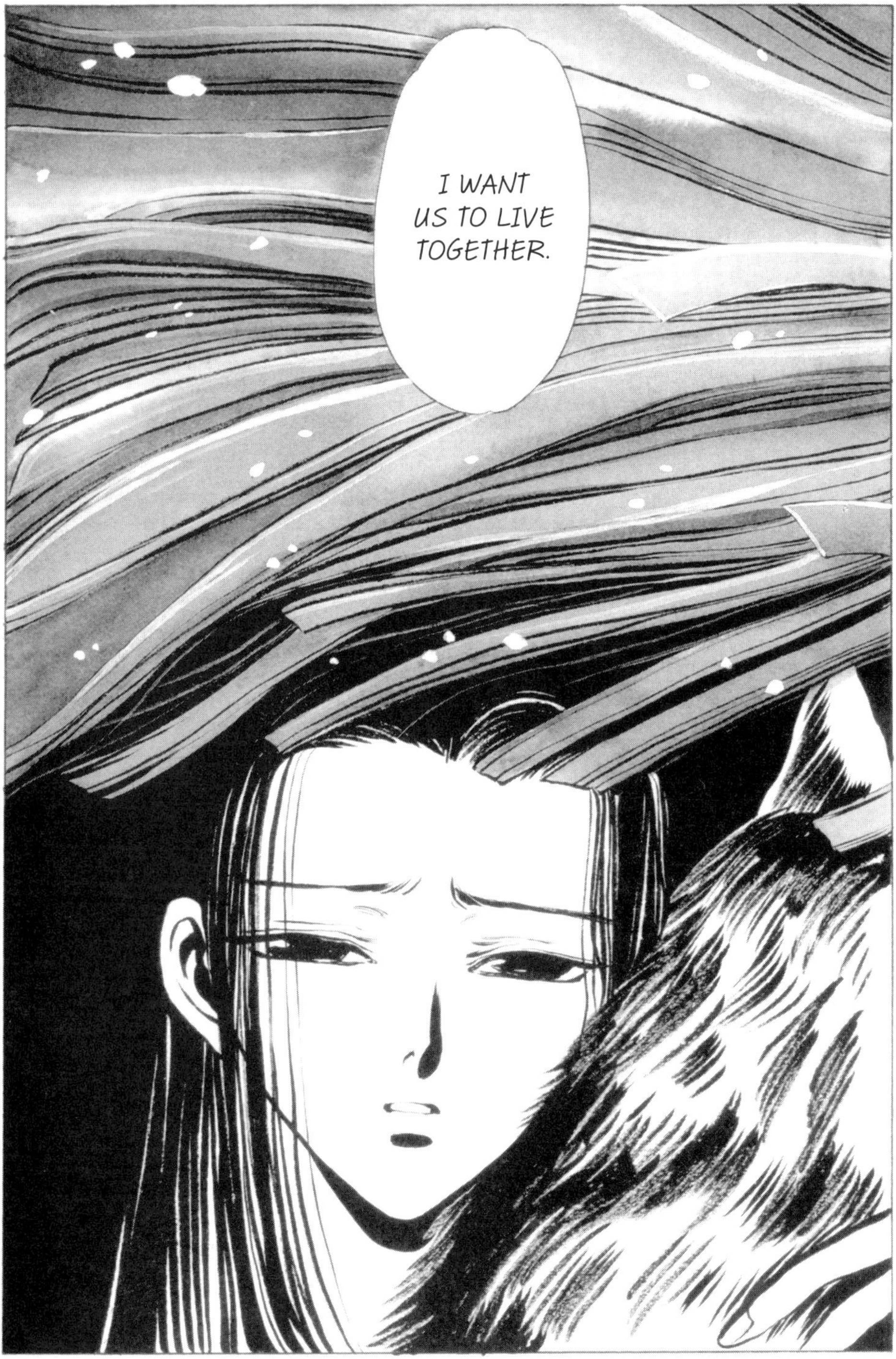
I WANT US TO LIVE TOGETHER.

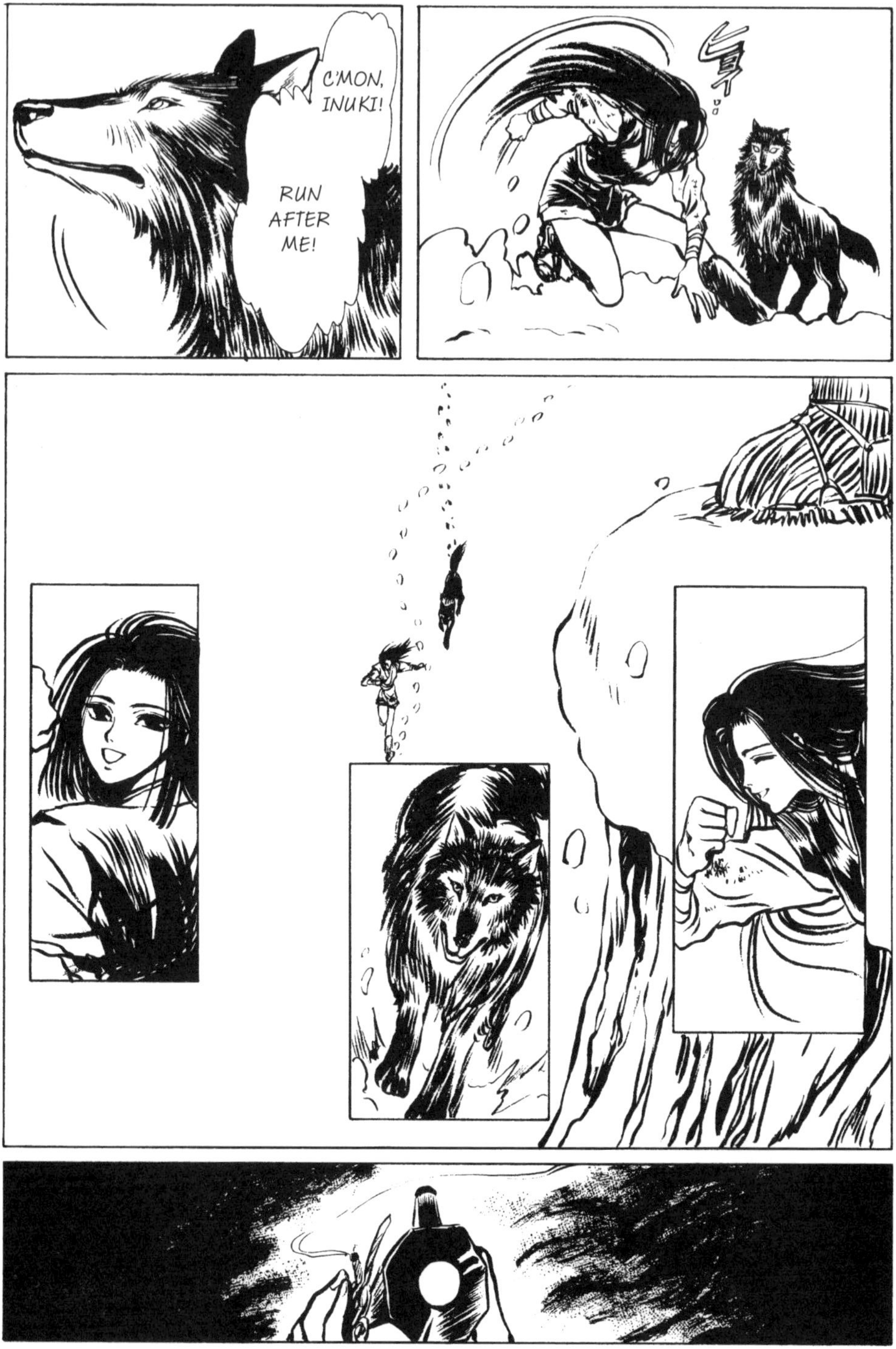
C'MON, INUKI!
RUN AFTER ME!

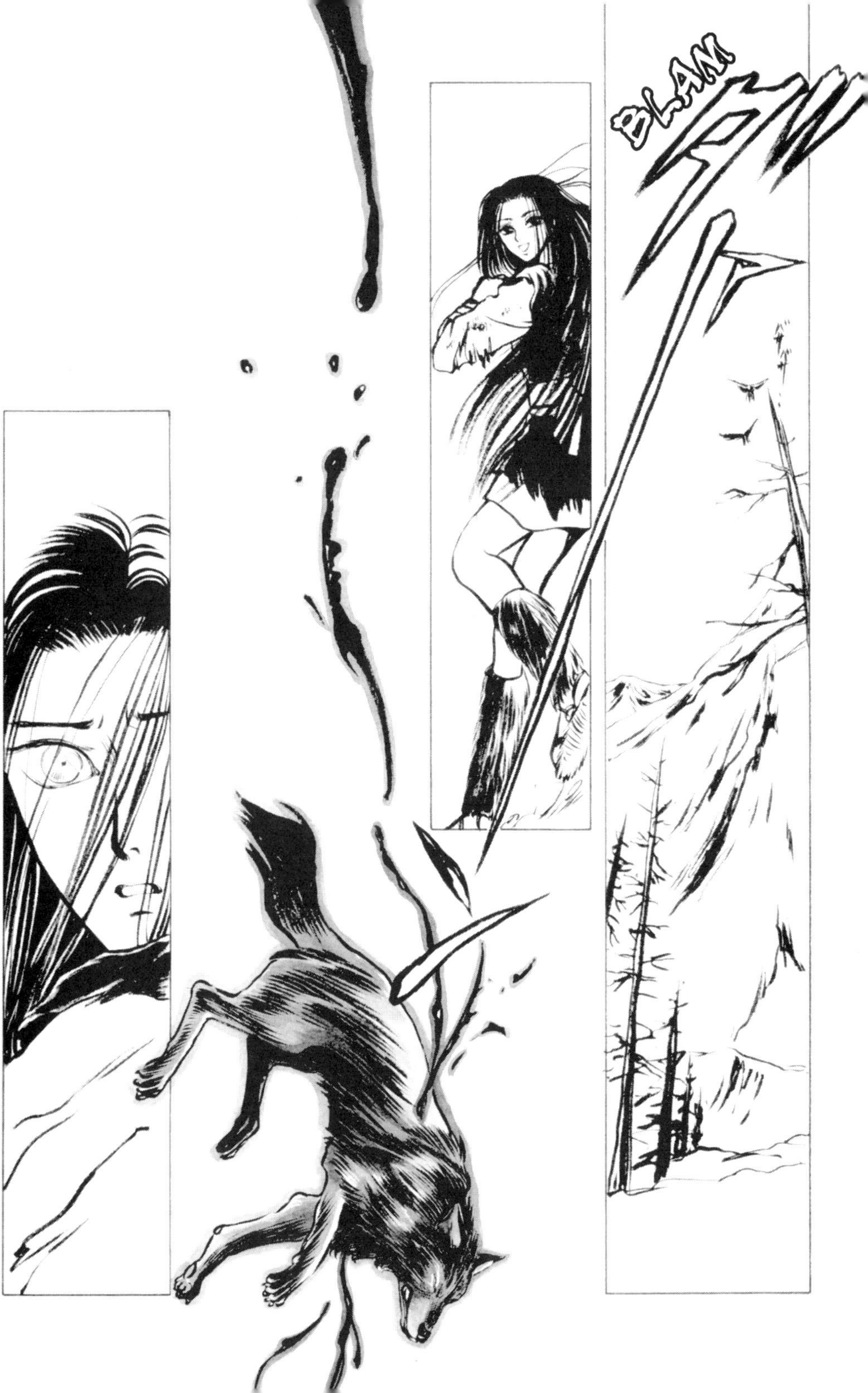
BLAM

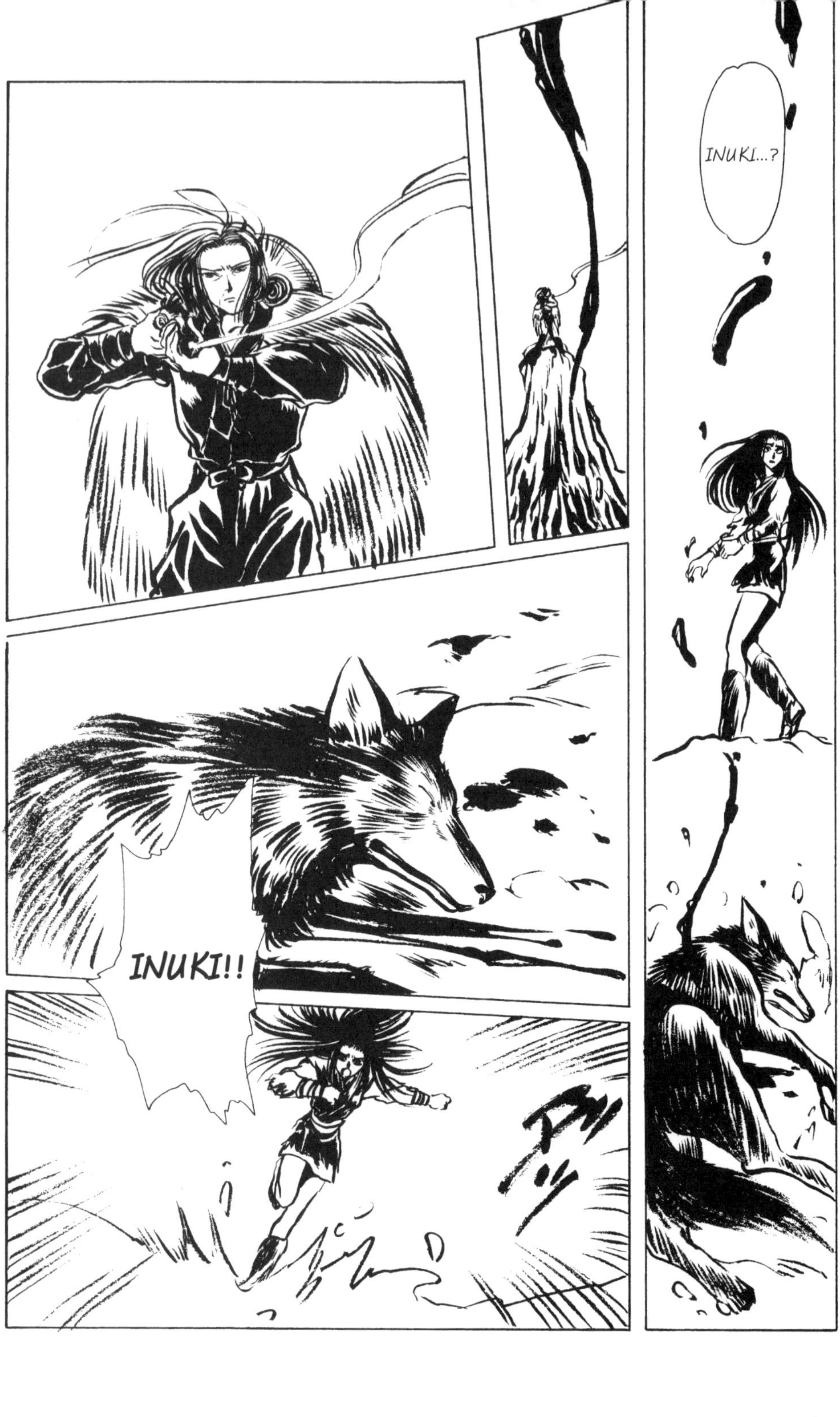
INUKI...?
INUKI!!

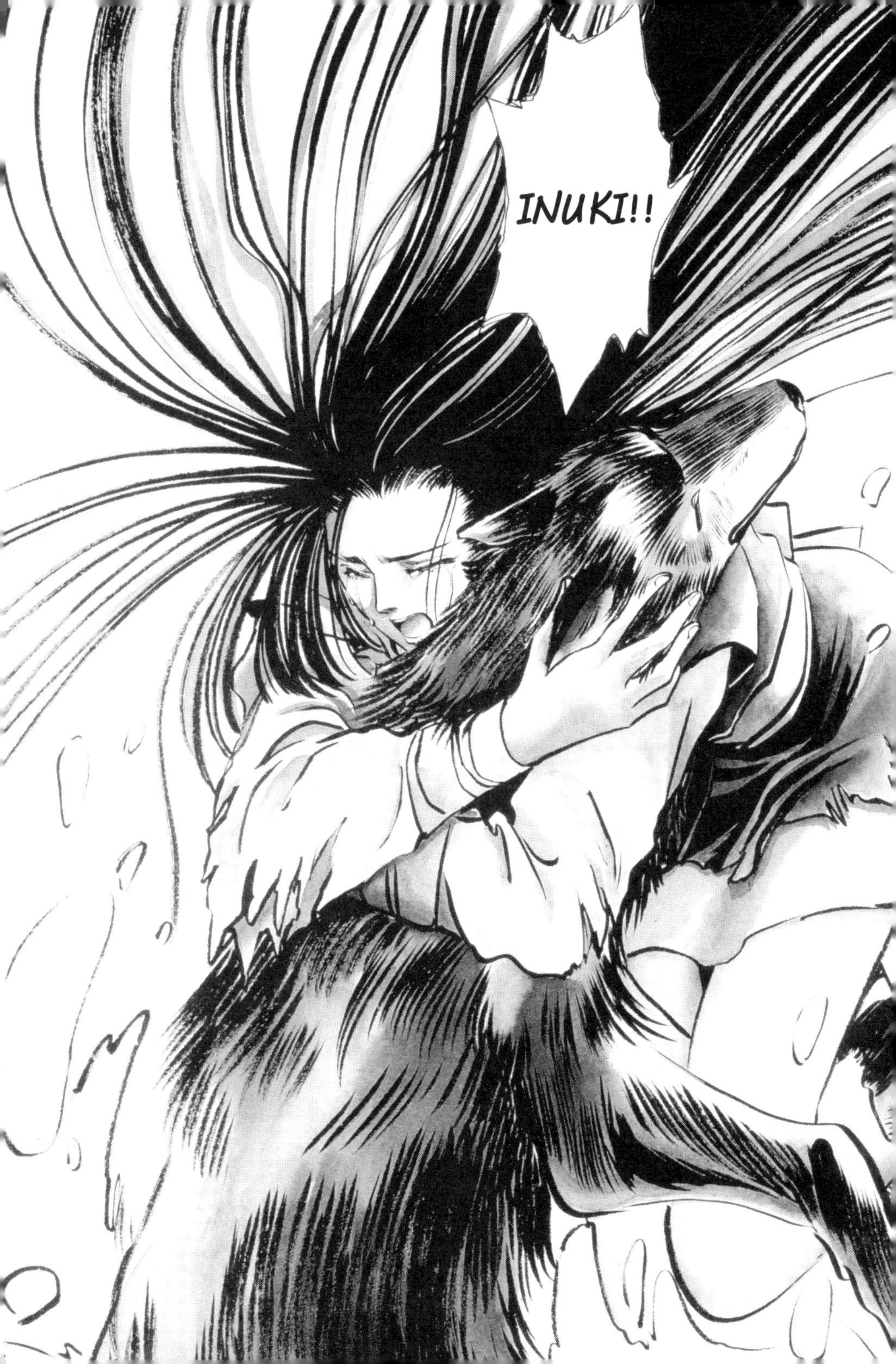
INUKI!!

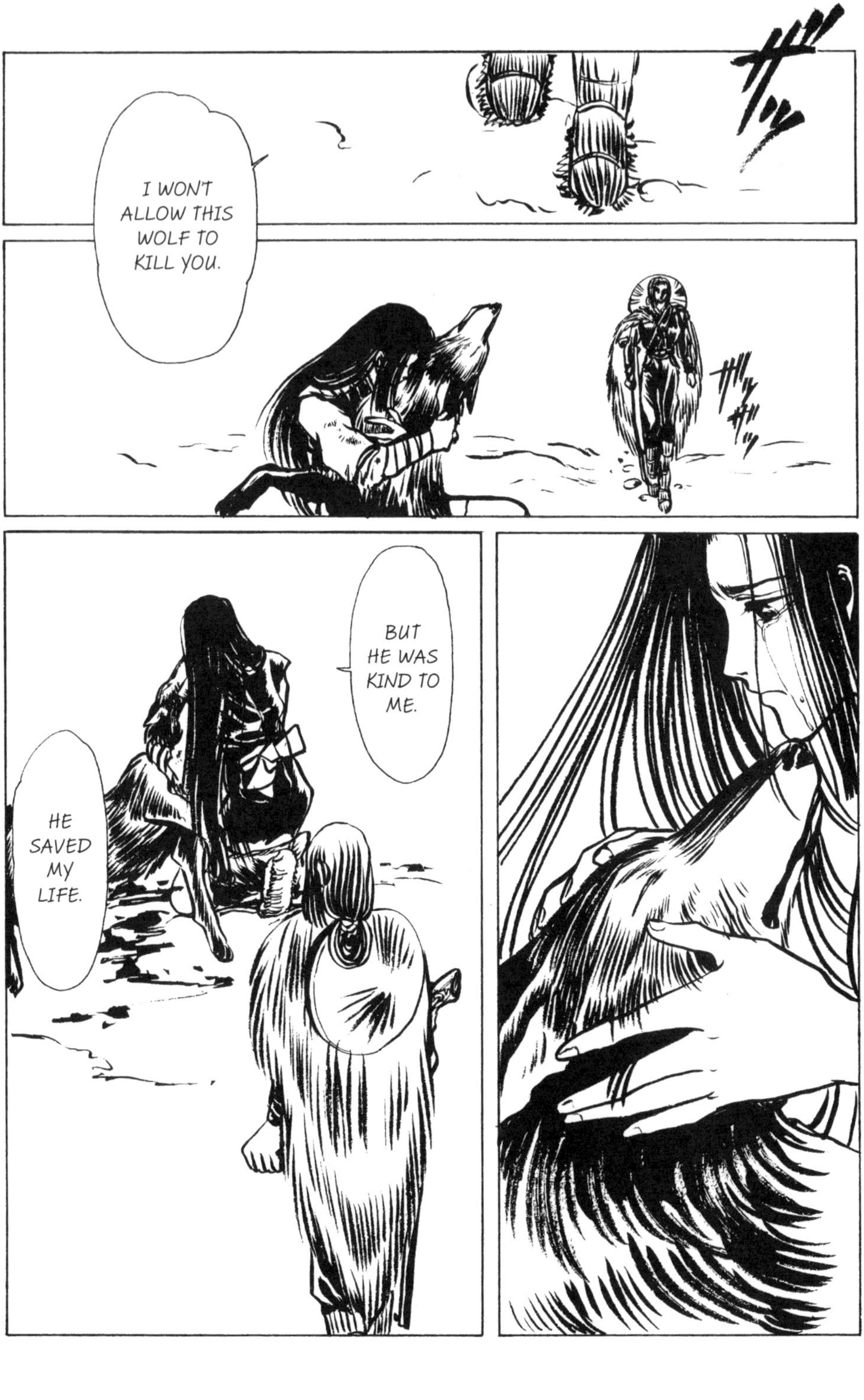
I WON'T ALLOW THIS WOLF TO KILL YOU.
BUT HE WAS KIND TO ME.
HE SAVED MY LIFE.

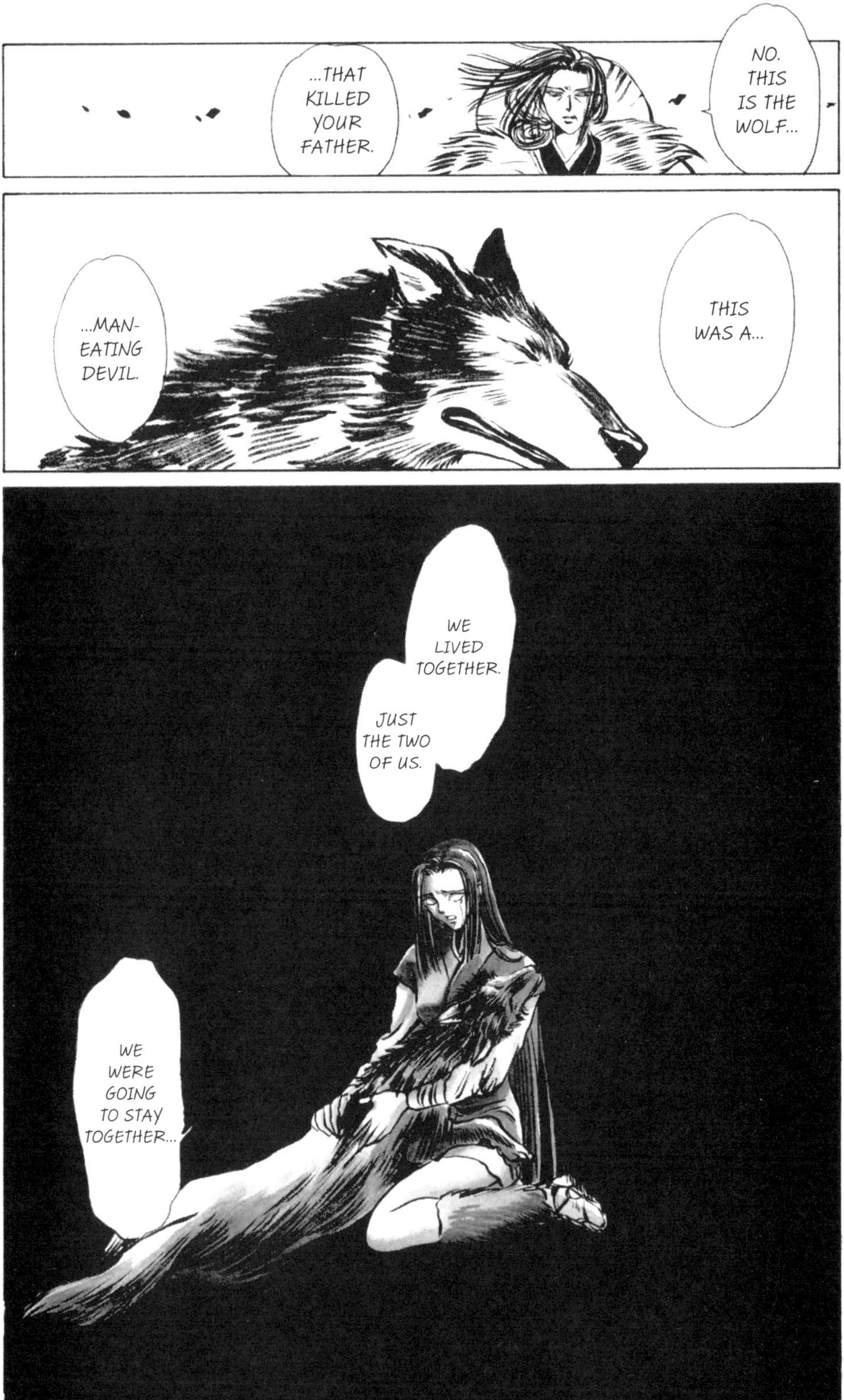
NO. THIS IS THE WOLF...
...THAT KILLED YOUR FATHER.
THIS WAS A...
...MAN-EATING DEVIL.
WE LIVED TOGETHER.
JUST THE TWO OF US.
WE WERE GOING TO STAY TOGETHER...

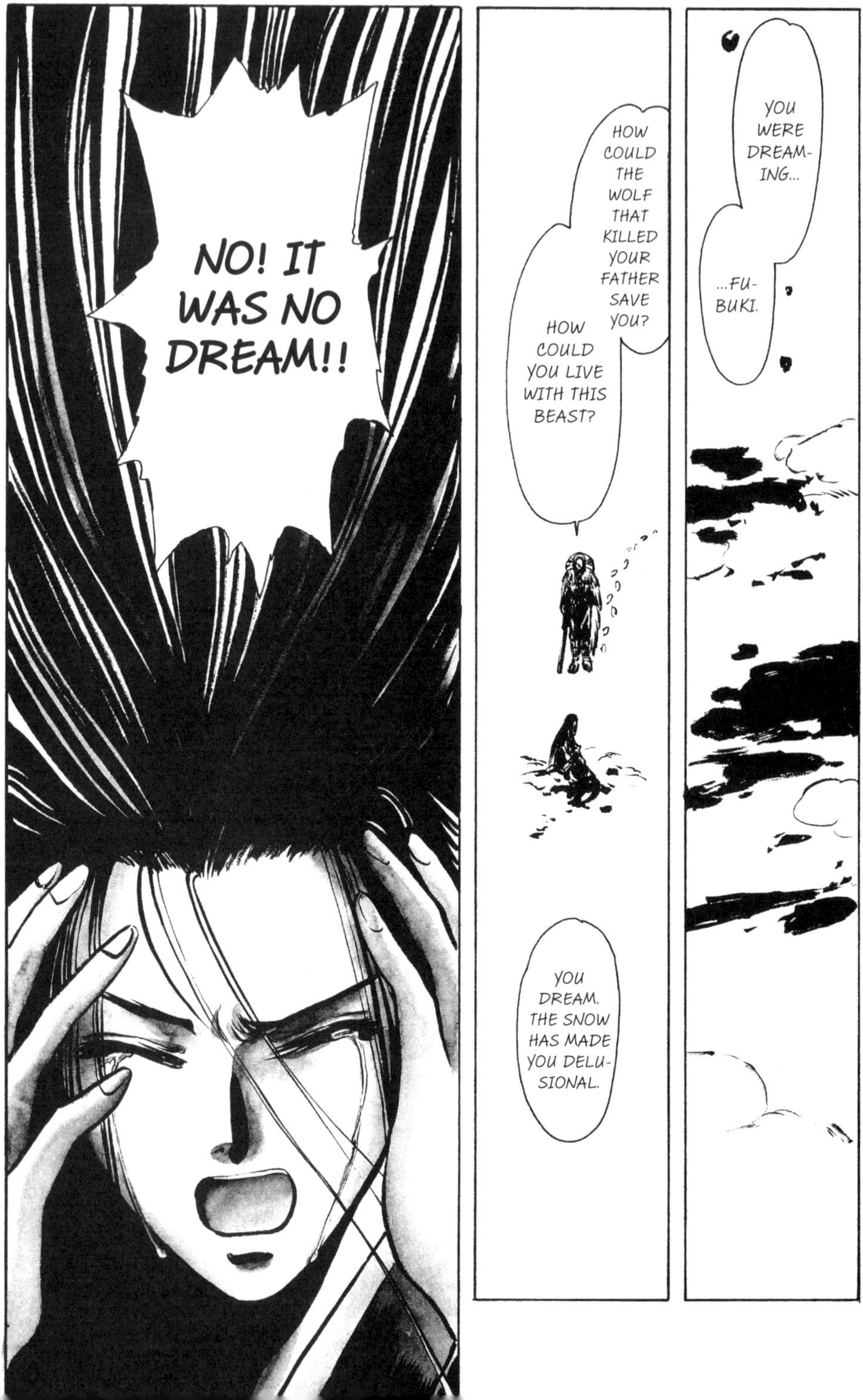

YOU WERE DREAMING...
...FUBUKI.
HOW COULD THE WOLF THAT KILLED YOUR FATHER SAVE YOU?
HOW COULD YOU LIVE WITH THIS BEAST?
YOU DREAM. THE SNOW HAS MADE YOU DELUSIONAL.
NO! IT WAS NO DREAM!!

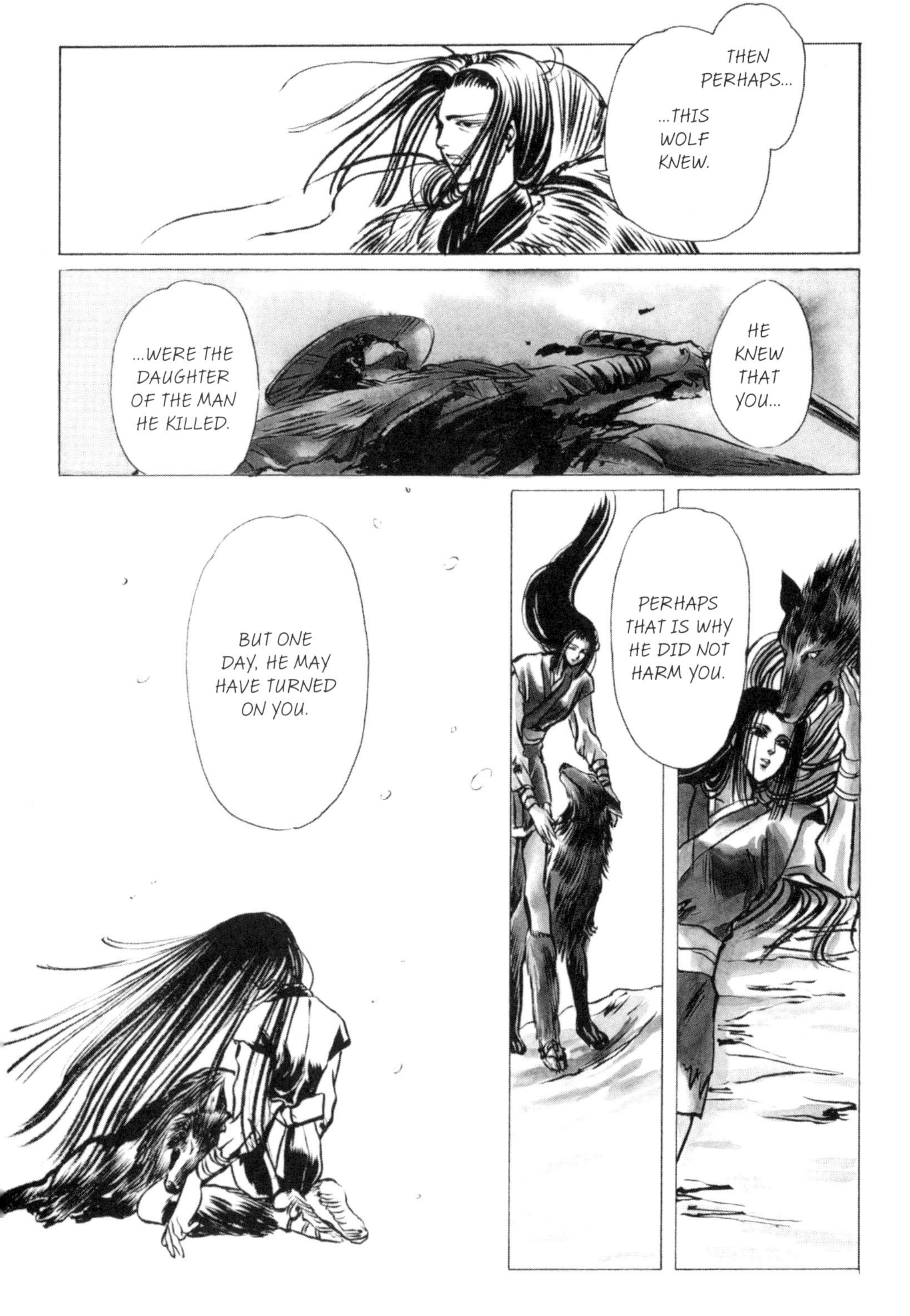
THEN PERHAPS...
...THIS WOLF KNEW.
HE KNEW THAT YOU...
...WERE THE DAUGHTER OF THE MAN HE KILLED.
PERHAPS THAT IS WHY HE DID NOT HARM YOU.
BUT ONE DAY, HE MAY HAVE TURNED ON YOU.

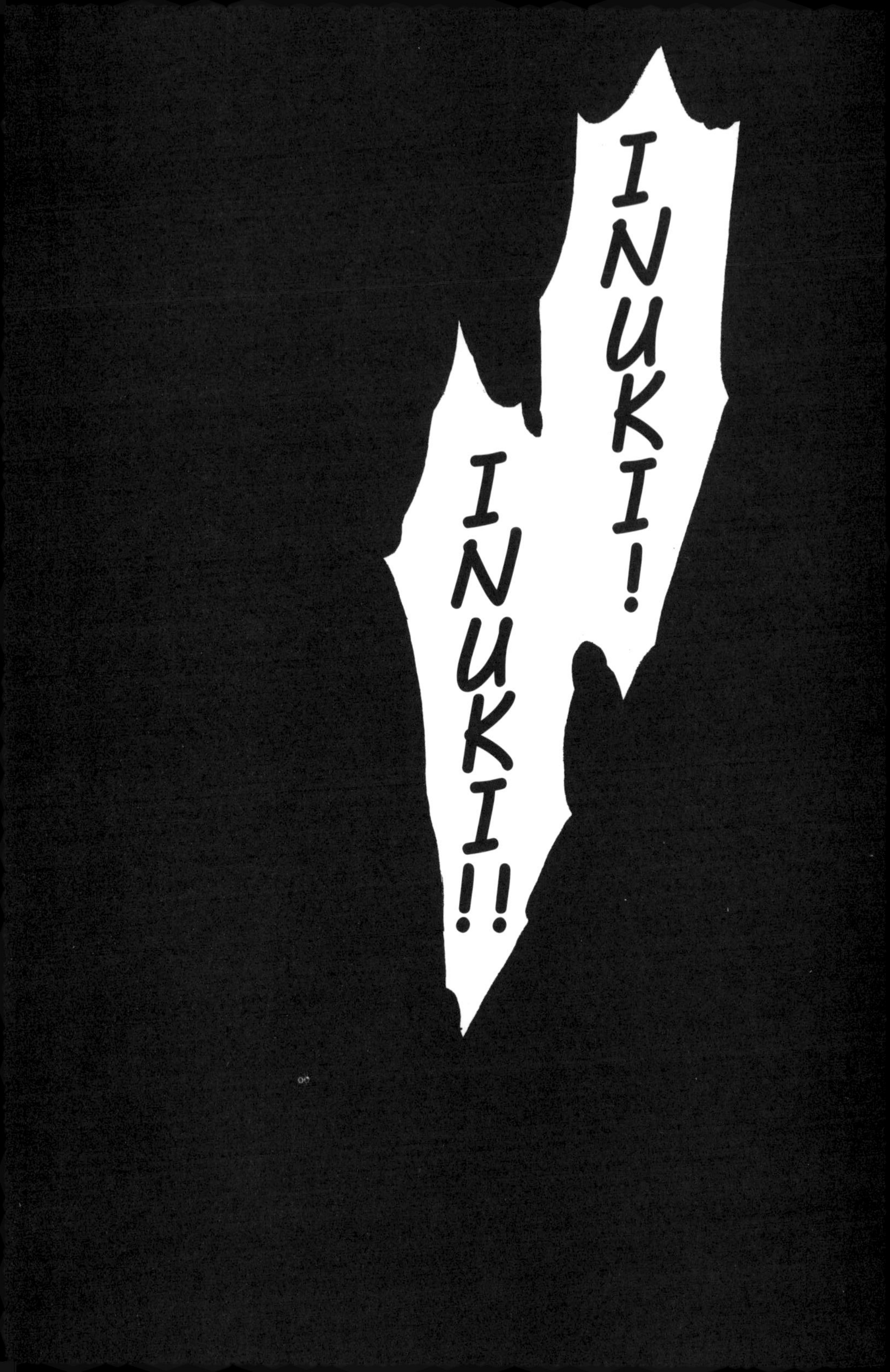
INUKI!
INUKI!!

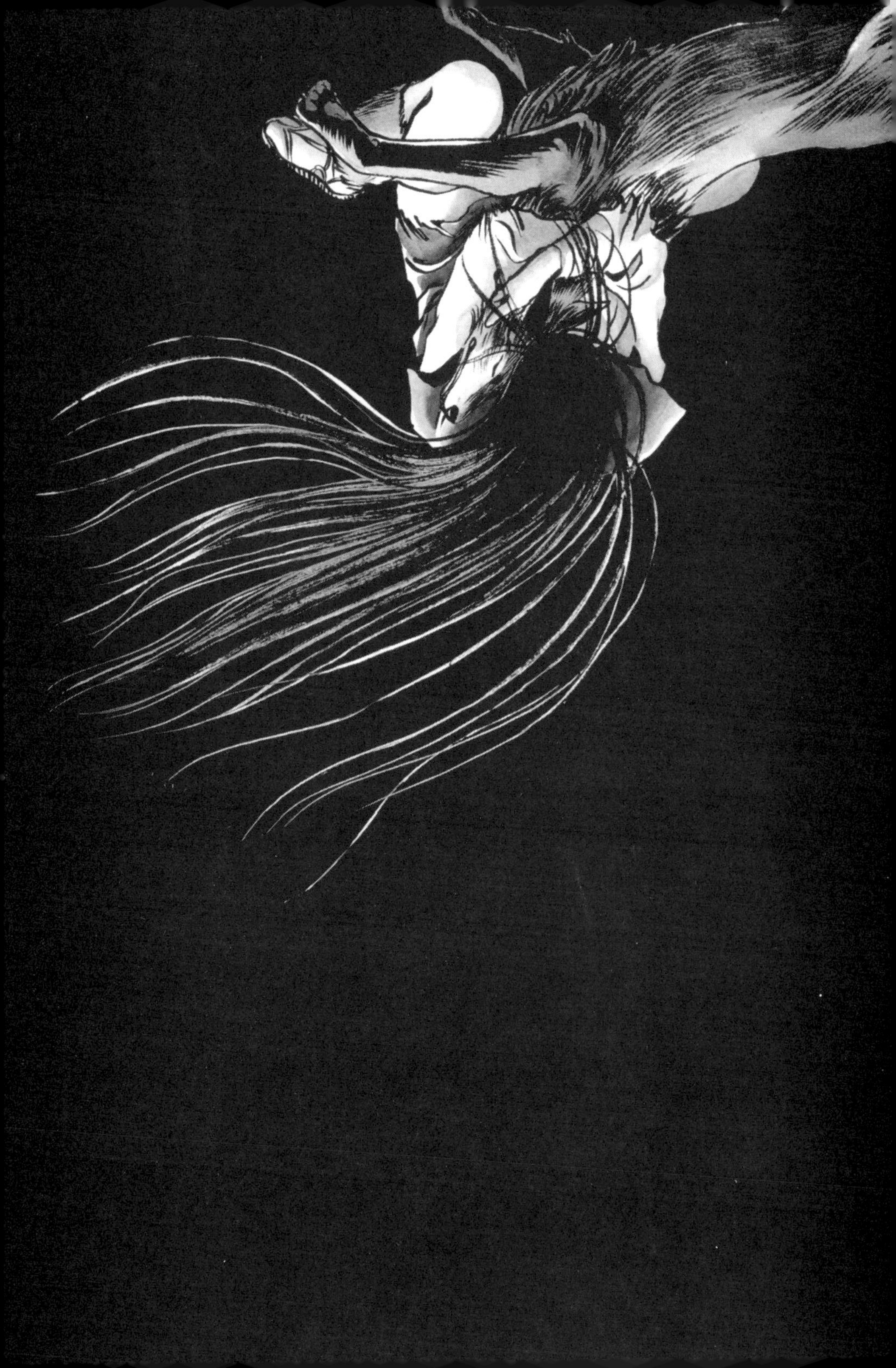

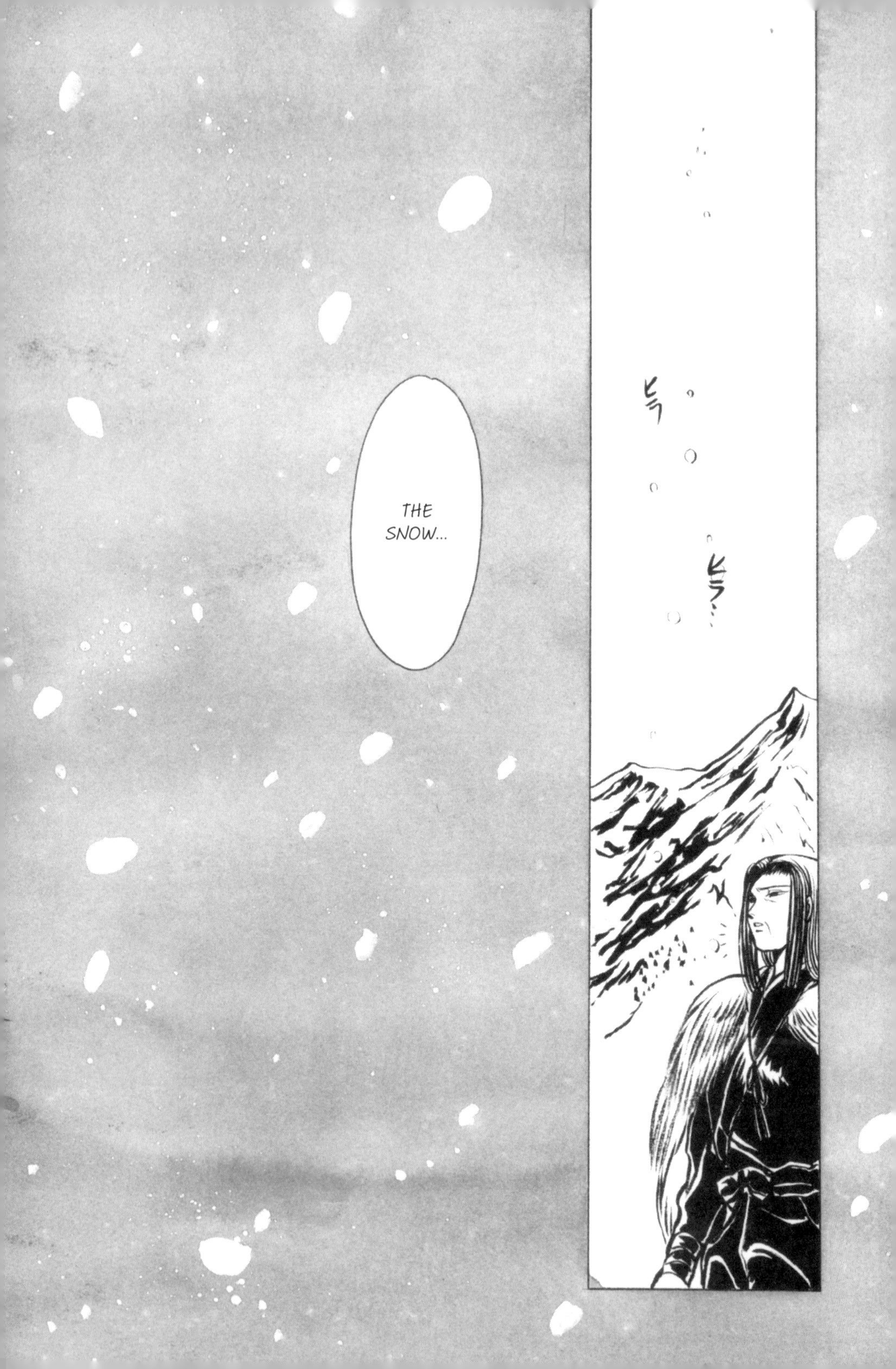
ヒラ…
ヒラ
THE SNOW...

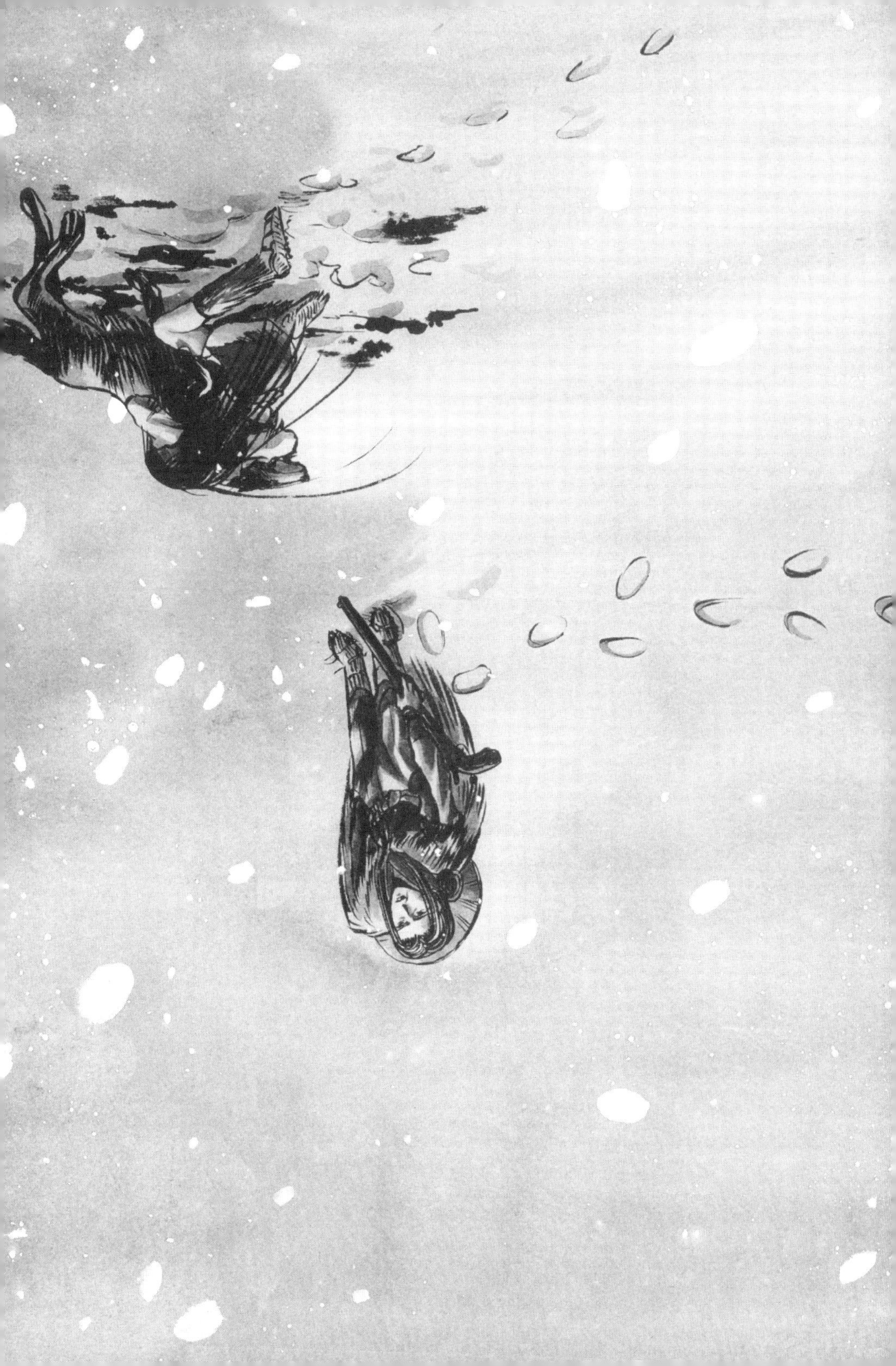

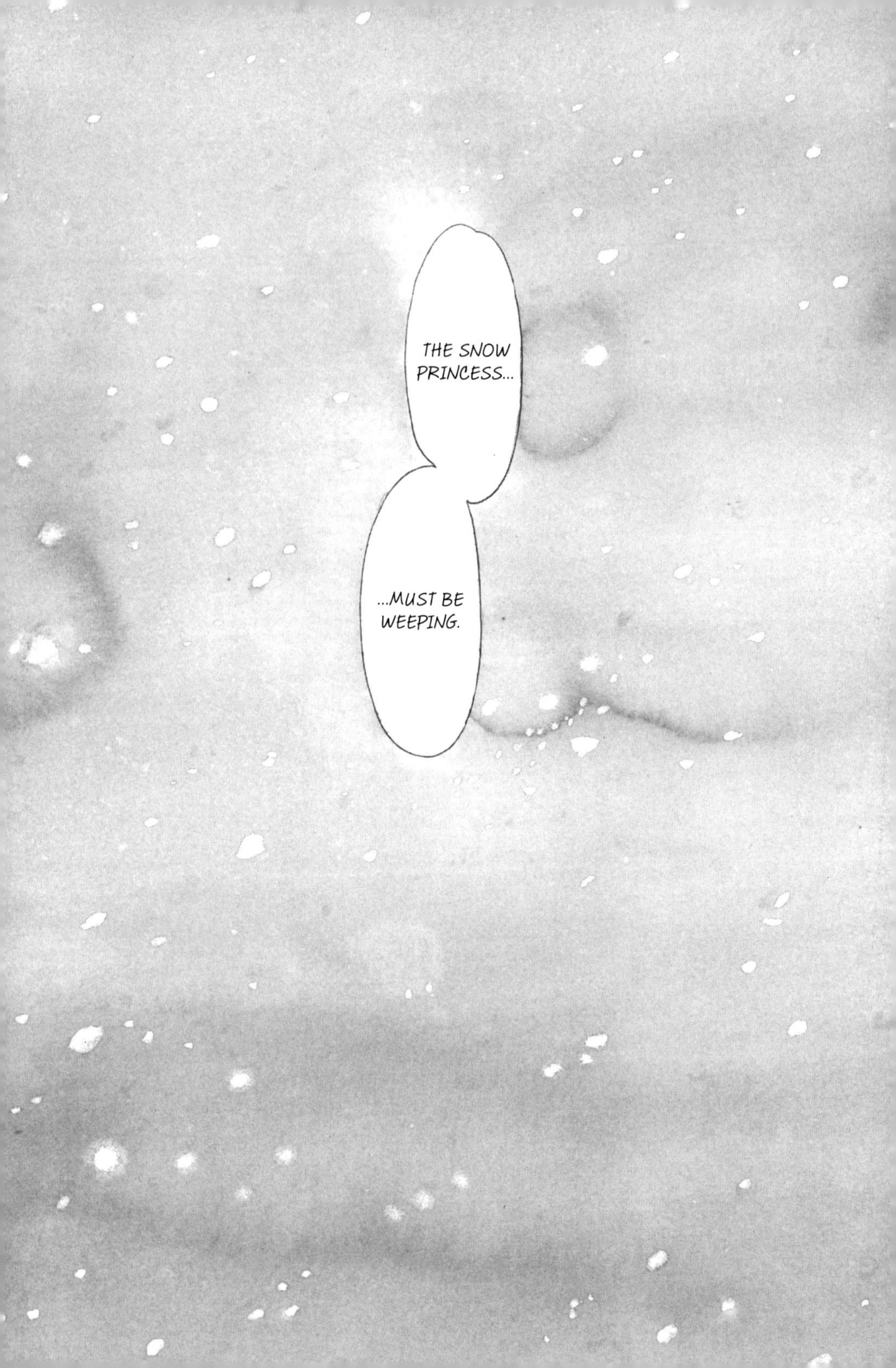
THE SNOW PRINCESS...
...MUST BE WEEPING.

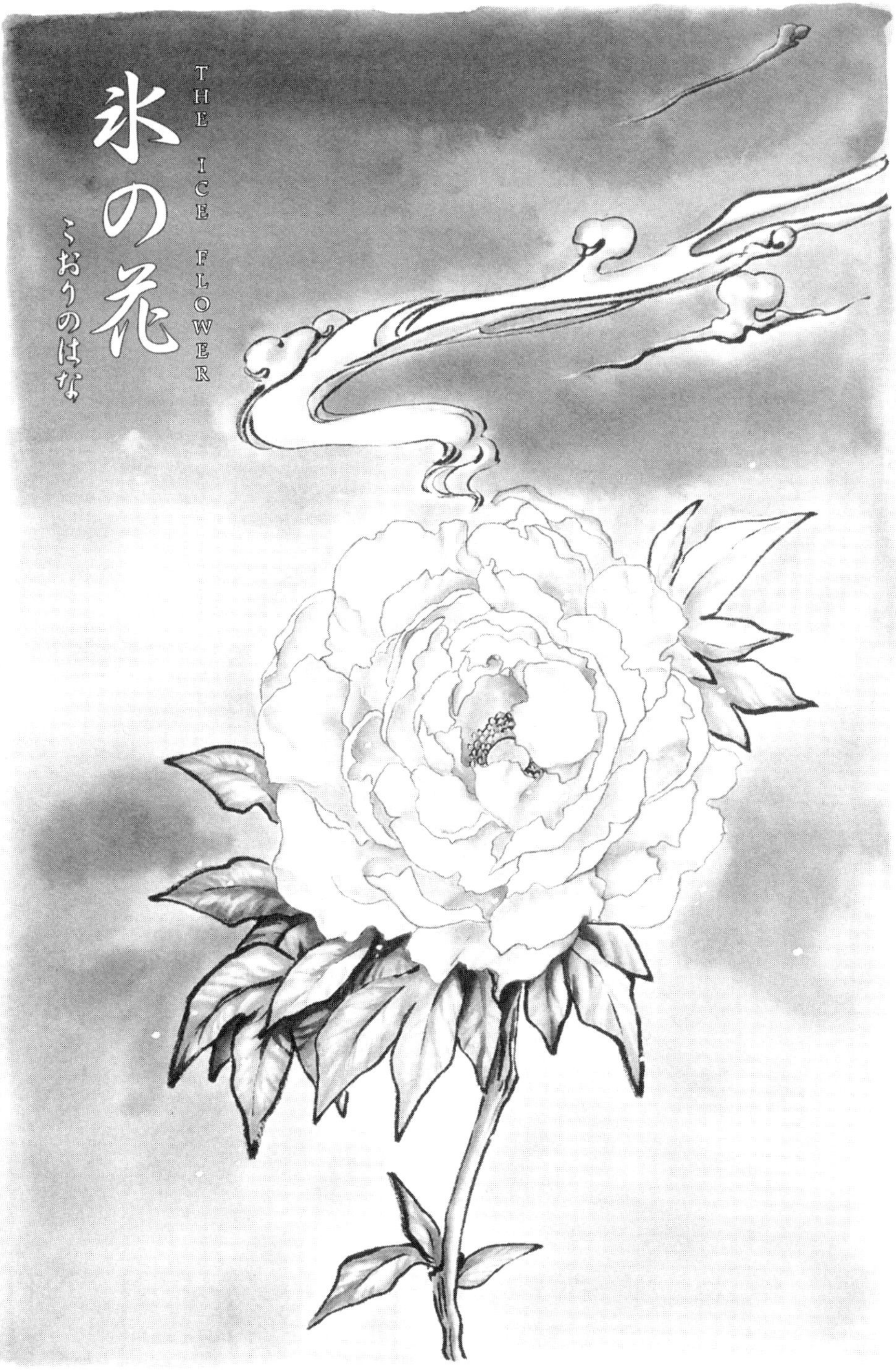
氷の花
THE ICE FLOWER
こおりのはな

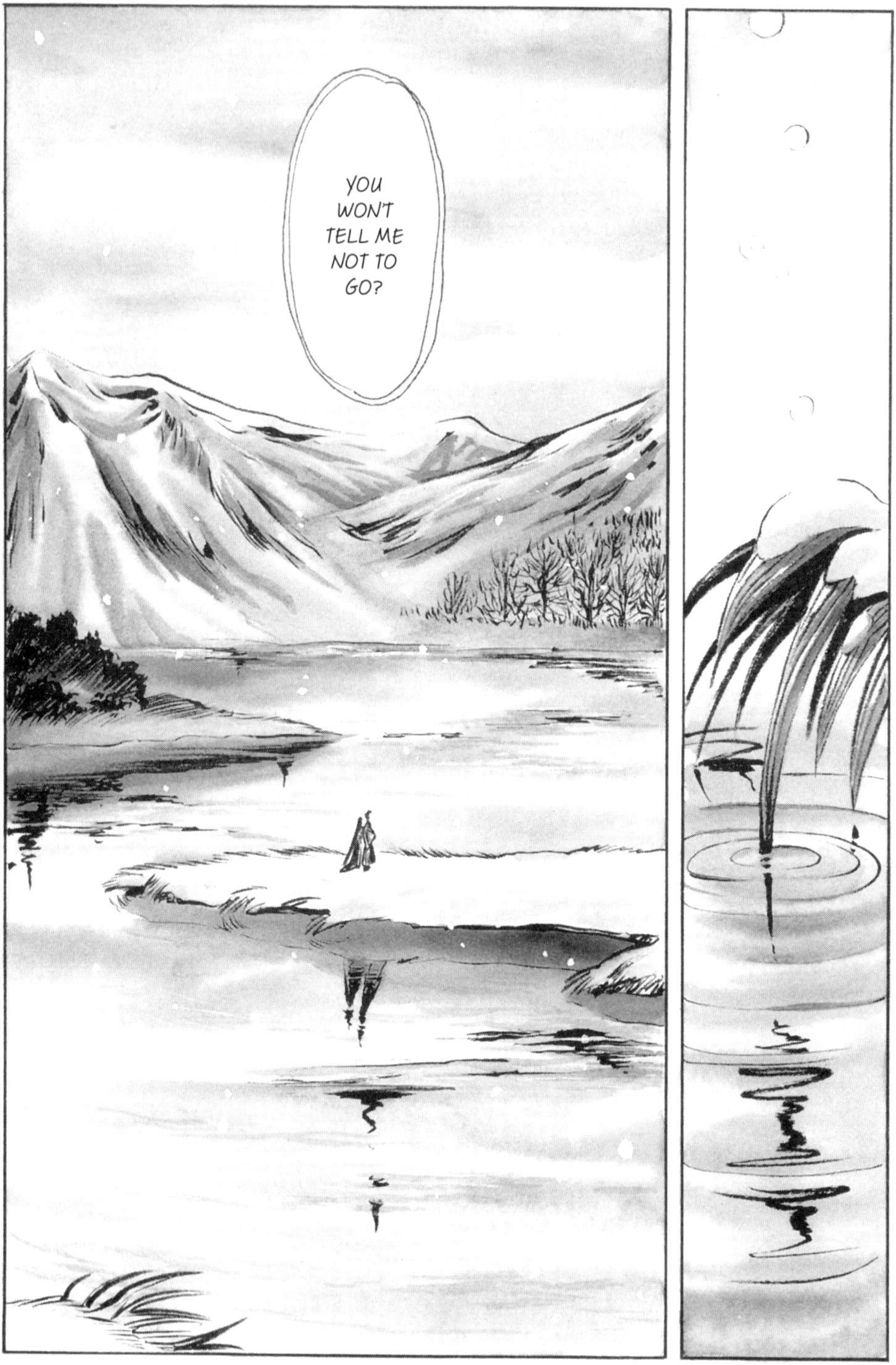
YOU WON'T TELL ME NOT TO GO?

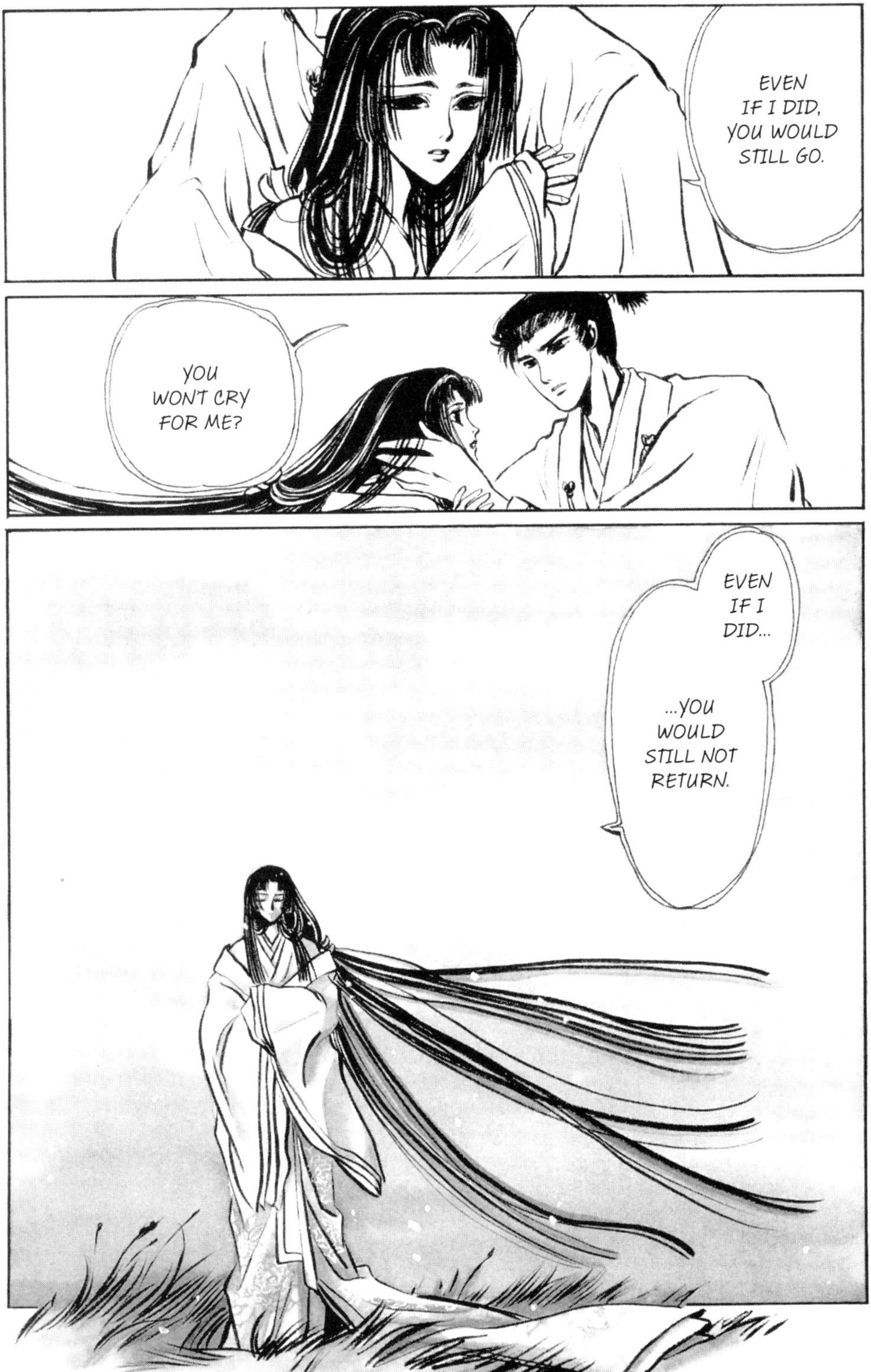
EVEN IF I DID, YOU WOULD STILL GO.
YOU WON'T CRY FOR ME?
EVEN IF I DID...
...YOU WOULD STILL NOT RETURN.

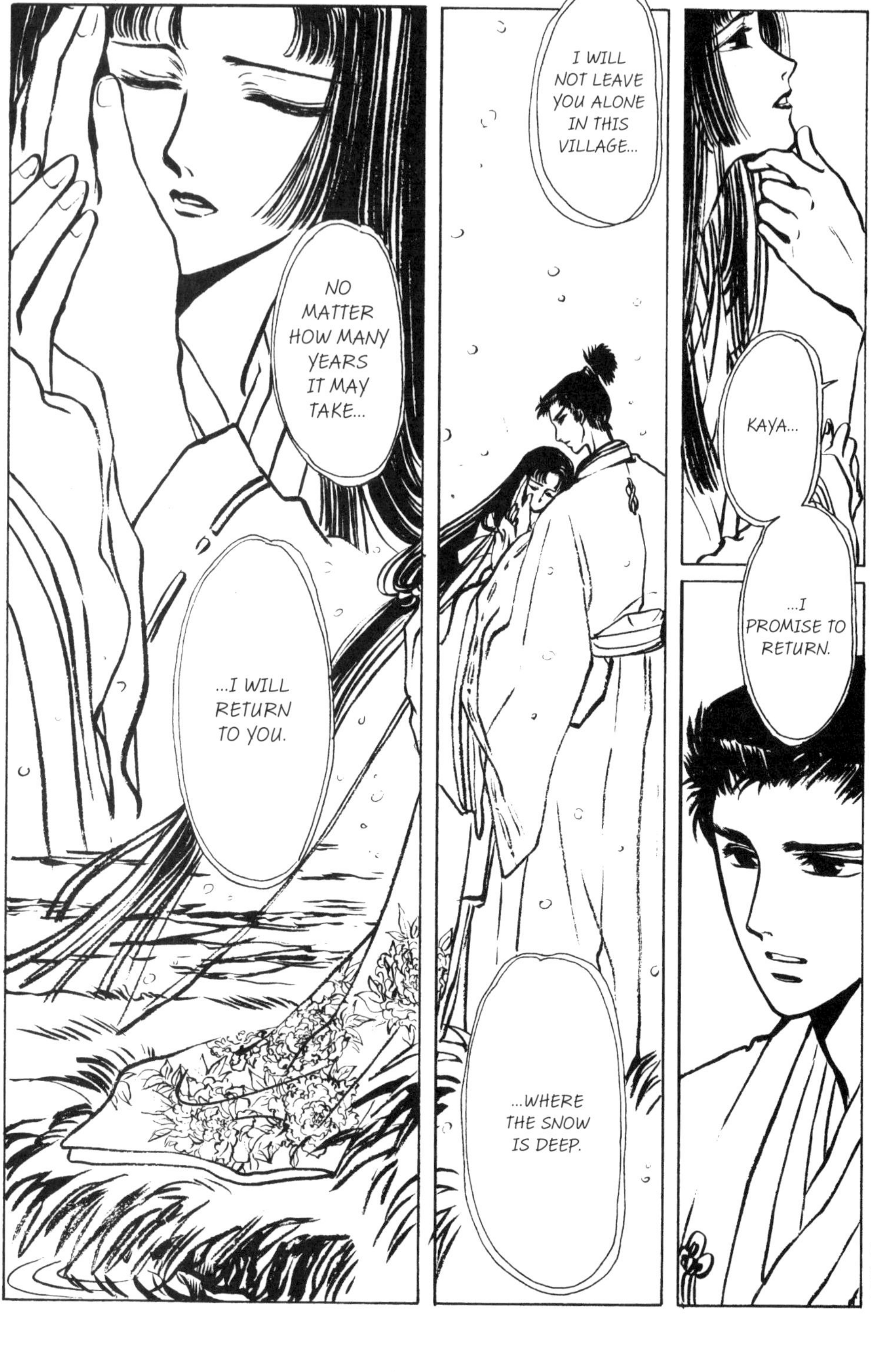
KAYA...
...I PROMISE TO RETURN.
I WILL NOT LEAVE YOU ALONE IN THIS VILLAGE...
...WHERE THE SNOW IS DEEP.
NO MATTER HOW MANY YEARS IT MAY TAKE...
...I WILL RETURN TO YOU.

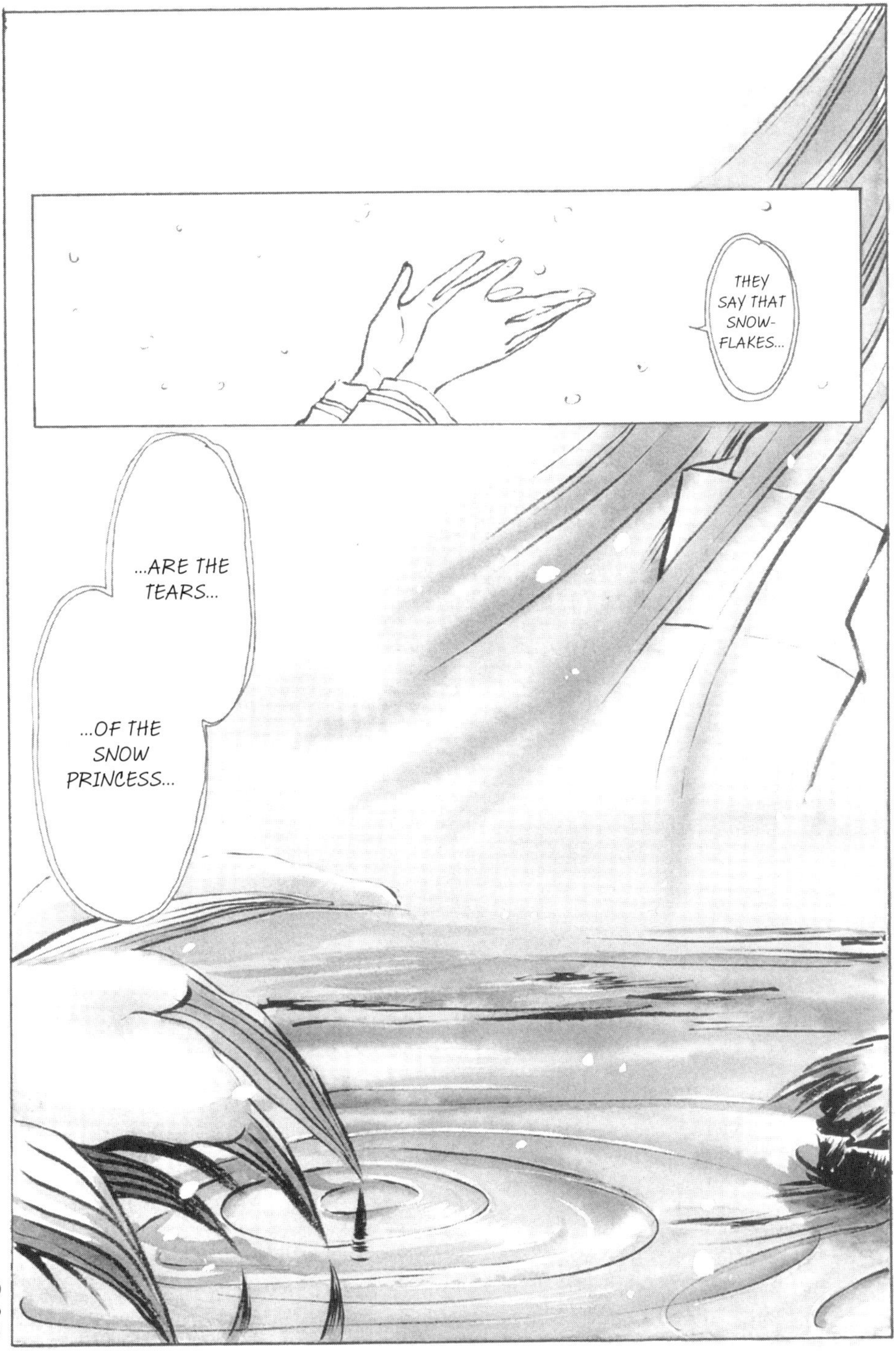
THEY SAY THAT SNOW-FLAKES...
...ARE THE TEARS...
...OF THE SNOW PRINCESS...

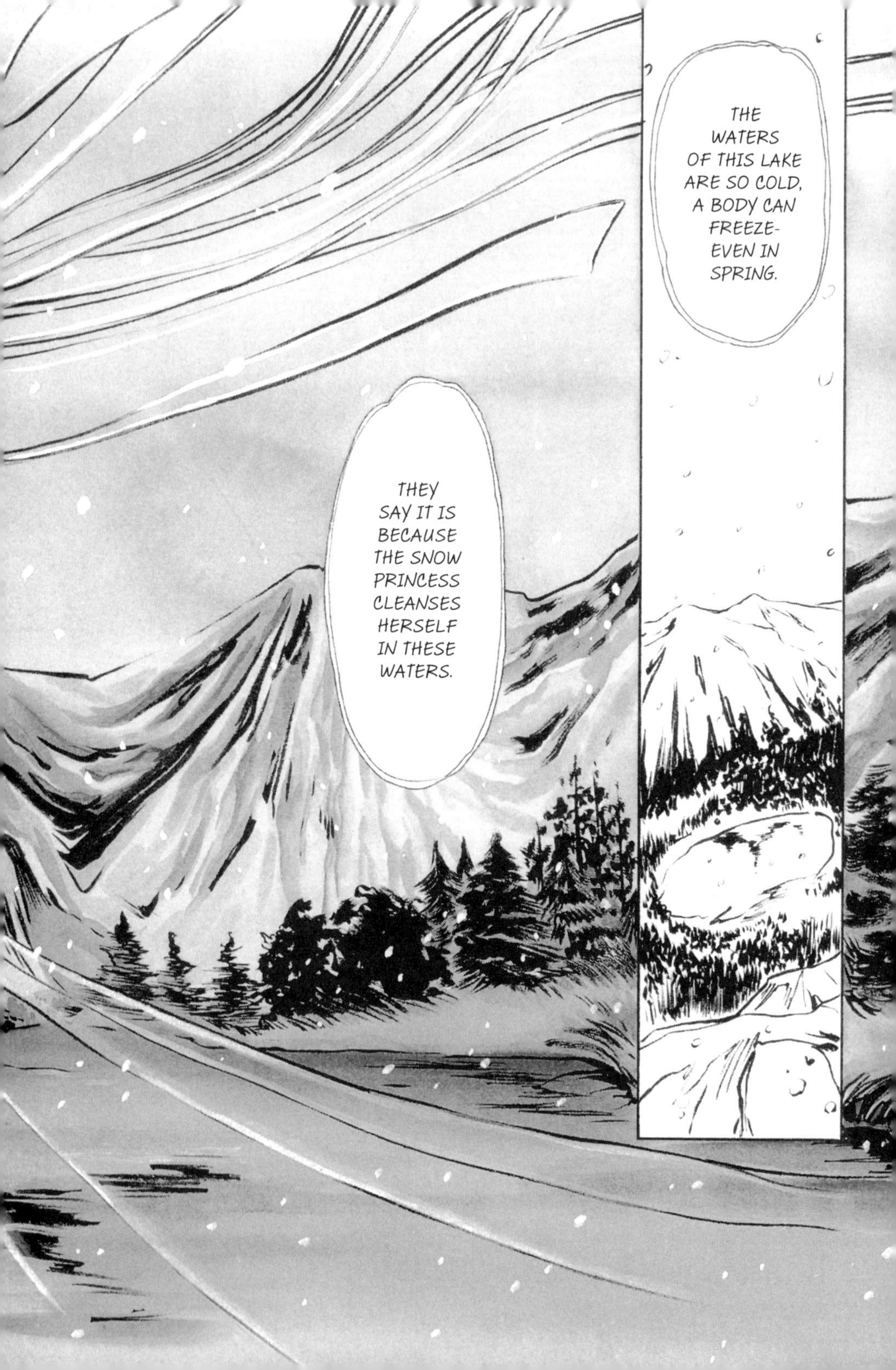
THE WATERS OF THIS LAKE ARE SO COLD, A BODY CAN FREEZE-EVEN IN SPRING.
THEY SAY IT IS BECAUSE THE SNOW PRINCESS CLEANSES HERSELF IN THESE WATERS.

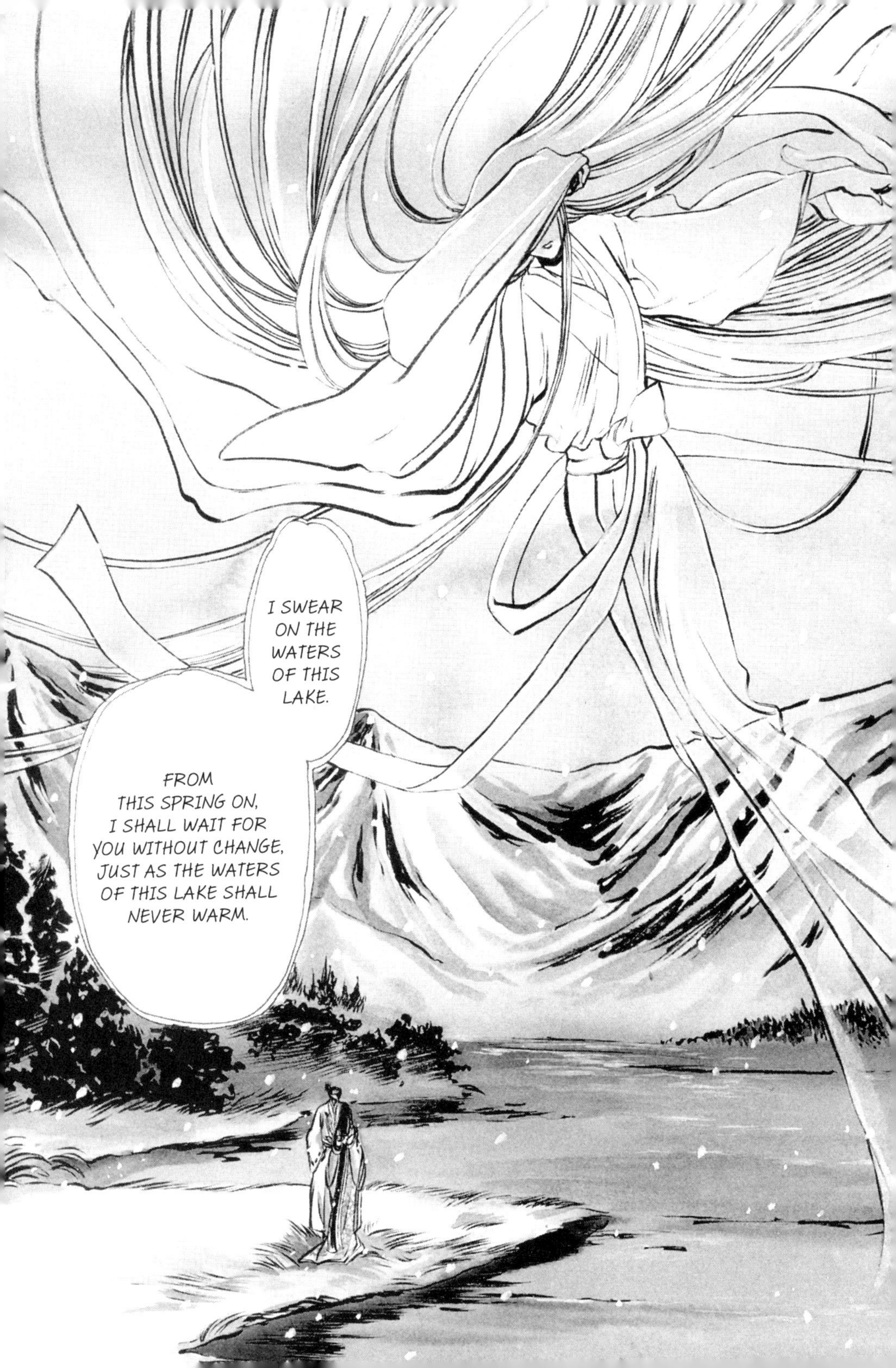
I SWEAR ON THE WATERS OF THIS LAKE.
FROM THIS SPRING ON, I SHALL WAIT FOR YOU WITHOUT CHANGE, JUST AS THE WATERS OF THIS LAKE SHALL NEVER WARM.

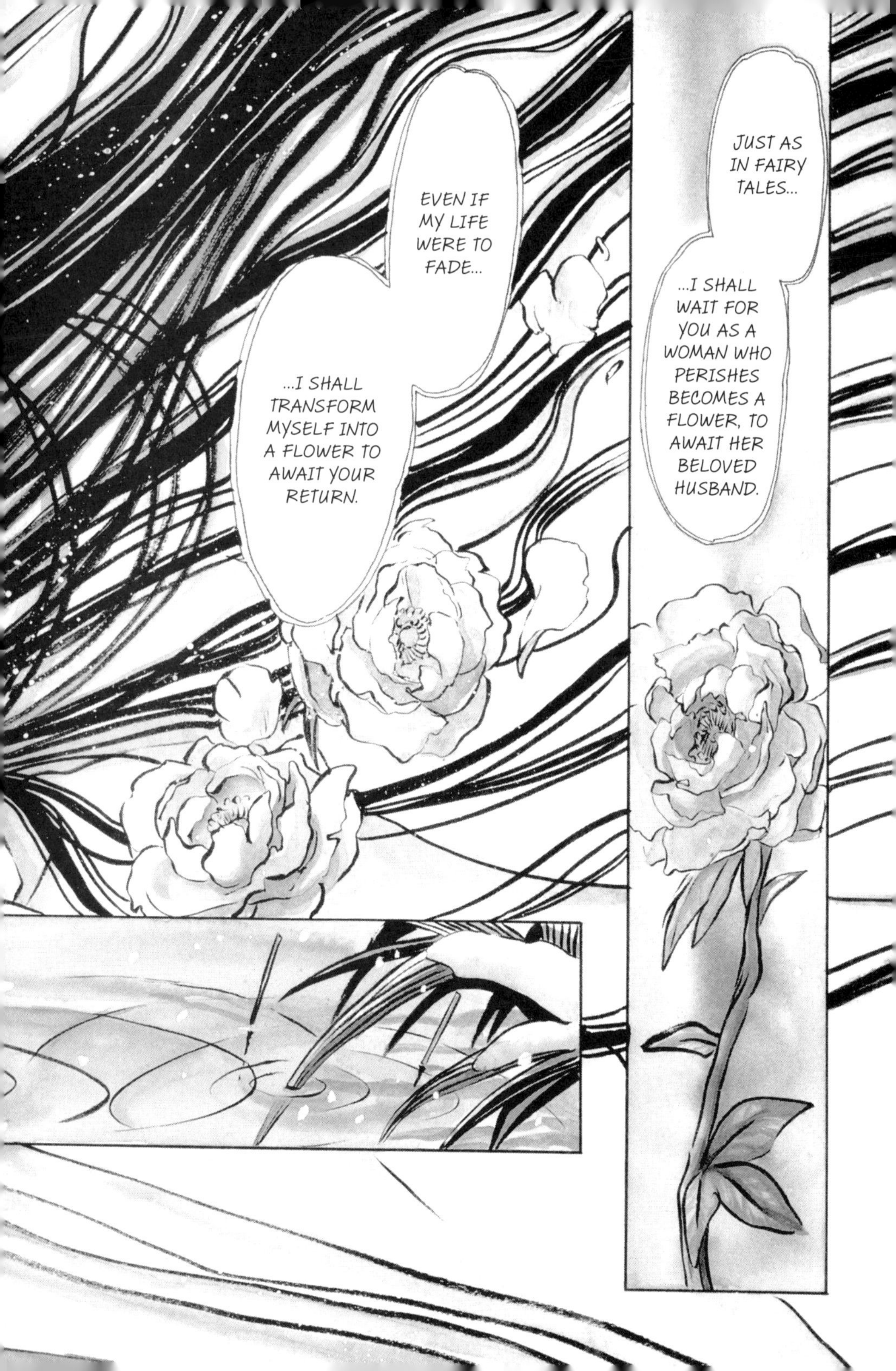
JUST AS IN FAIRY TALES...
...I SHALL WAIT FOR YOU AS A WOMAN WHO PERISHES BECOMES A FLOWER, TO AWAIT HER BELOVED HUSBAND.
EVEN IF MY LIFE WERE TO FADE...
...I SHALL TRANSFORM MYSELF INTO A FLOWER TO AWAIT YOUR RETURN.

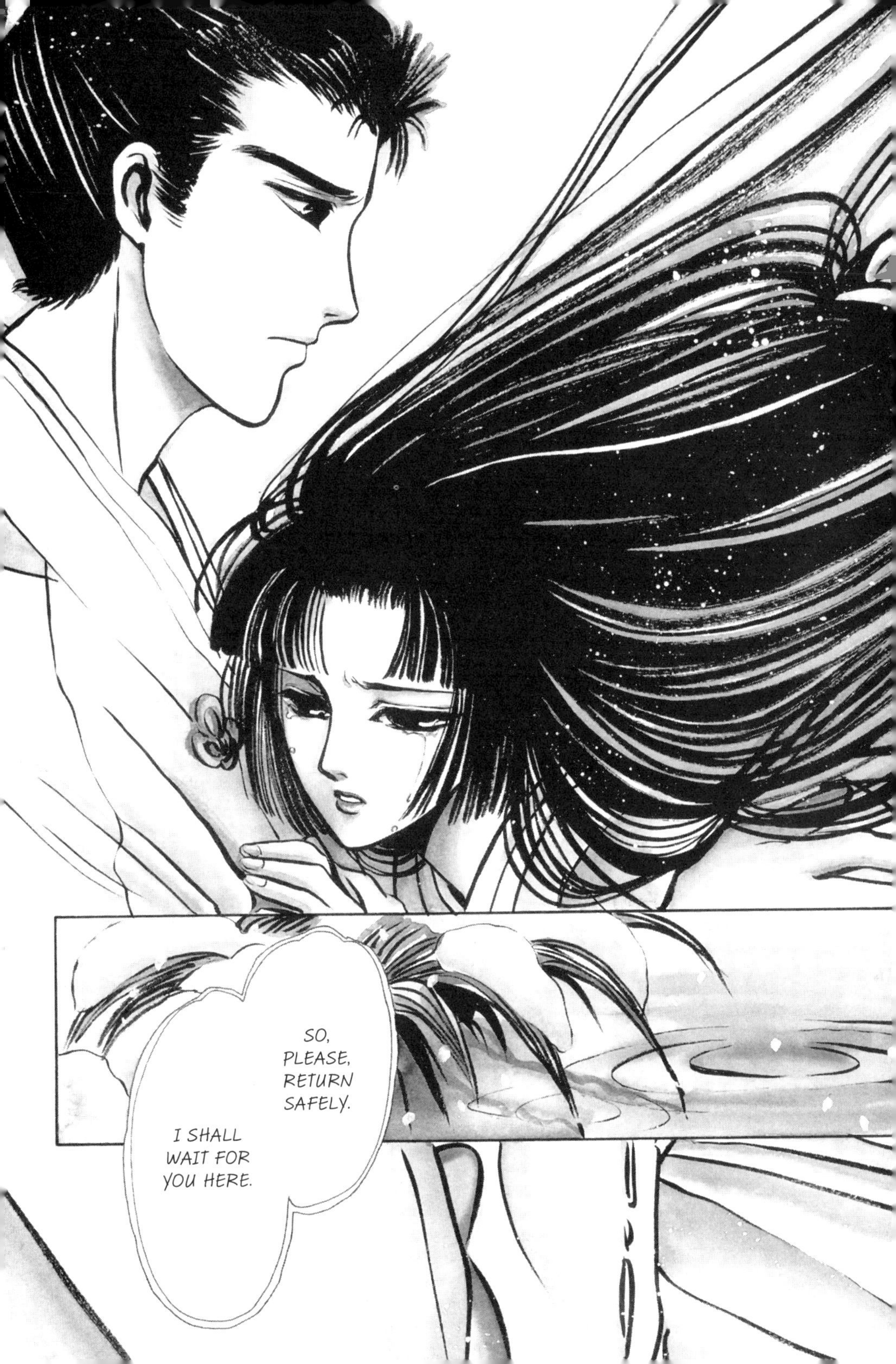
SO, PLEASE, RETURN SAFELY.
I SHALL WAIT FOR YOU HERE.

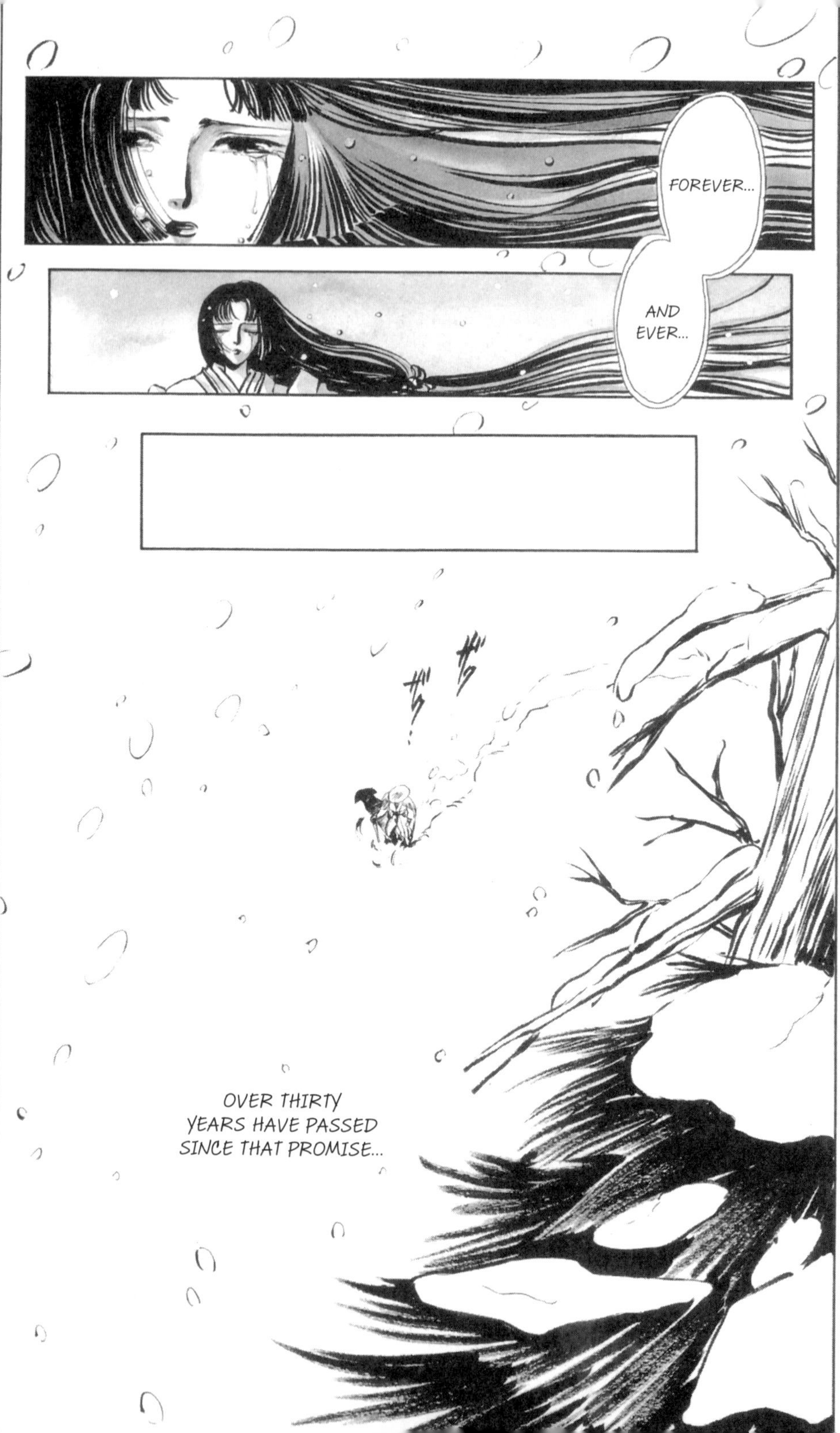
FOREVER...
AND EVER...
OVER THIRTY YEARS HAVE PASSED SINCE THAT PROMISE...

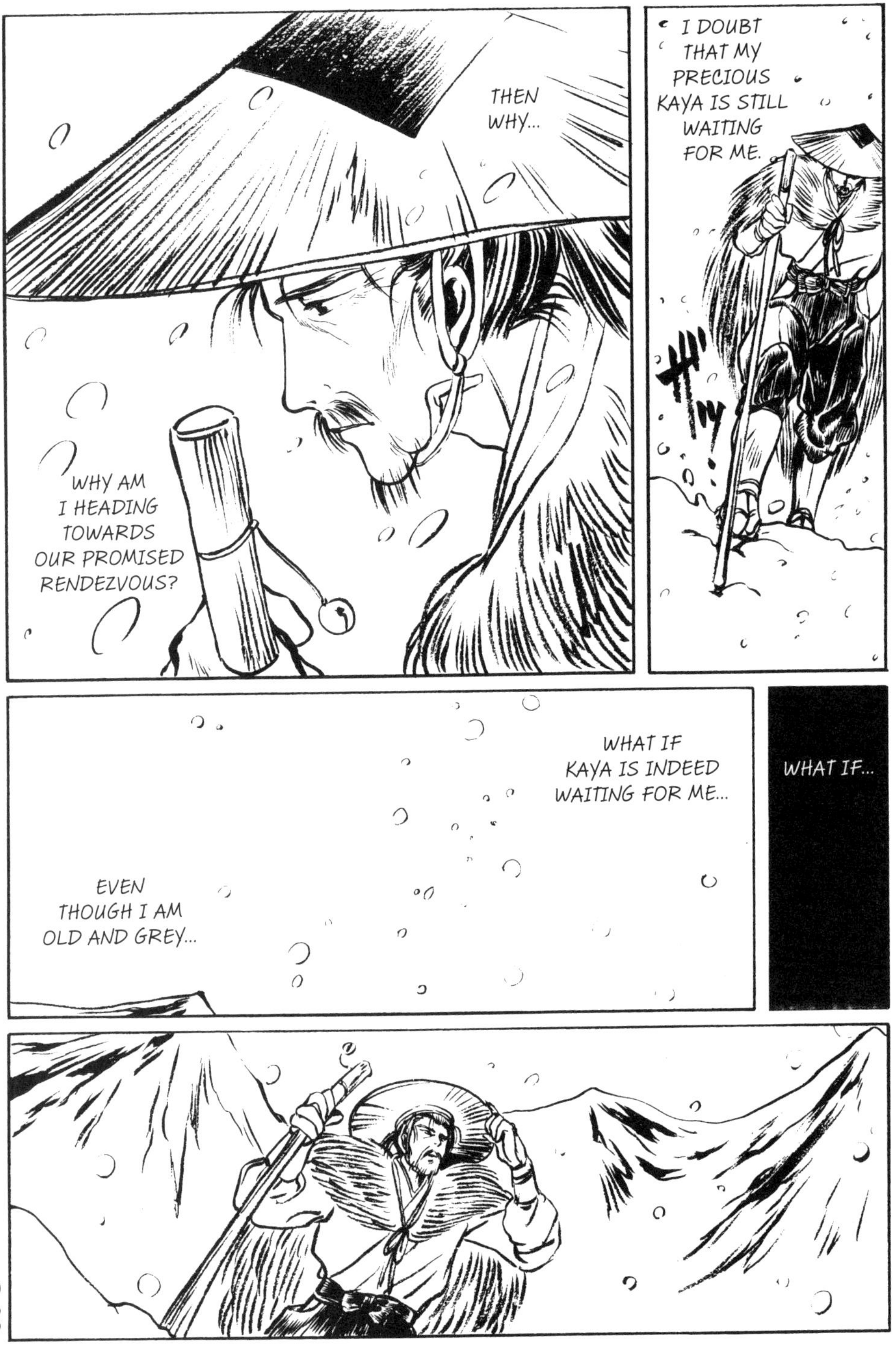
I DOUBT THAT MY PRECIOUS KAYA IS STILL WAITING FOR ME.
THEN WHY...
WHY AM I HEADING TOWARDS OUR PROMISED RENDEZVOUS?
WHAT IF...
WHAT IF KAYA IS INDEED WAITING FOR ME...
EVEN THOUGH I AM OLD AND GREY...

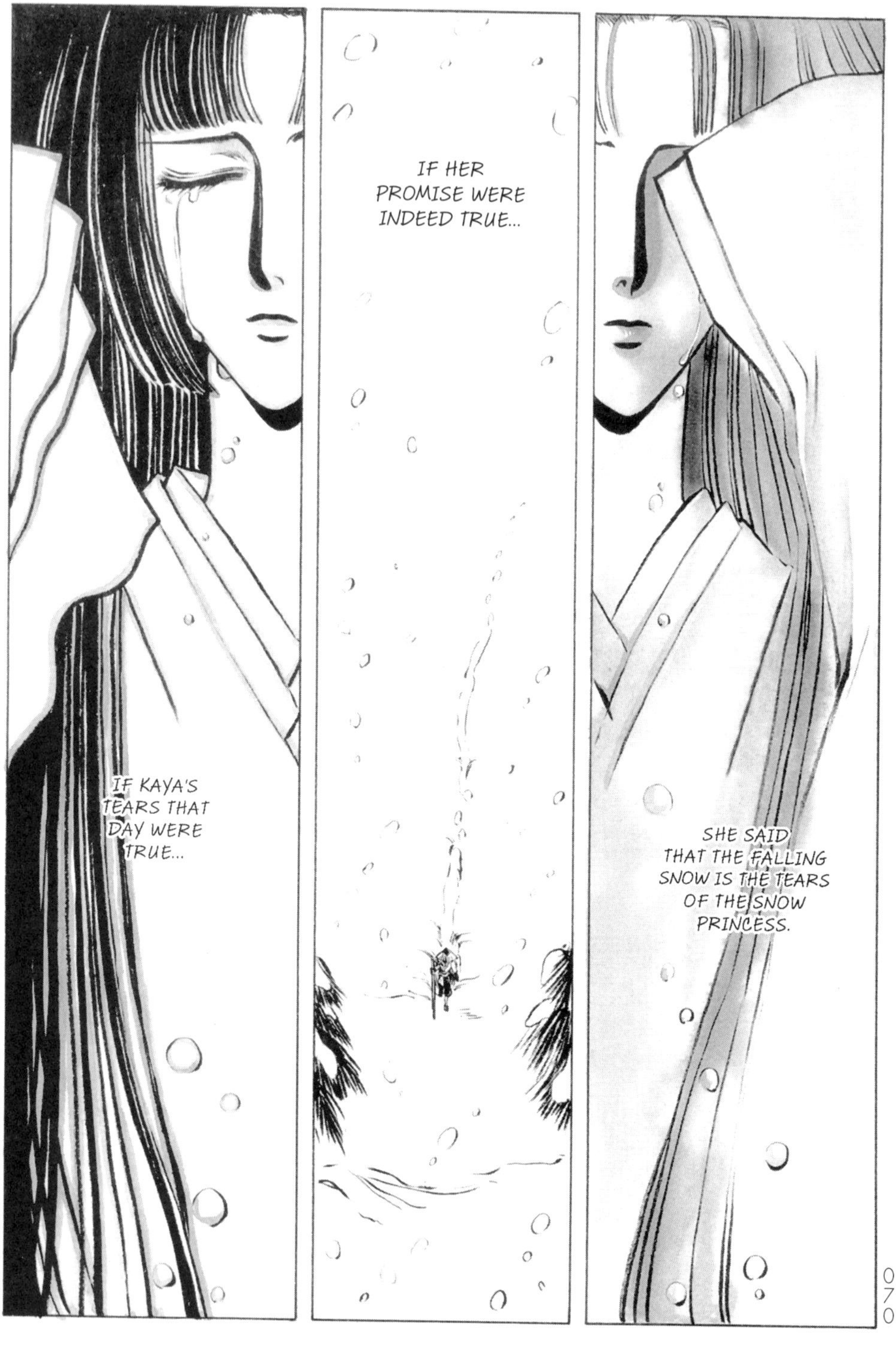
SHE SAID THAT THE FALLING SNOW IS THE TEARS OF THE SNOW PRINCESS.
IF HER PROMISE WERE INDEED TRUE...
IF KAYA'S TEARS THAT DAY WERE TRUE...

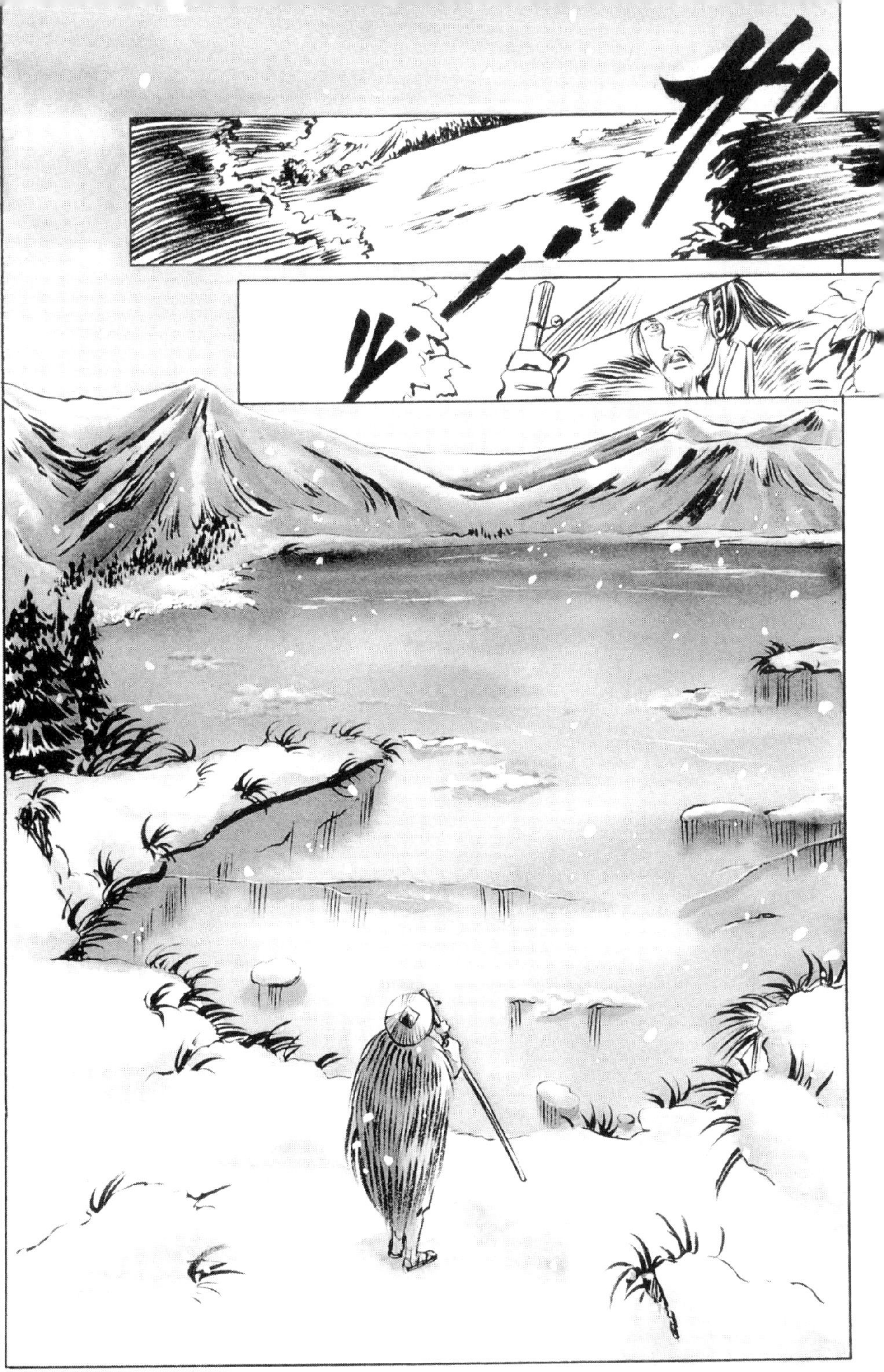
ザッ

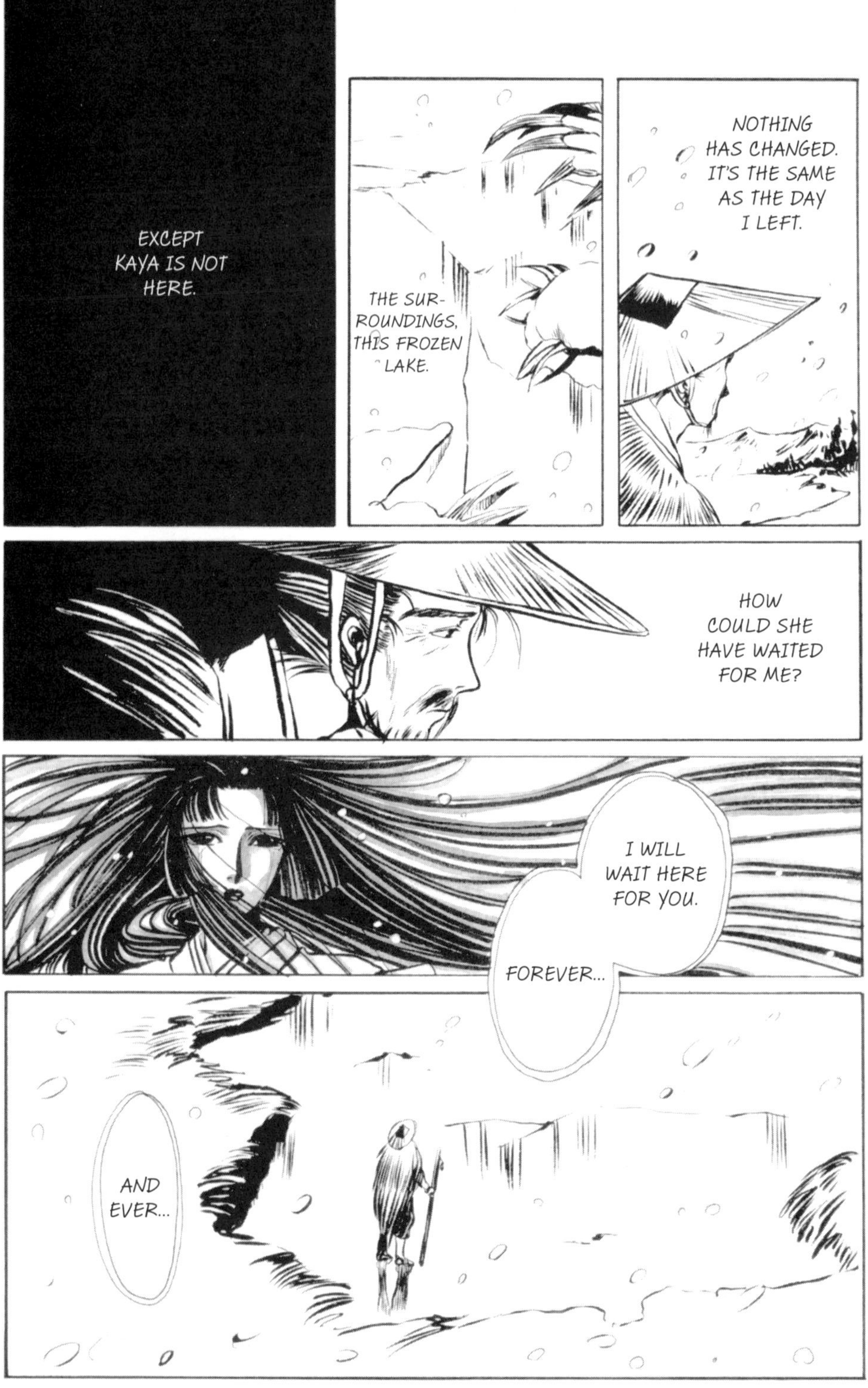
NOTHING HAS CHANGED. IT'S THE SAME AS THE DAY I LEFT.
THE SUR-ROUNDINGS, THIS FROZEN LAKE.
EXCEPT KAYA IS NOT HERE.
HOW COULD SHE HAVE WAITED FOR ME?
I WILL WAIT HERE FOR YOU.
FOREVER...
AND EVER...

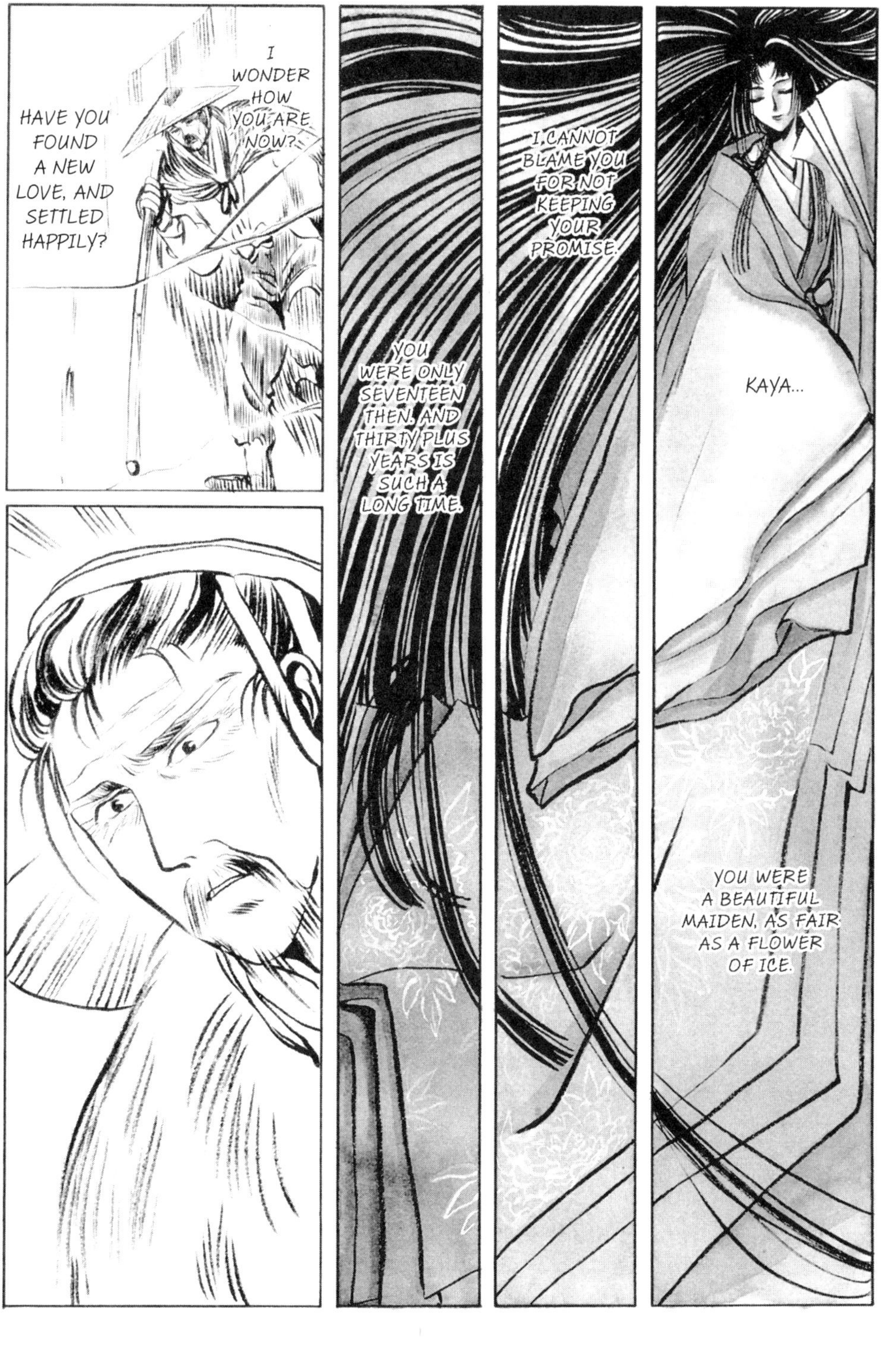
KAYA...
YOU WERE A BEAUTIFUL MAIDEN, AS FAIR AS A FLOWER OF ICE.
I CANNOT BLAME YOU FOR NOT KEEPING YOUR PROMISE.
YOU WERE ONLY SEVENTEEN THEN. AND THIRTY PLUS YEARS IS SUCH A LONG TIME.
I WONDER HOW YOU ARE NOW?
HAVE YOU FOUND A NEW LOVE, AND SETTLED HAPPILY?

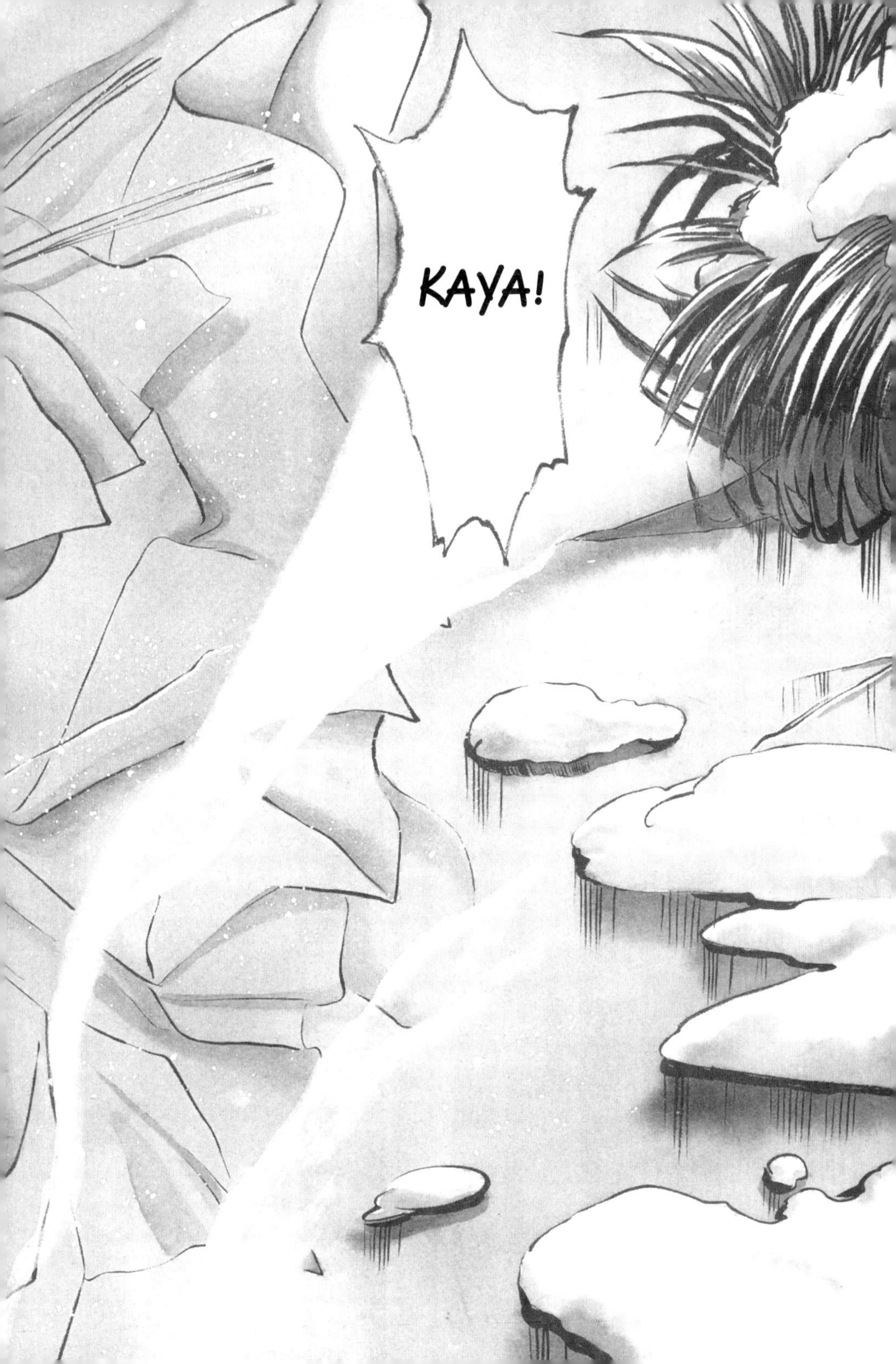
KAYA!

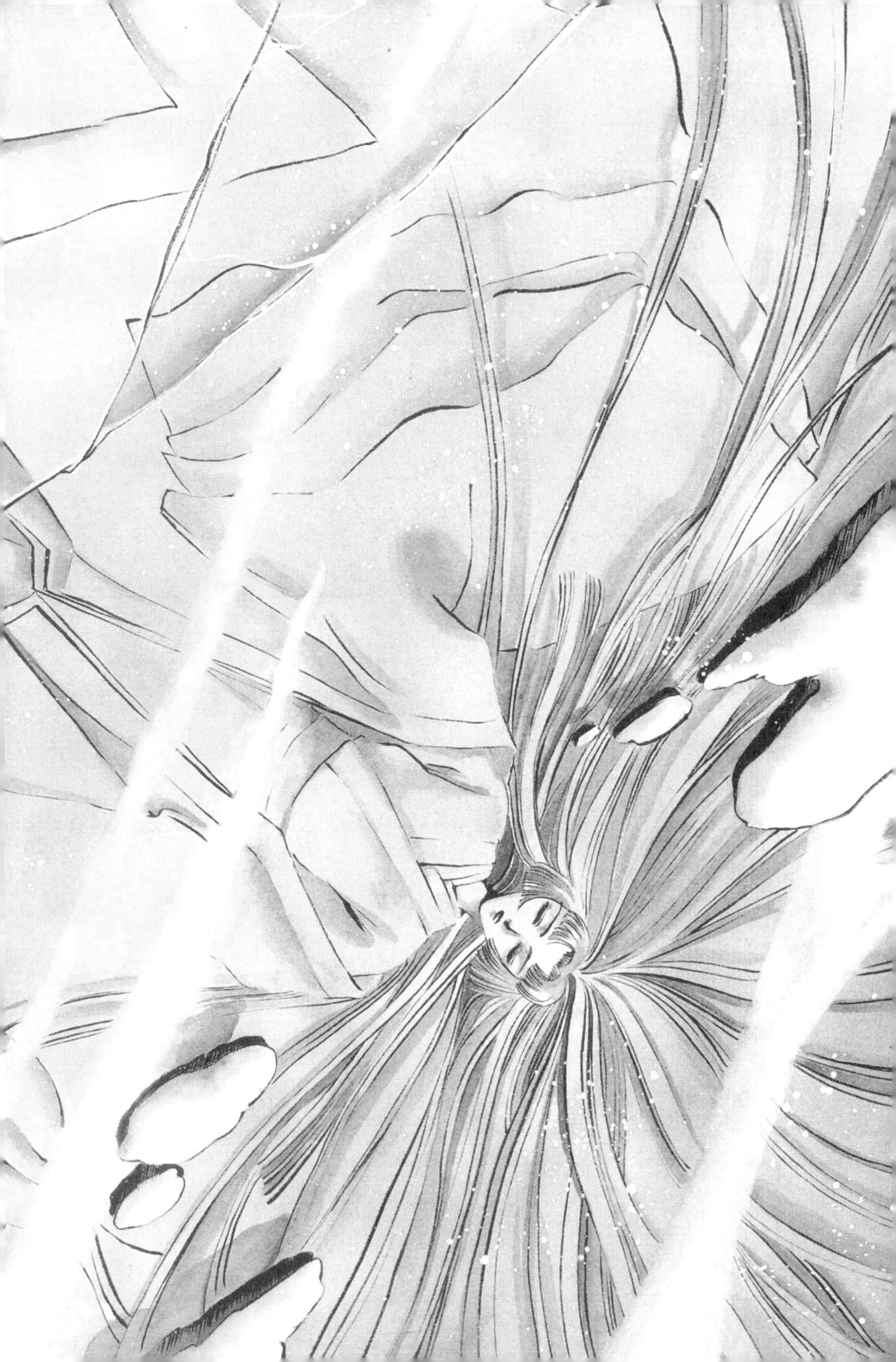

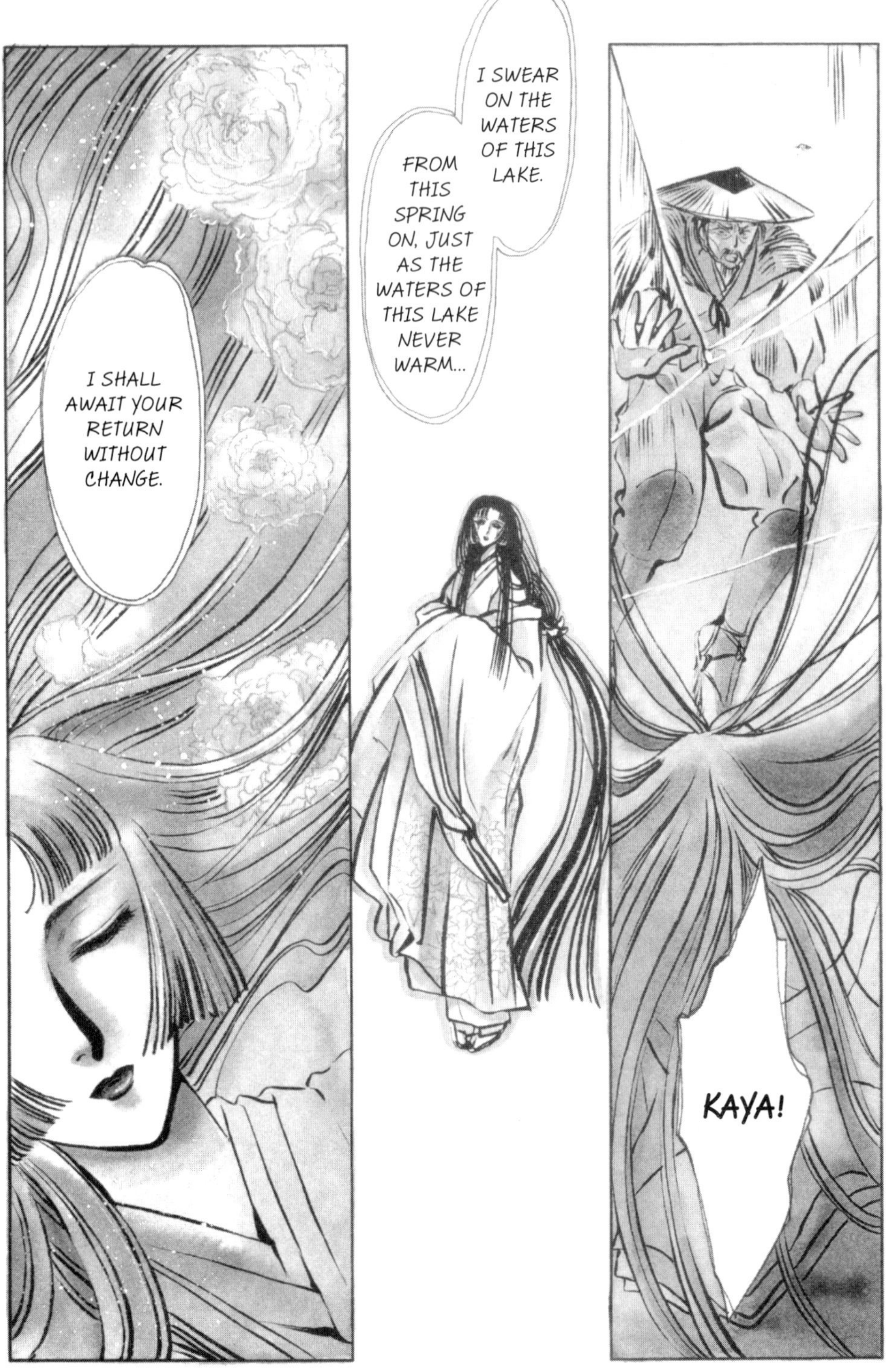
KAYA!
I SWEAR ON THE WATERS OF THIS LAKE.
FROM THIS SPRING ON, JUST AS THE WATERS OF THIS LAKE NEVER WARM...
I SHALL AWAIT YOUR RETURN WITHOUT CHANGE.

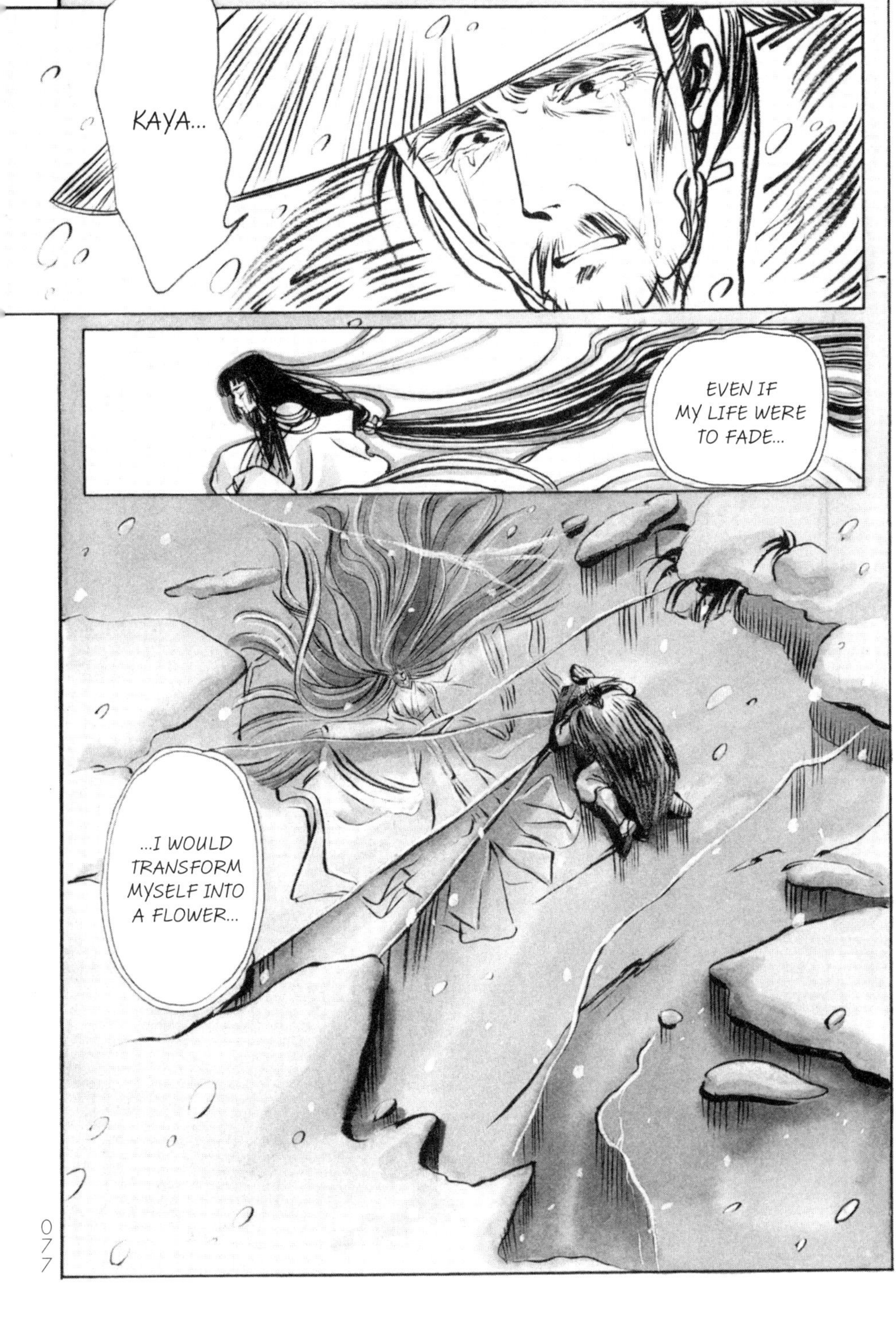
KAYA...
EVEN IF MY LIFE WERE TO FADE...
...I WOULD TRANSFORM MYSELF INTO A FLOWER...

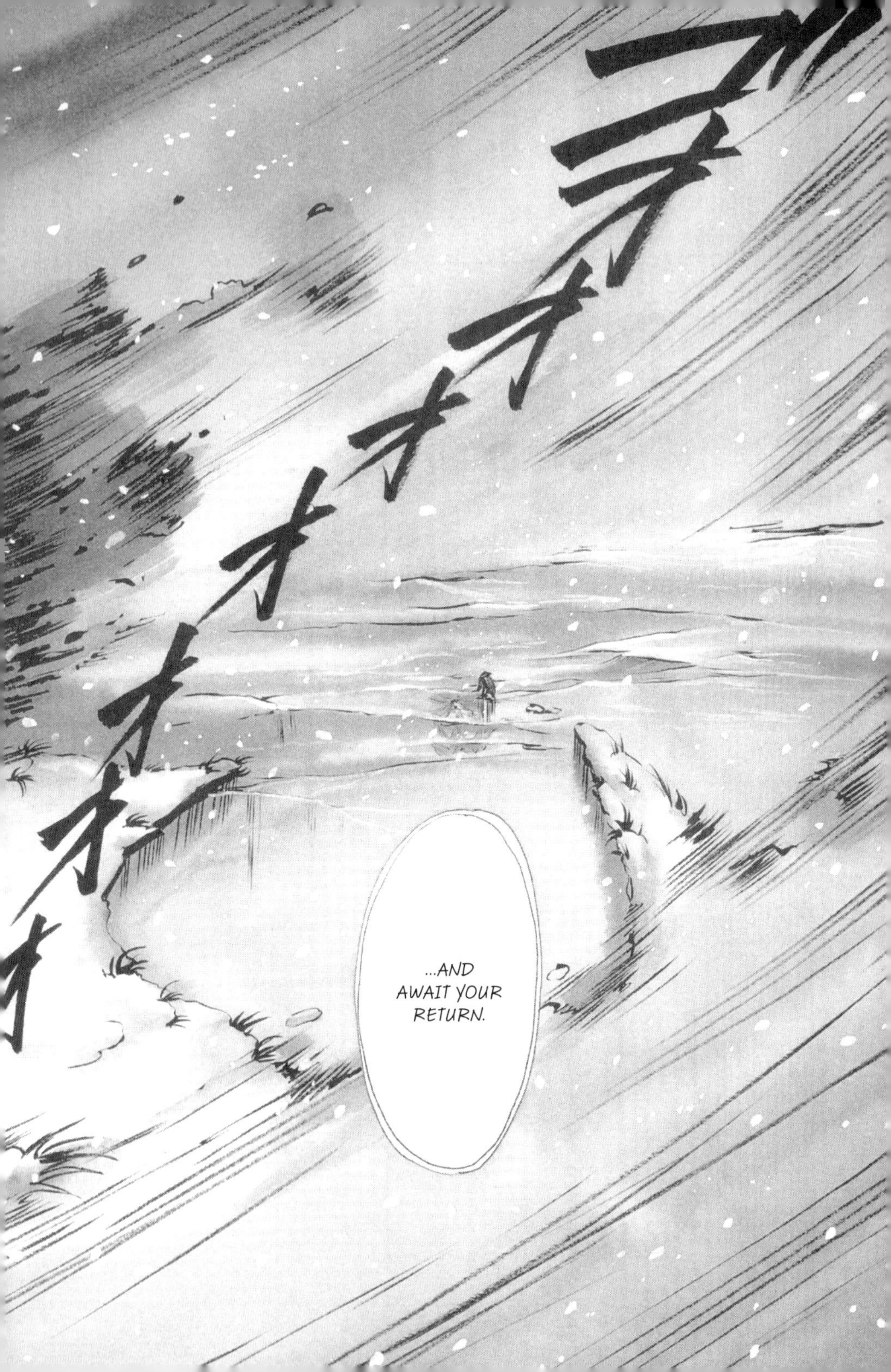
...AND AWAIT YOUR RETURN.

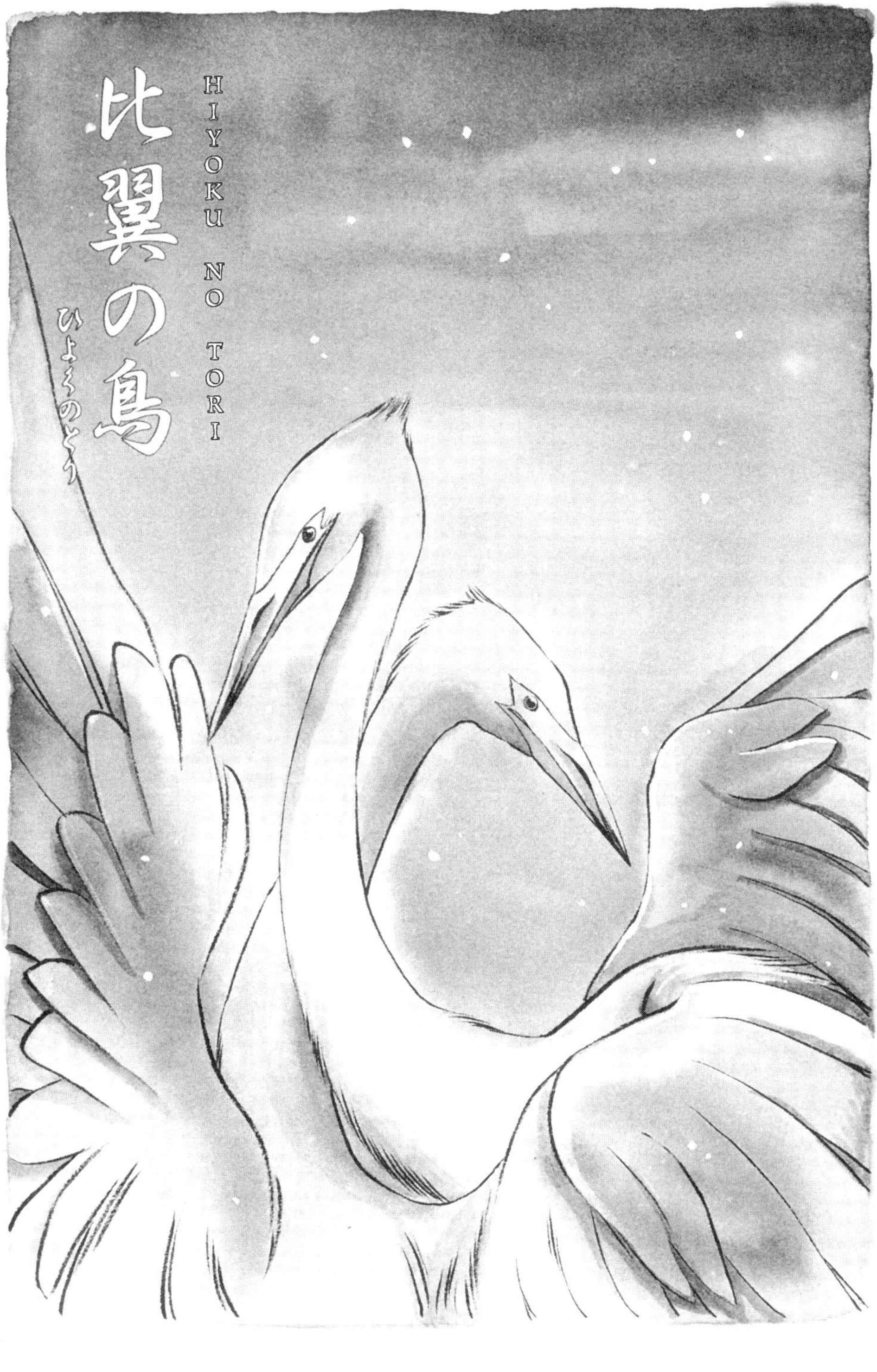

比翼の鳥
ひよくのとり
HIYOKU NO TORI

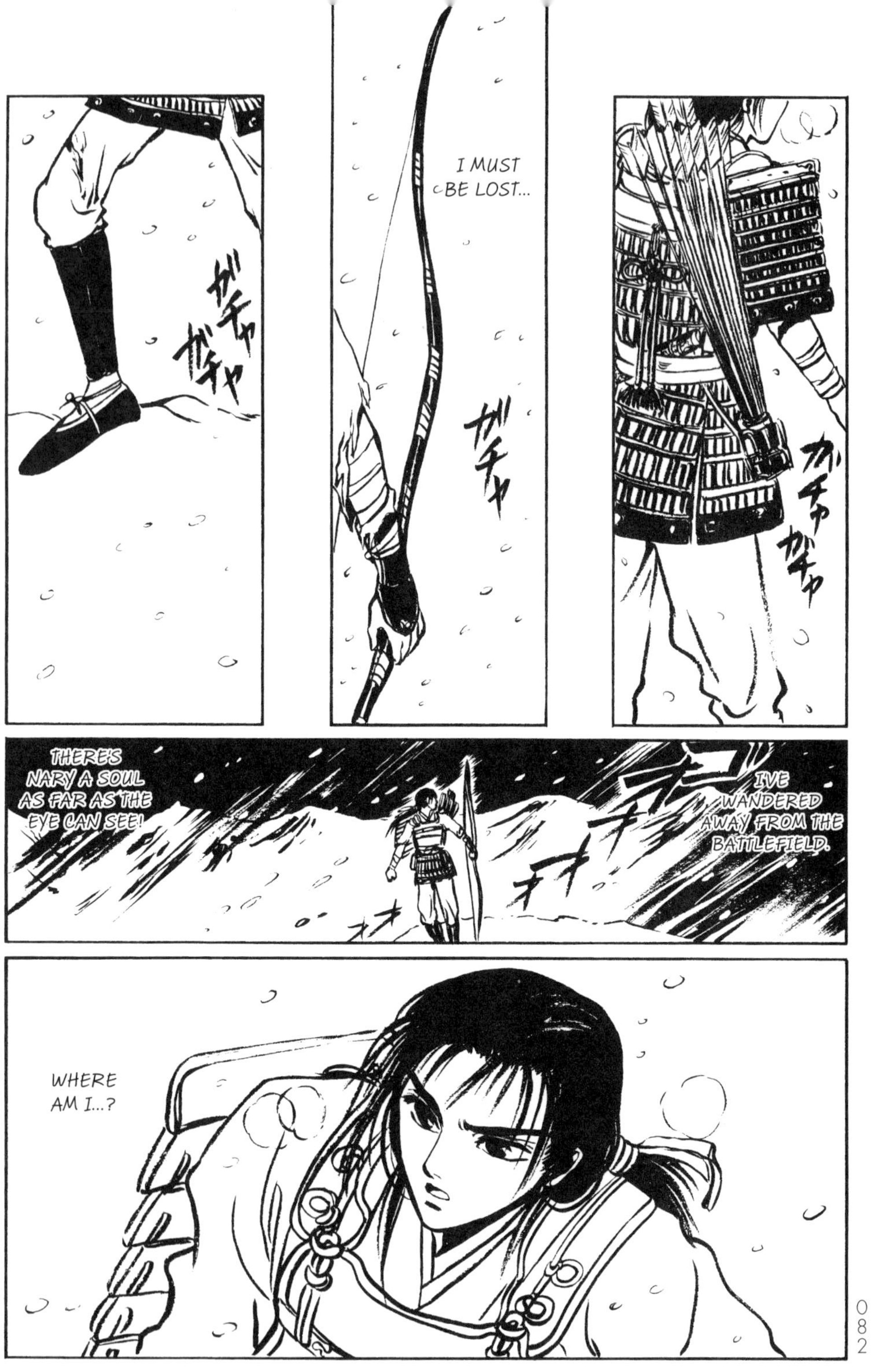
ガチャ
ガチャ
I MUST BE LOST...
ガチャ
ガチャ
ガチャ
I'VE WANDERED AWAY FROM THE BATTLEFIELD.
THERE'S NARY A SOUL AS FAR AS THE EYE CAN SEE!
WHERE AM I...?

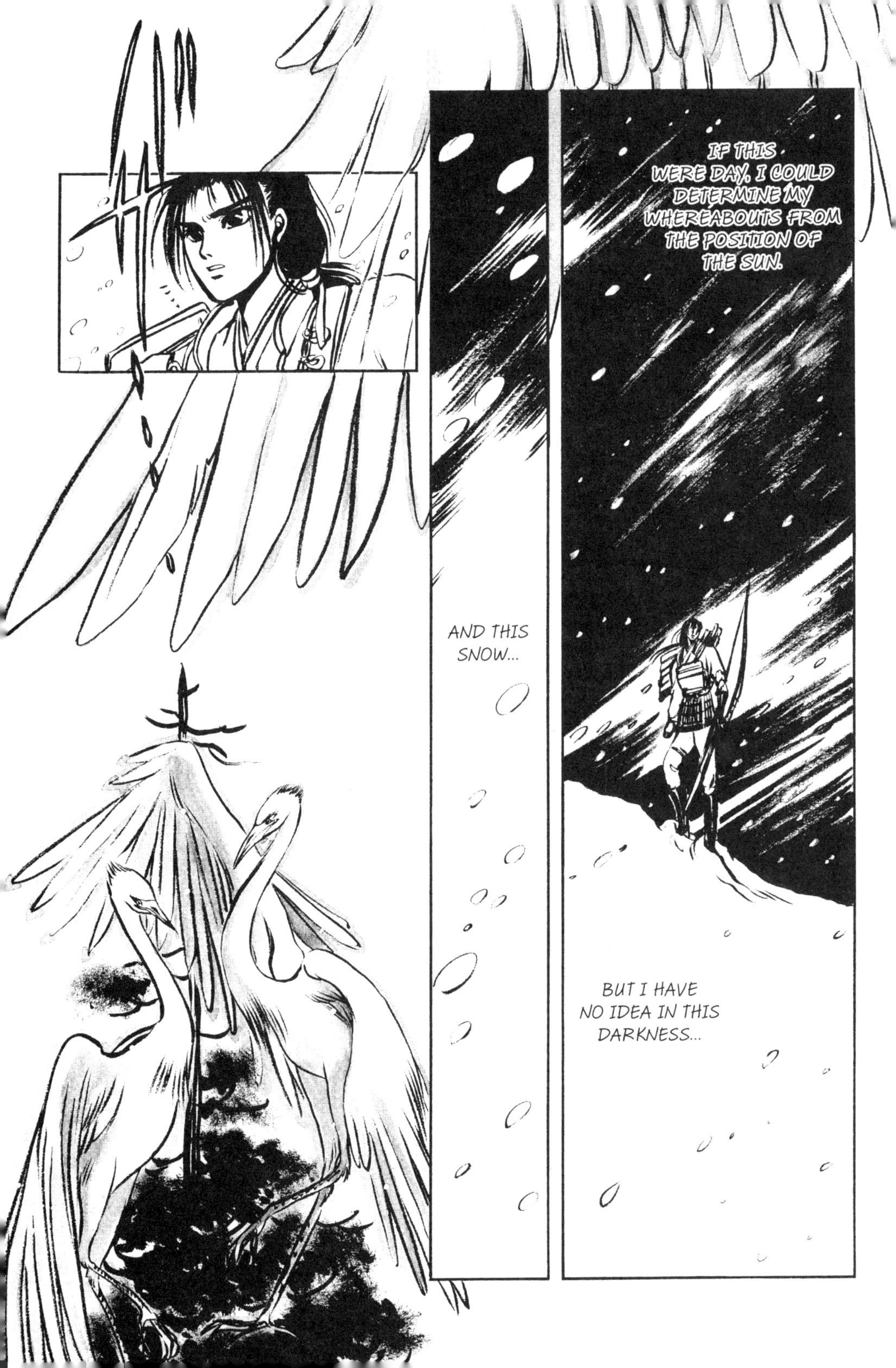
IF THIS WERE DAY, I COULD DETERMINE MY WHEREABOUTS FROM THE POSITION OF THE SUN.
BUT I HAVE NO IDEA IN THIS DARKNESS...
AND THIS SNOW...

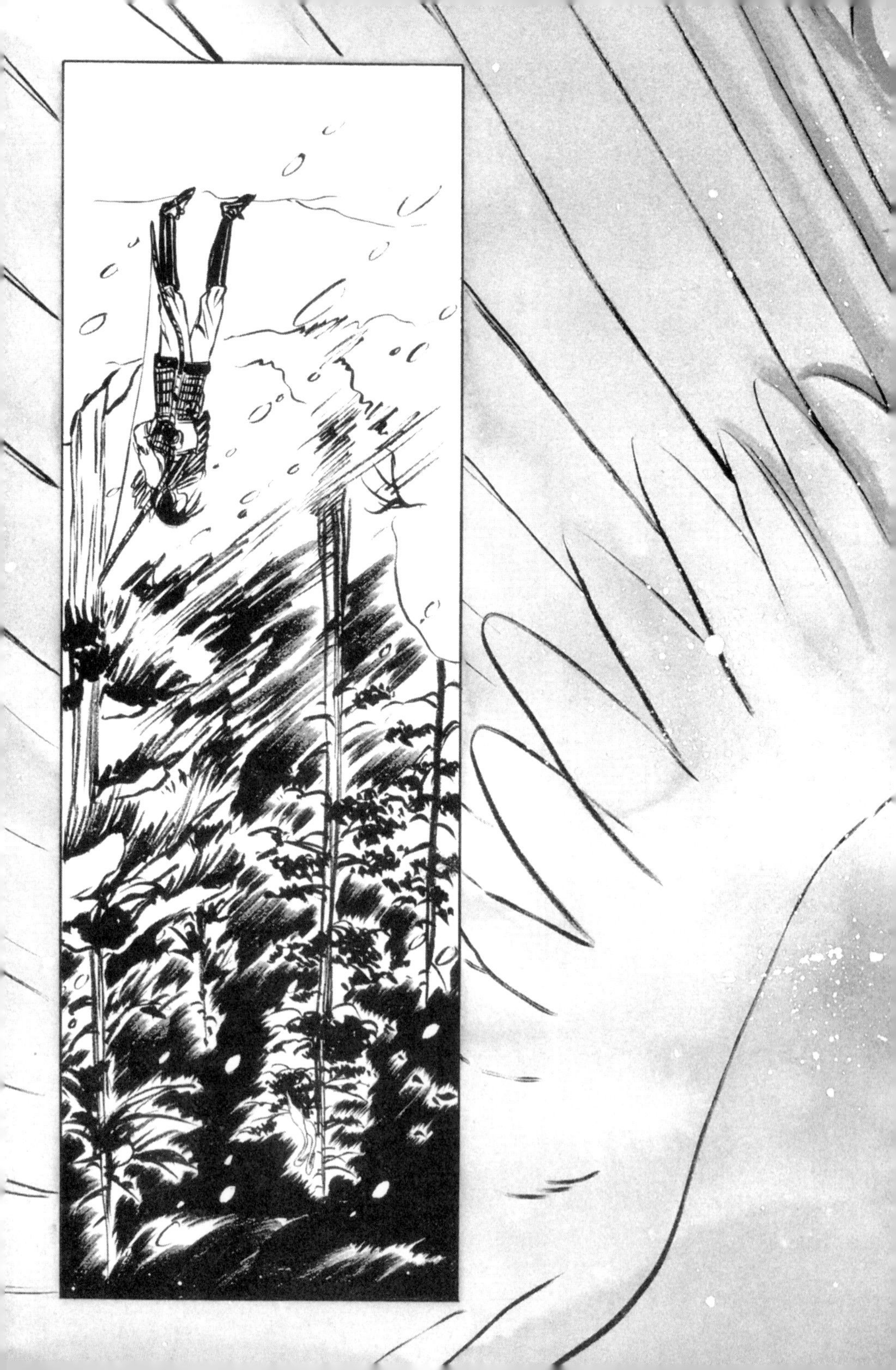

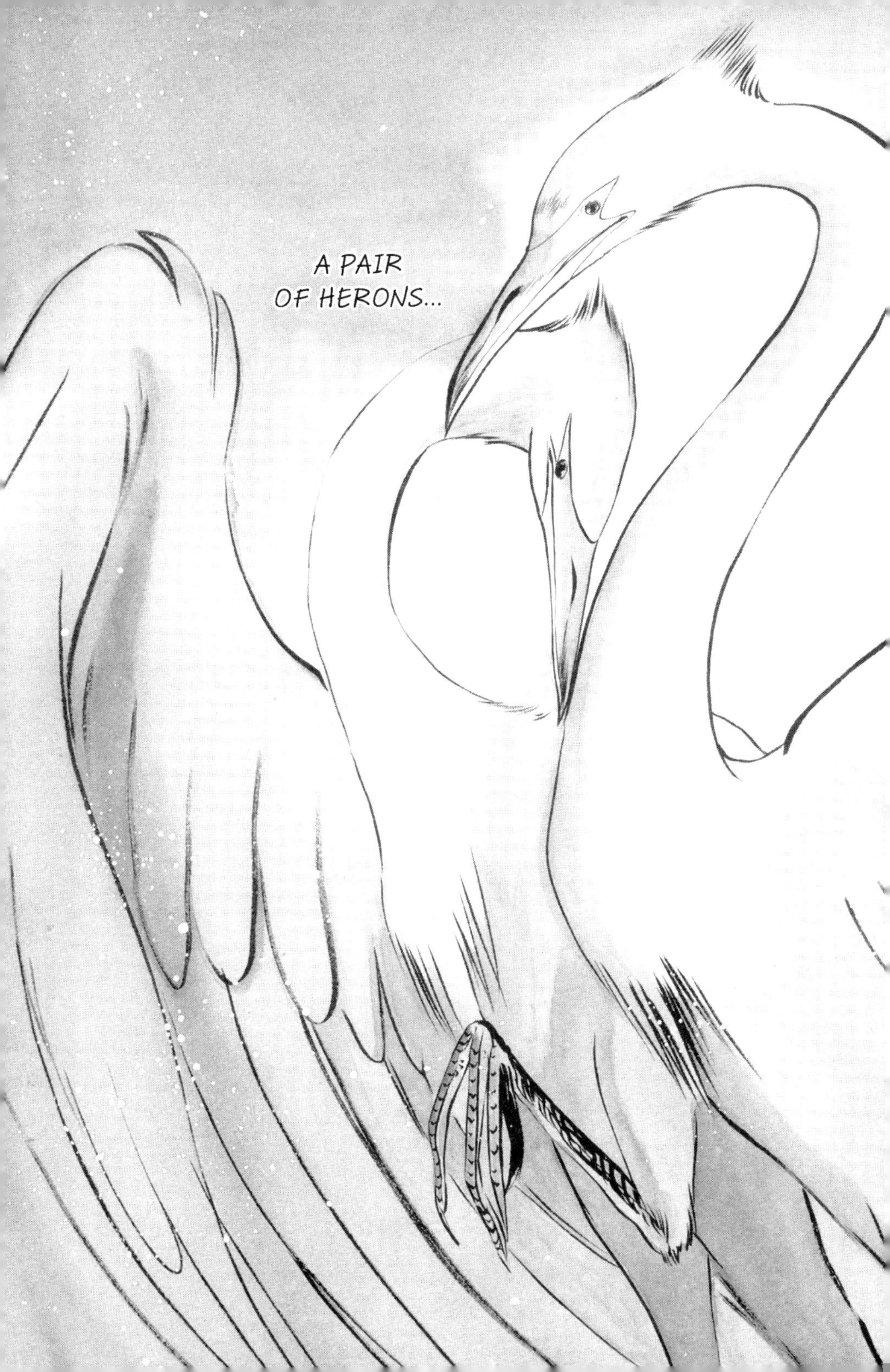
A PAIR
OF HERONS...

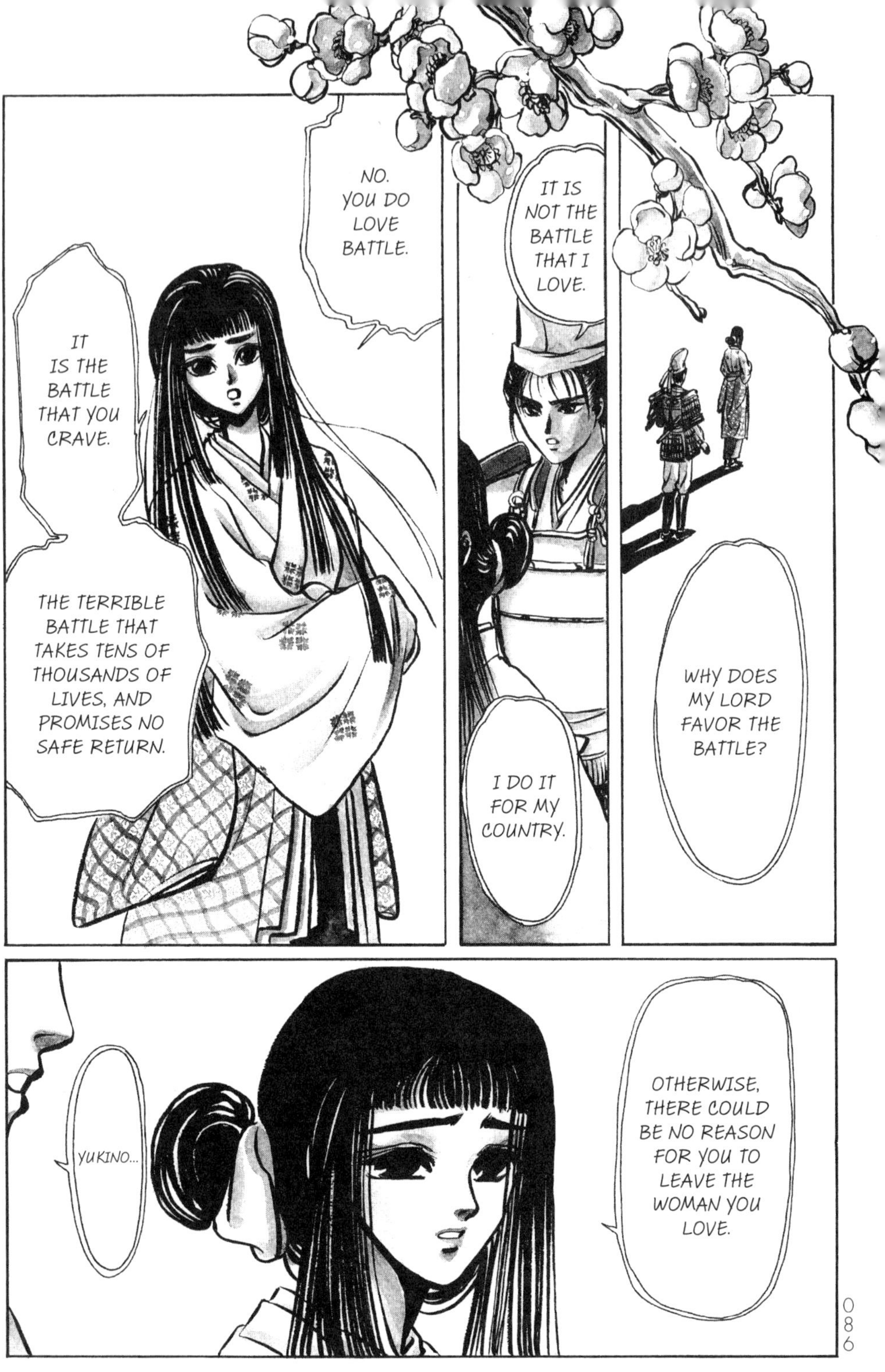
WHY DOES MY LORD FAVOR THE BATTLE?
I DO IT FOR MY COUNTRY.
IT IS NOT THE BATTLE THAT I LOVE.
NO. YOU DO LOVE BATTLE.
IT IS THE BATTLE THAT YOU CRAVE.
THE TERRIBLE BATTLE THAT TAKES TENS OF THOUSANDS OF LIVES, AND PROMISES NO SAFE RETURN.
OTHERWISE, THERE COULD BE NO REASON FOR YOU TO LEAVE THE WOMAN YOU LOVE.
YUKINO...

IF I FIGHT HONORABLY, YOUR FATHER WILL ACCEPT ME.

AND THEN HE MAY FINALLY AGREE TO OUR MARRIAGE.

HUG

FOR YOUR LOVE...

...FOR OUR HAPPINESS...

...I WILL FIGHT.

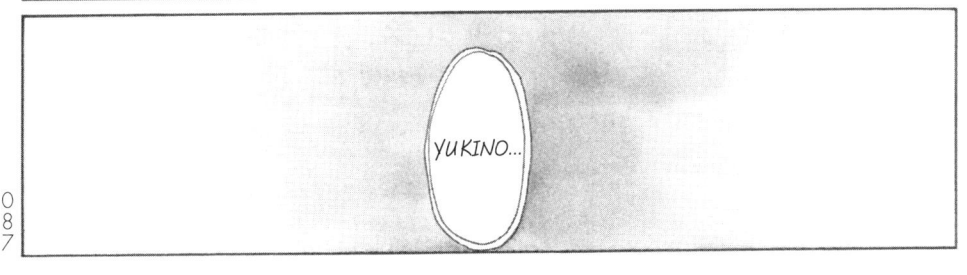

YUKINO...

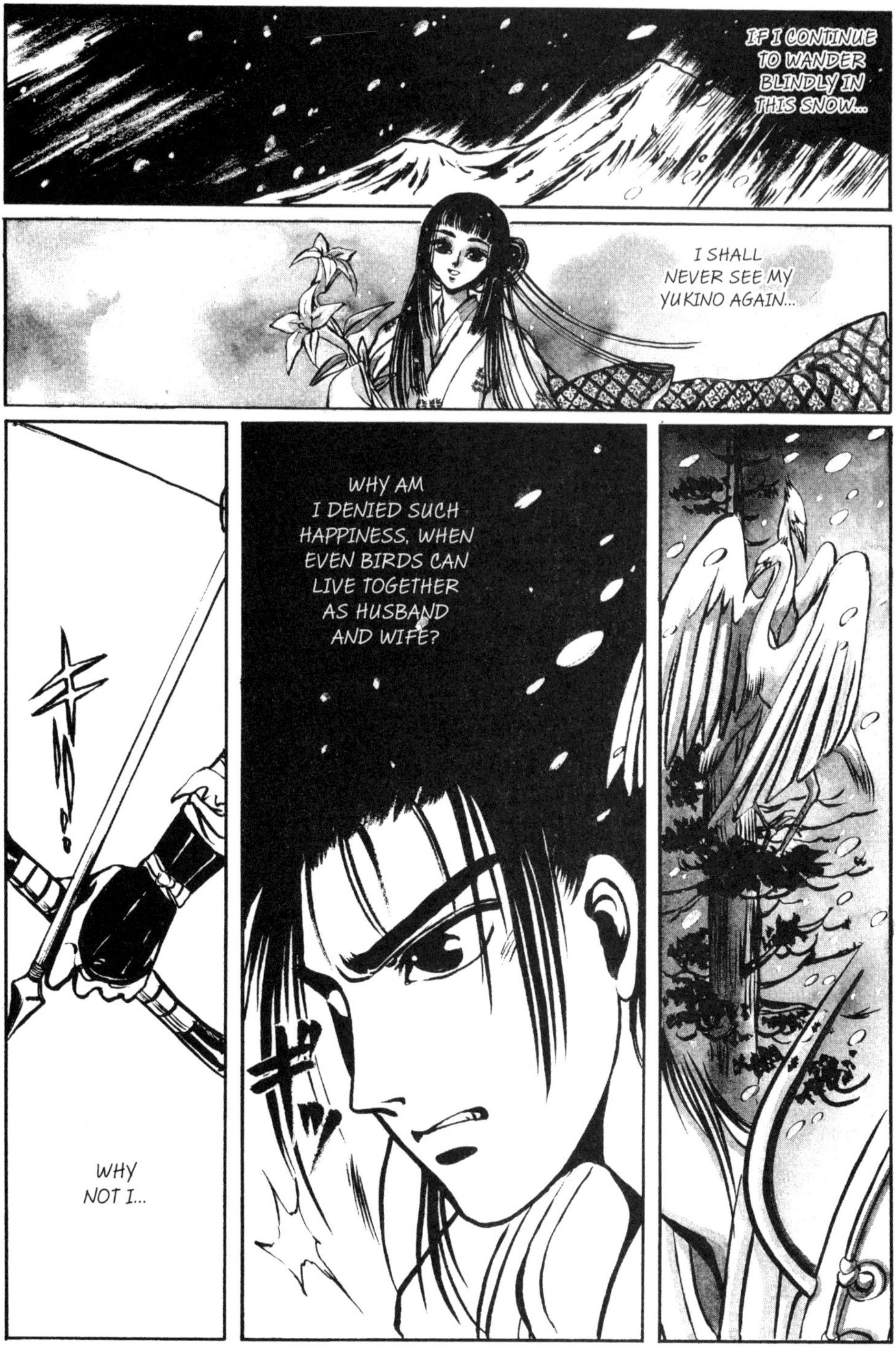
IF I CONTINUE TO WANDER BLINDLY IN THIS SNOW...
I SHALL NEVER SEE MY YUKINO AGAIN...
WHY AM I DENIED SUCH HAPPINESS, WHEN EVEN BIRDS CAN LIVE TOGETHER AS HUSBAND AND WIFE?
WHY NOT I...

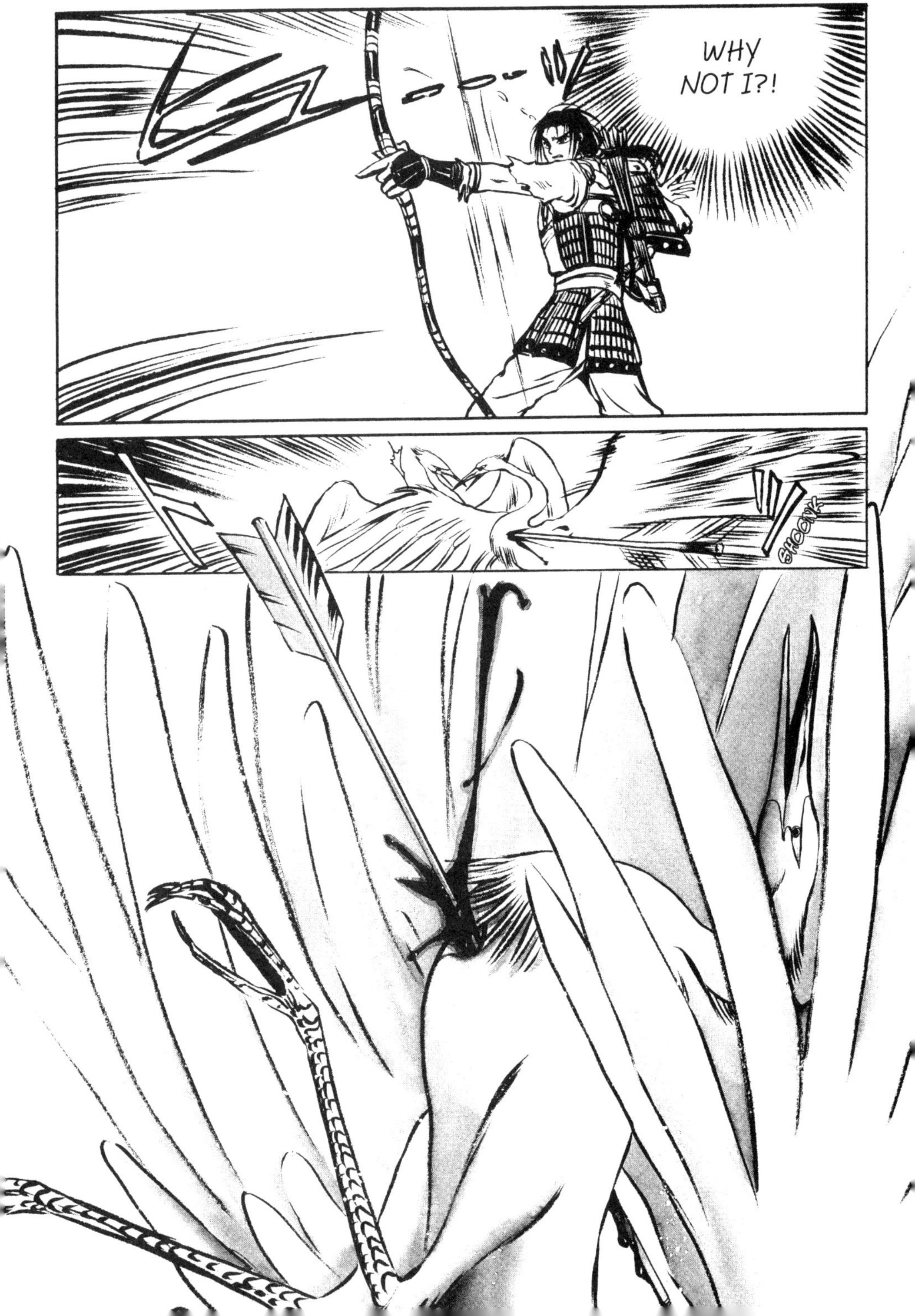
WHY NOT I?!
SHOONK

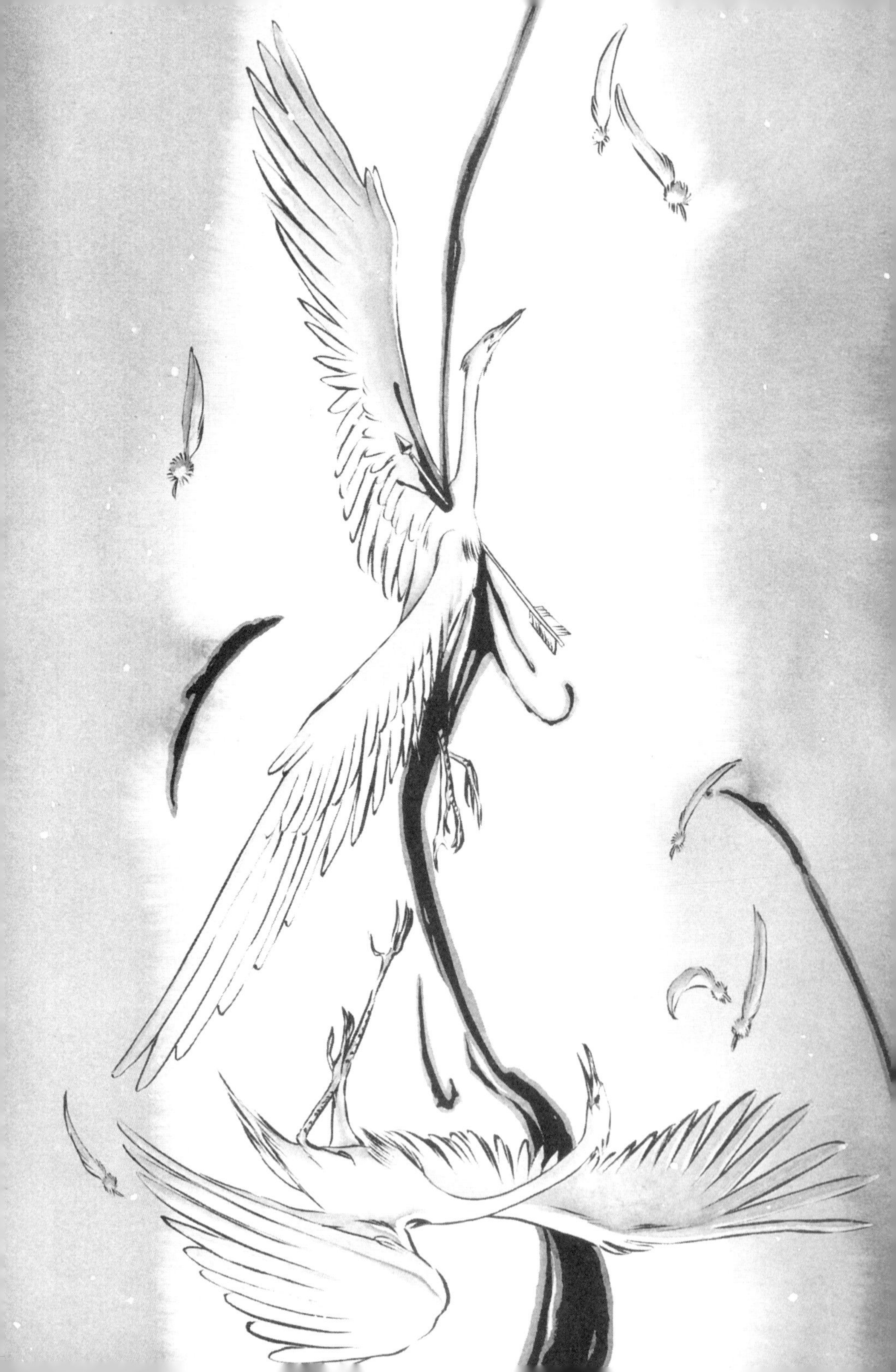

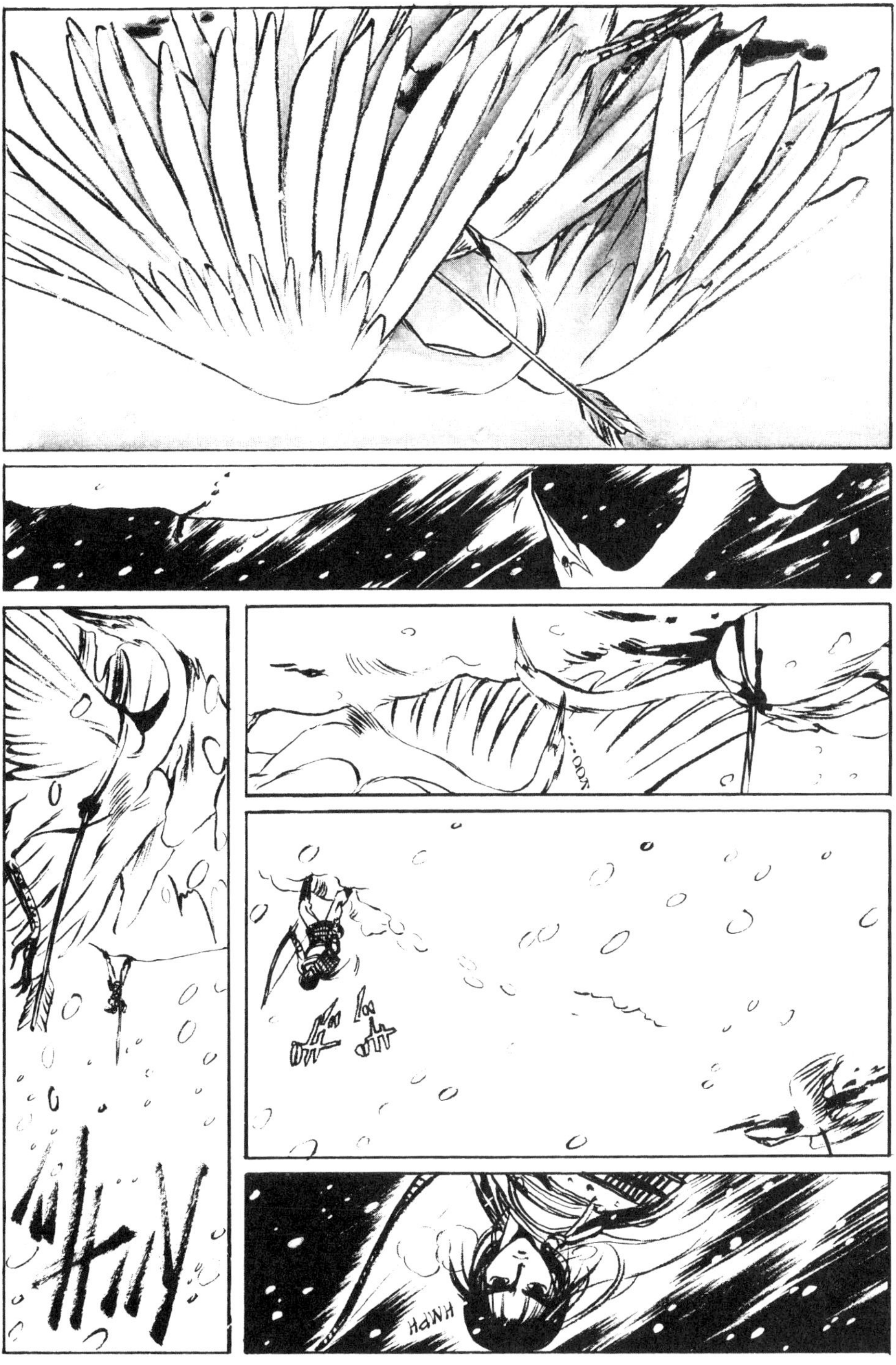
HMPH

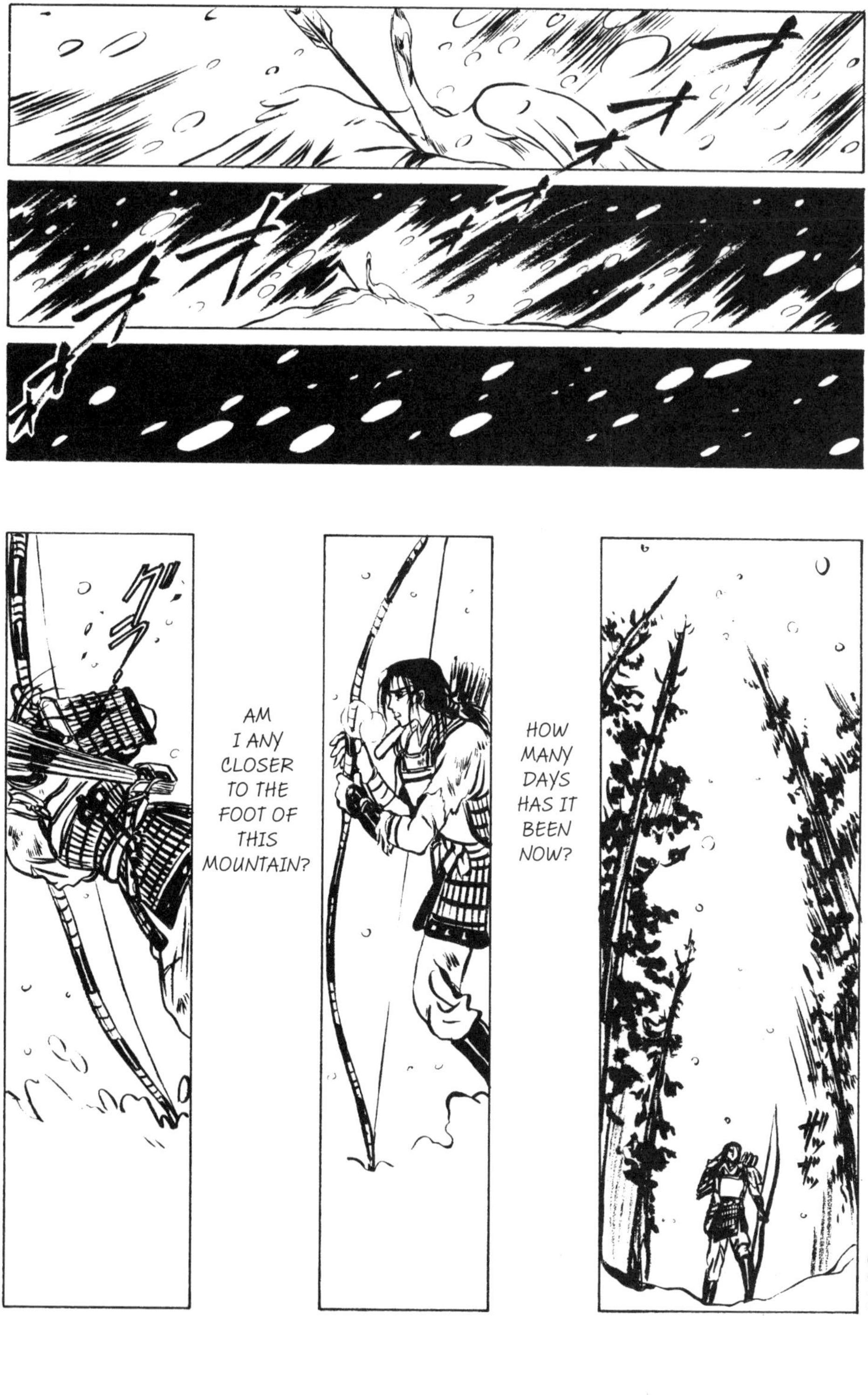
HOW MANY DAYS HAS IT BEEN NOW?
AM I ANY CLOSER TO THE FOOT OF THIS MOUNTAIN?

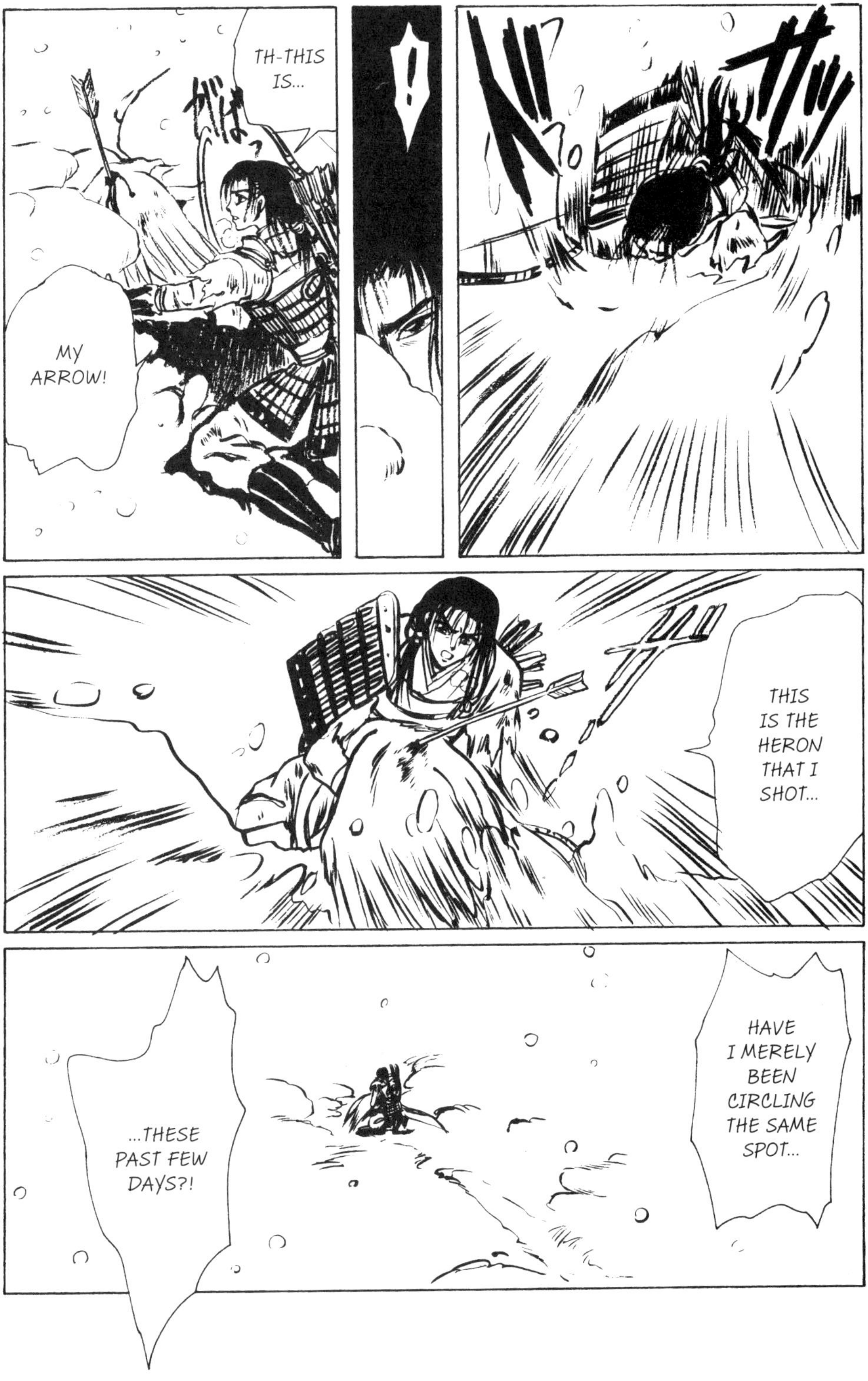
!
TH-THIS IS...
がばっ
MY ARROW!
THIS IS THE HERON THAT I SHOT...
HAVE I MERELY BEEN CIRCLING THE SAME SPOT...
...THESE PAST FEW DAYS?!

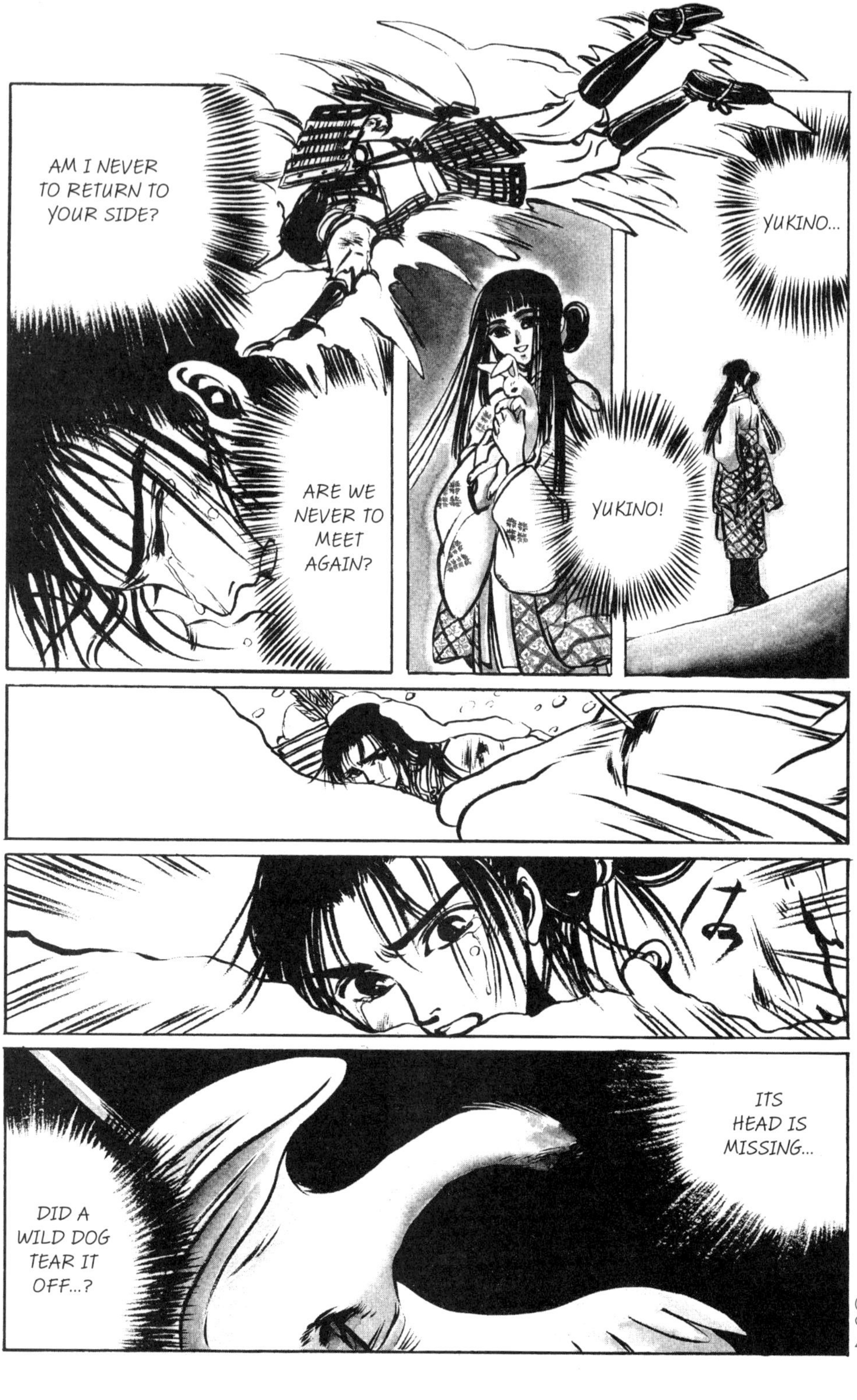
YUKINO...
YUKINO!
AM I NEVER TO RETURN TO YOUR SIDE?
ARE WE NEVER TO MEET AGAIN?
ITS HEAD IS MISSING...
DID A WILD DOG TEAR IT OFF...?

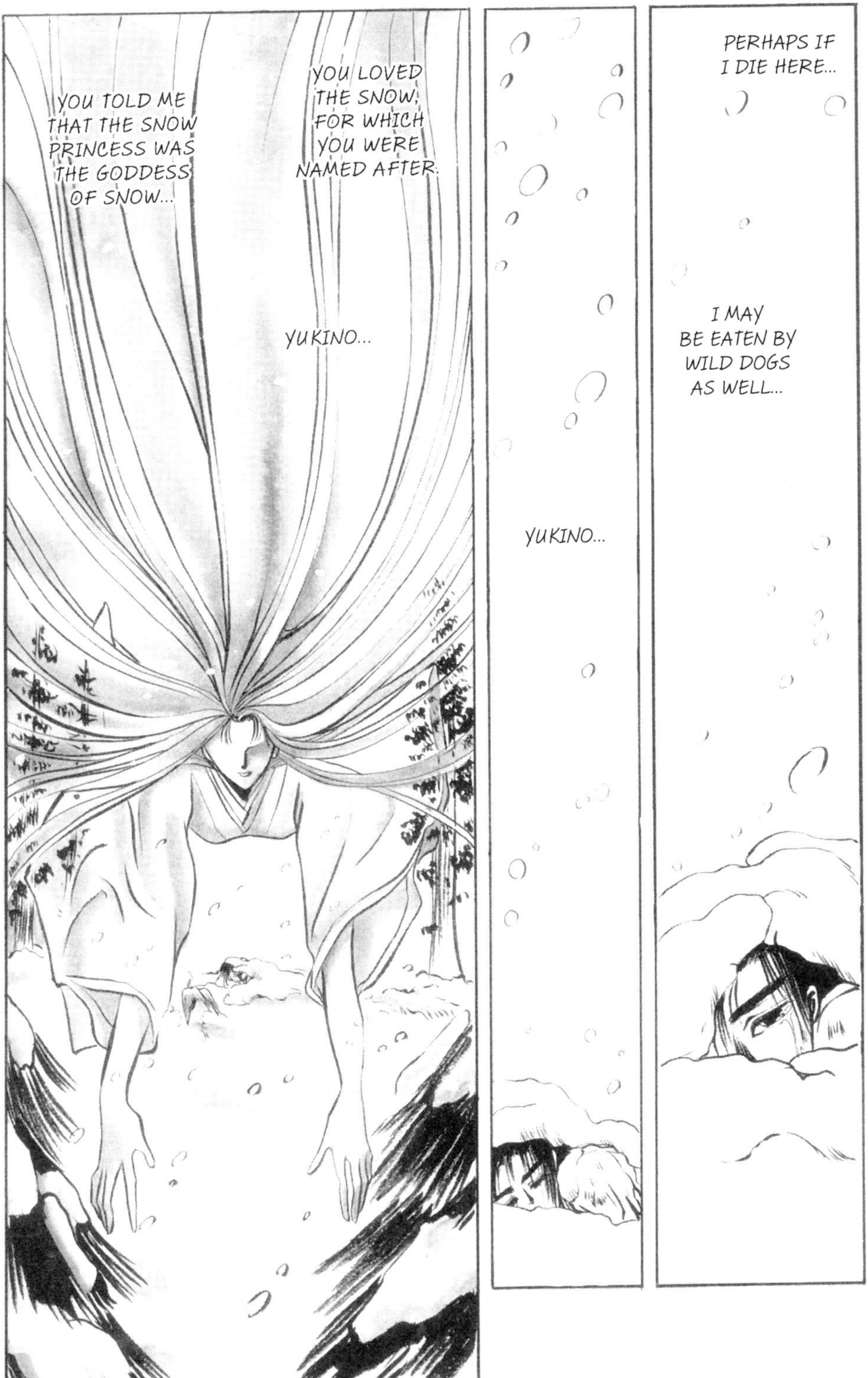
PERHAPS IF I DIE HERE...
I MAY BE EATEN BY WILD DOGS AS WELL...
YUKINO...
YOU LOVED THE SNOW, FOR WHICH YOU WERE NAMED AFTER.
YOU TOLD ME THAT THE SNOW PRINCESS WAS THE GODDESS OF SNOW...
YUKINO...

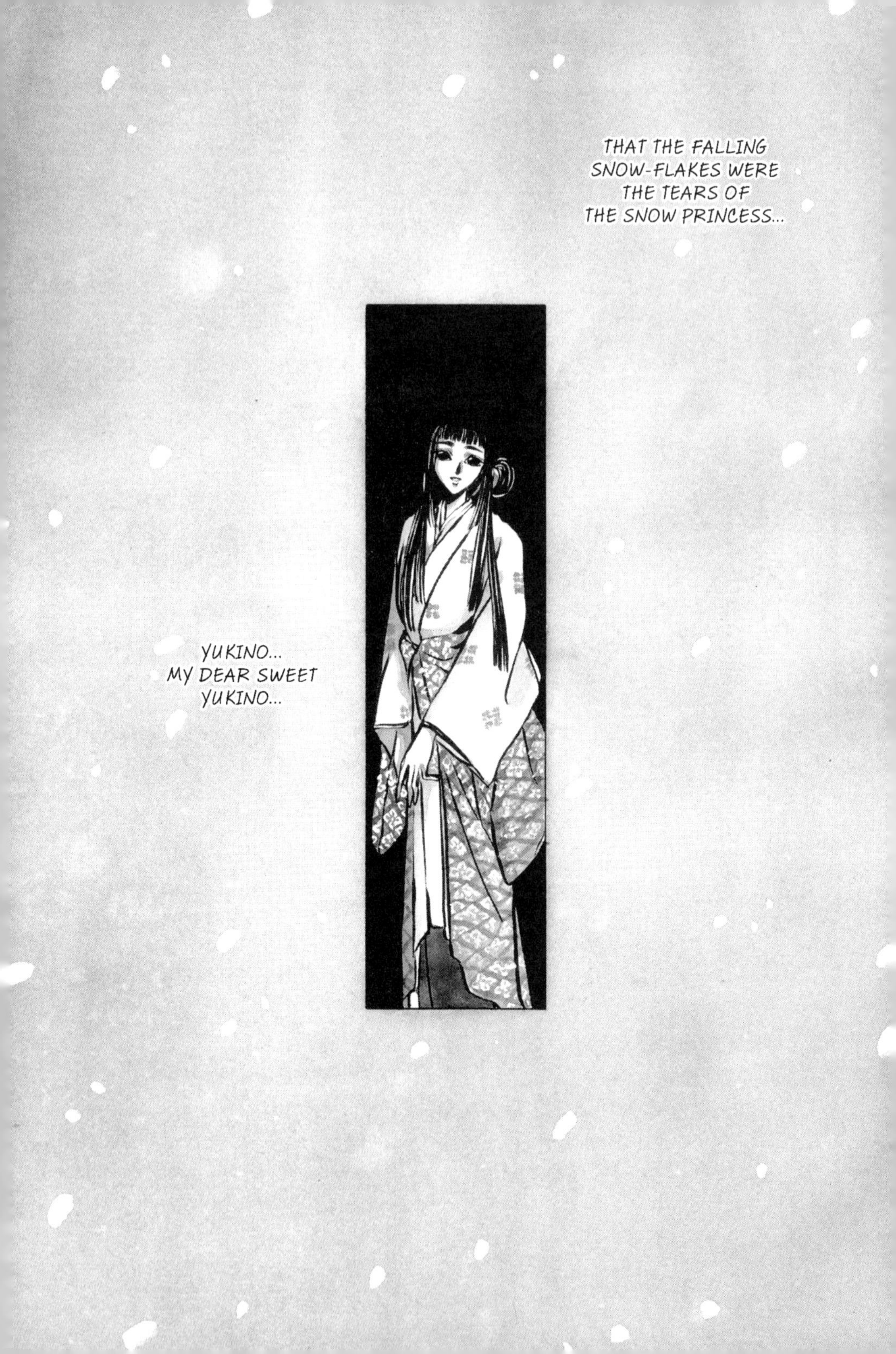
THAT THE FALLING SNOW-FLAKES WERE THE TEARS OF THE SNOW PRINCESS...
YUKINO... MY DEAR SWEET YUKINO...

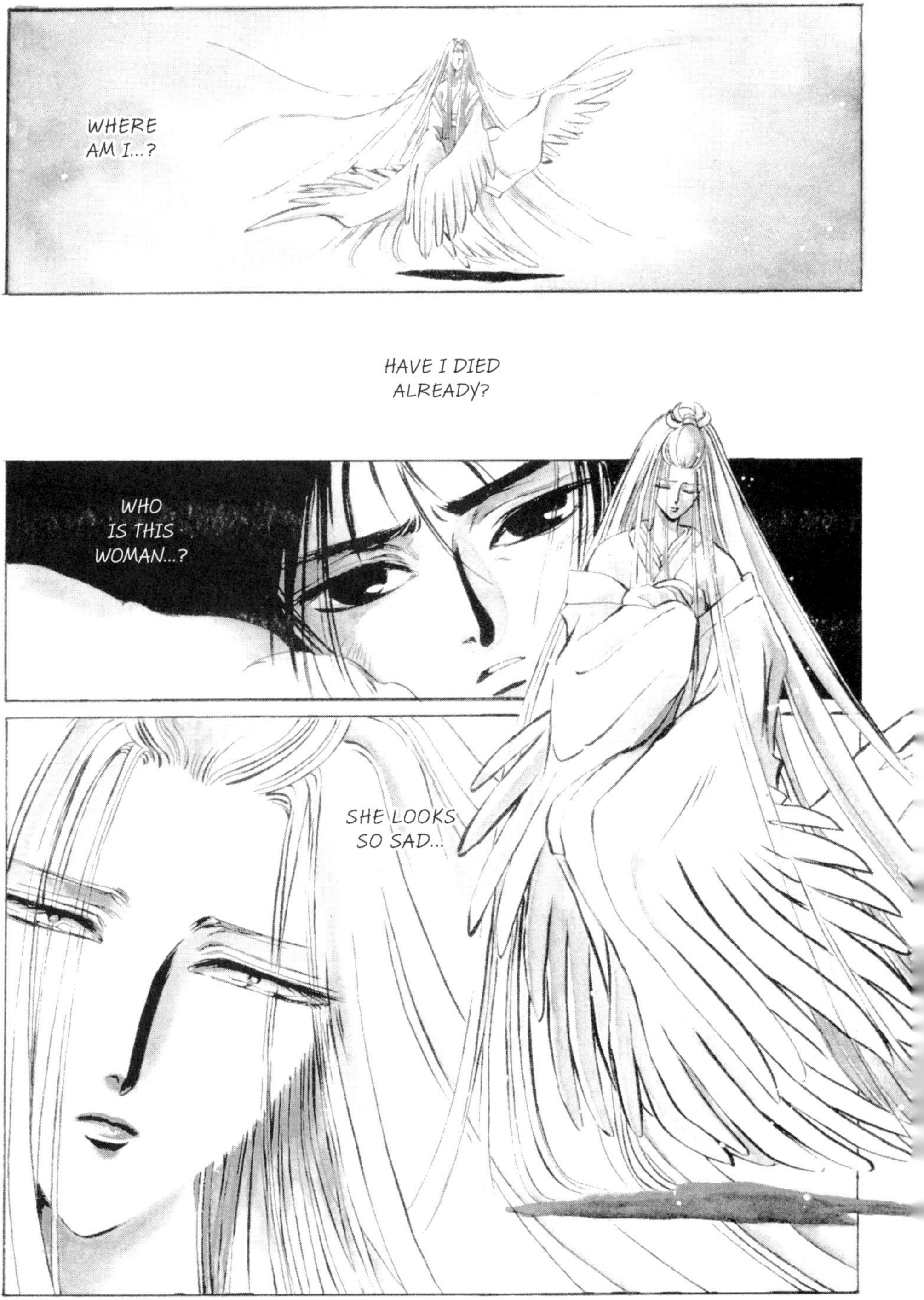
WHERE AM I...?
HAVE I DIED ALREADY?
WHO IS THIS WOMAN...?
SHE LOOKS SO SAD...

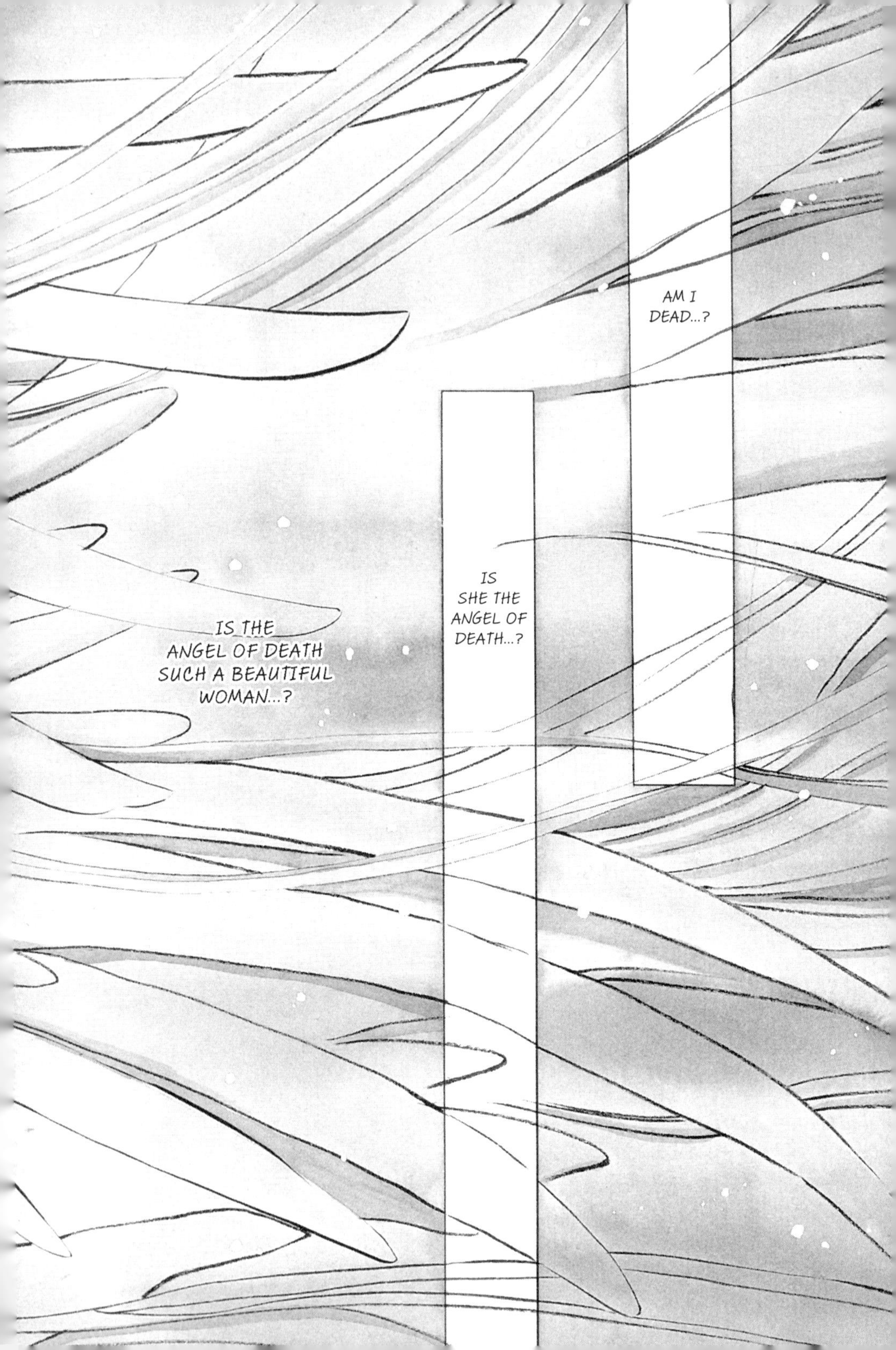
AM I DEAD...?
IS SHE THE ANGEL OF DEATH...?
IS THE ANGEL OF DEATH SUCH A BEAUTIFUL WOMAN...?

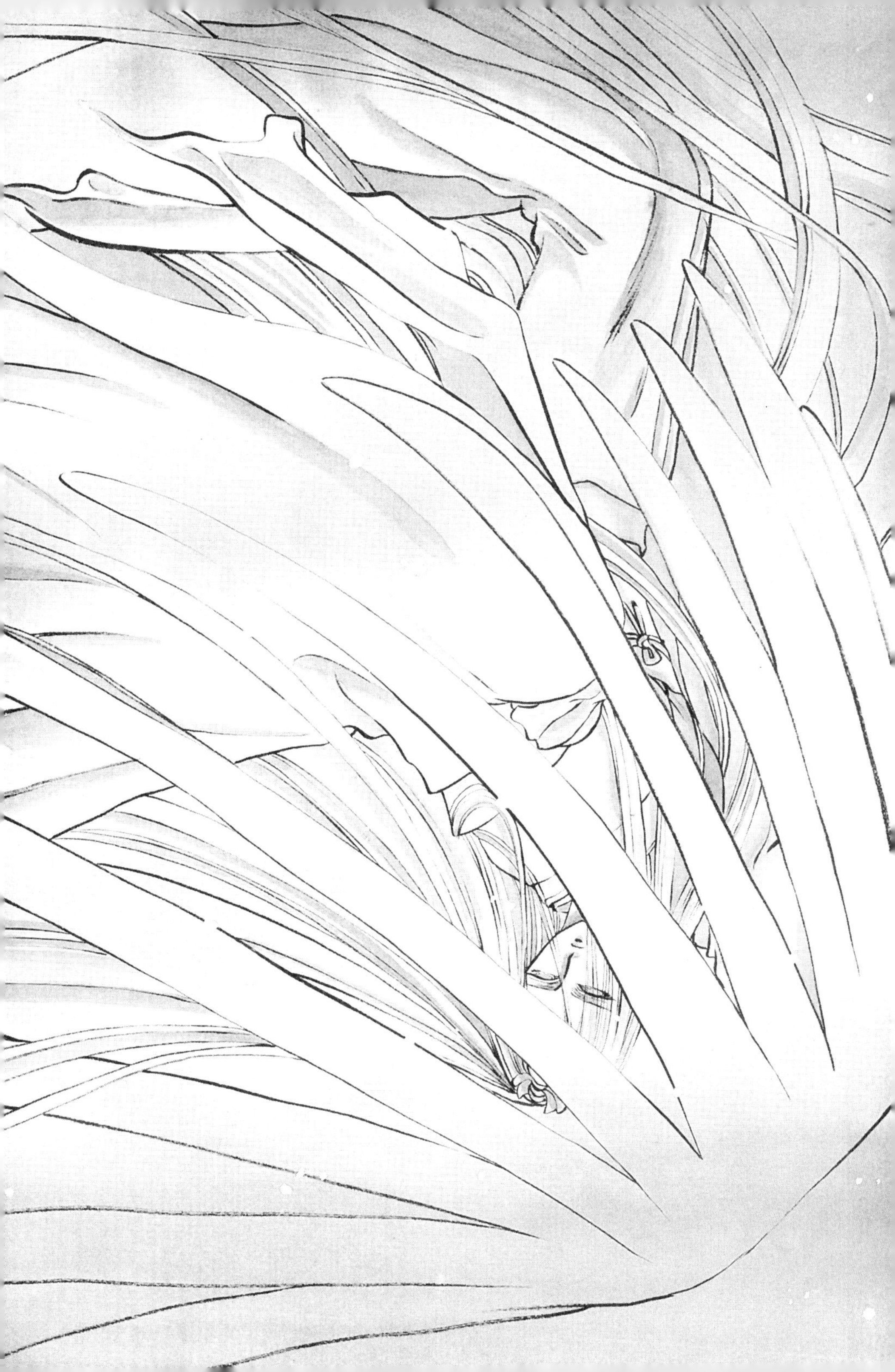

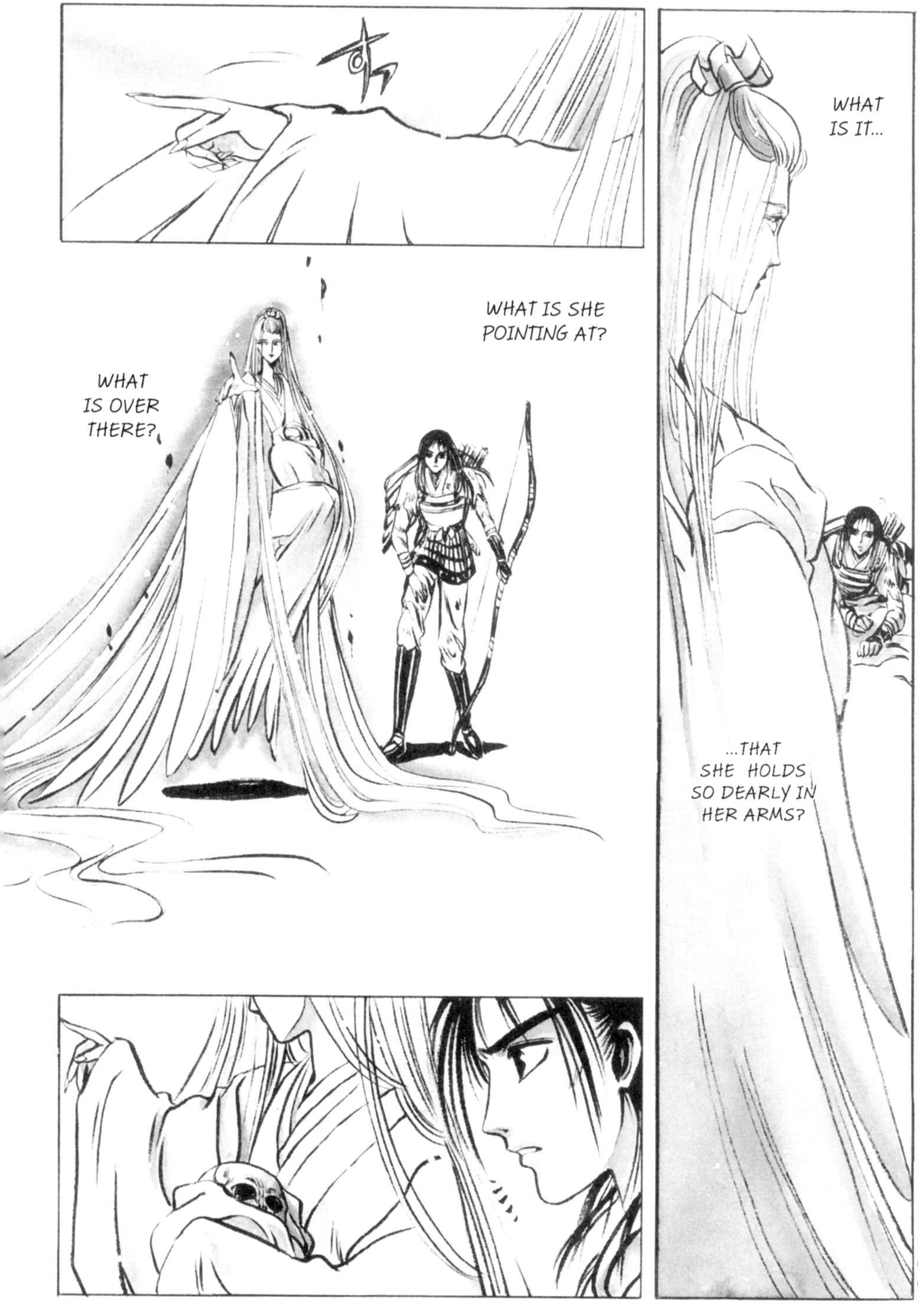
WHAT IS IT...
...THAT SHE HOLDS SO DEARLY IN HER ARMS?
WHAT IS SHE POINTING AT?
WHAT IS OVER THERE?

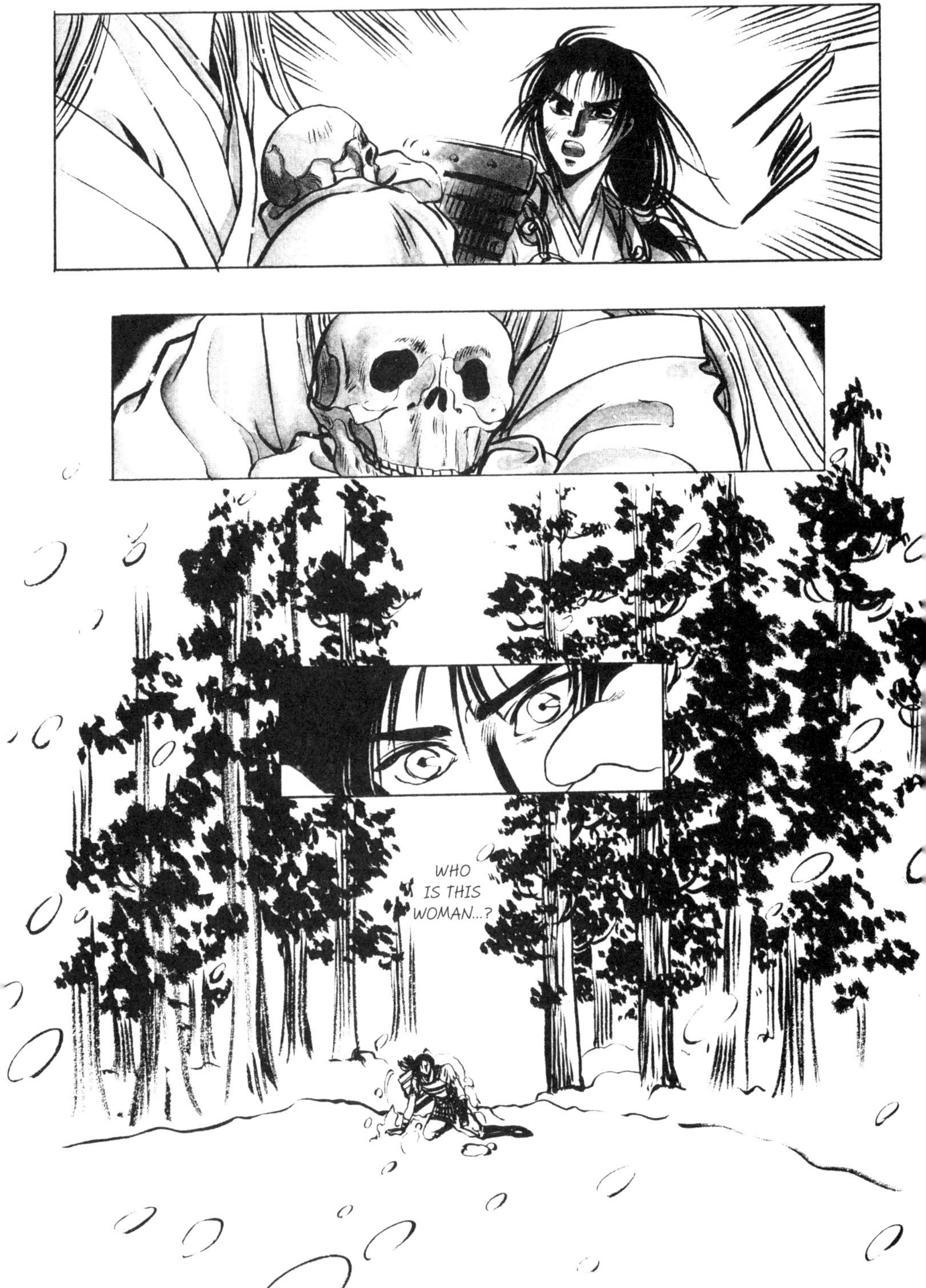
WHO IS THIS WOMAN...?

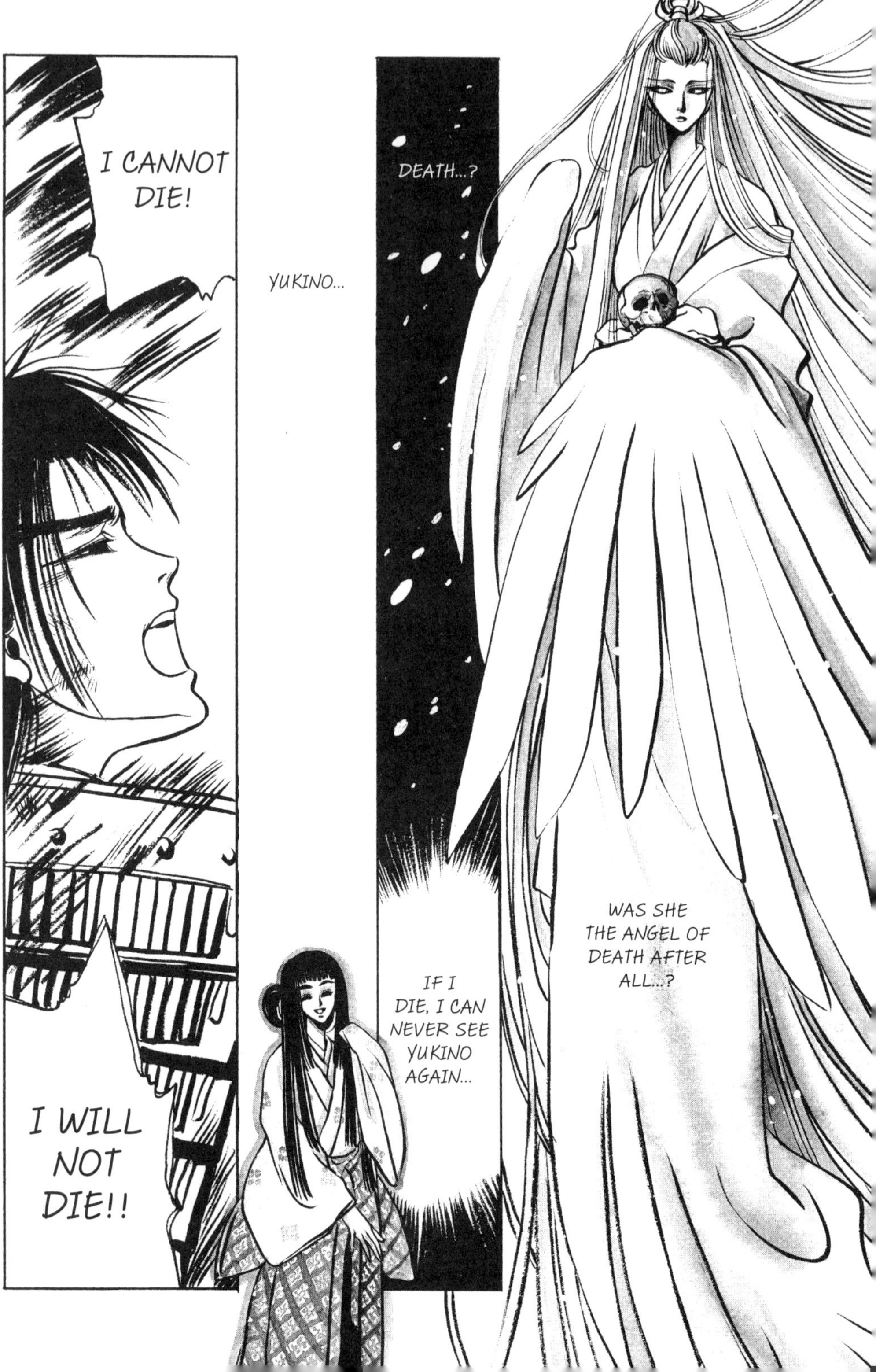
WAS SHE THE ANGEL OF DEATH AFTER ALL...?
DEATH...?
IF I DIE, I CAN NEVER SEE YUKINO AGAIN...
YUKINO...
I CANNOT DIE!
I WILL NOT DIE!!

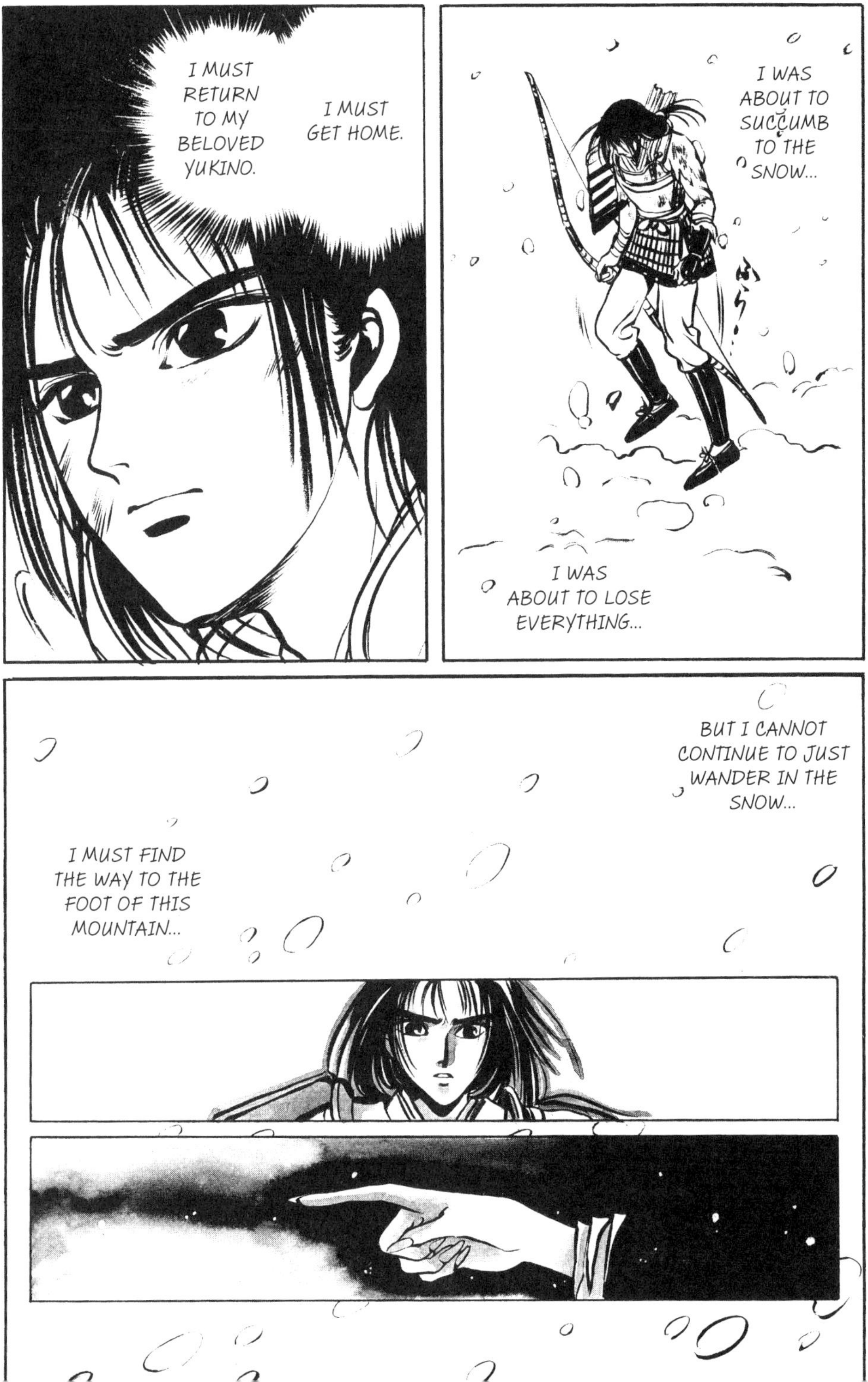
I WAS ABOUT TO SUCCUMB TO THE SNOW...
I WAS ABOUT TO LOSE EVERYTHING...
I MUST RETURN TO MY BELOVED YUKINO.
I MUST GET HOME.
BUT I CANNOT CONTINUE TO JUST WANDER IN THE SNOW...
I MUST FIND THE WAY TO THE FOOT OF THIS MOUNTAIN...

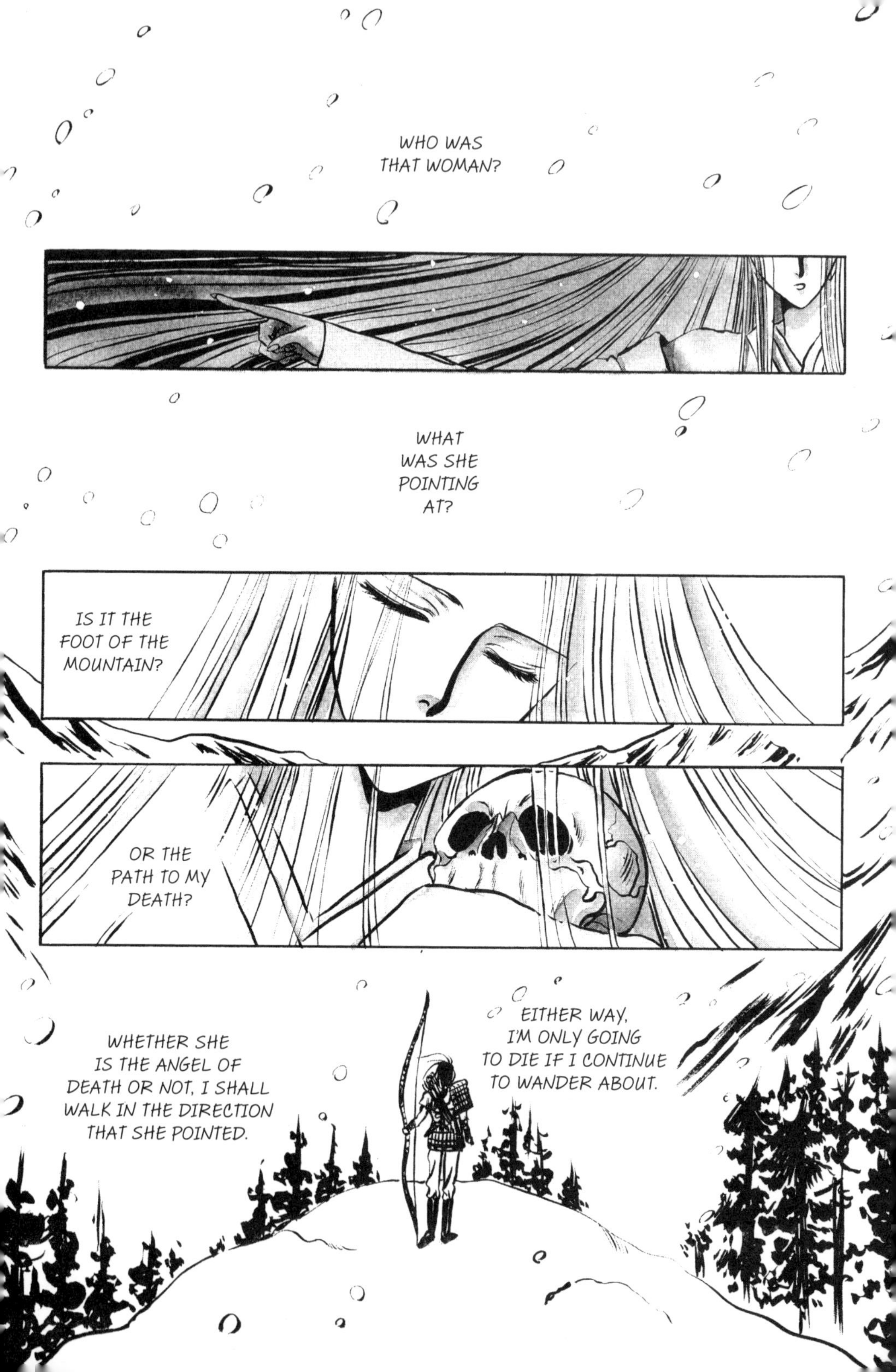
WHO WAS THAT WOMAN?
WHAT WAS SHE POINTING AT?
IS IT THE FOOT OF THE MOUNTAIN?
OR THE PATH TO MY DEATH?
EITHER WAY, I'M ONLY GOING TO DIE IF I CONTINUE TO WANDER ABOUT.
WHETHER SHE IS THE ANGEL OF DEATH OR NOT, I SHALL WALK IN THE DIRECTION THAT SHE POINTED.

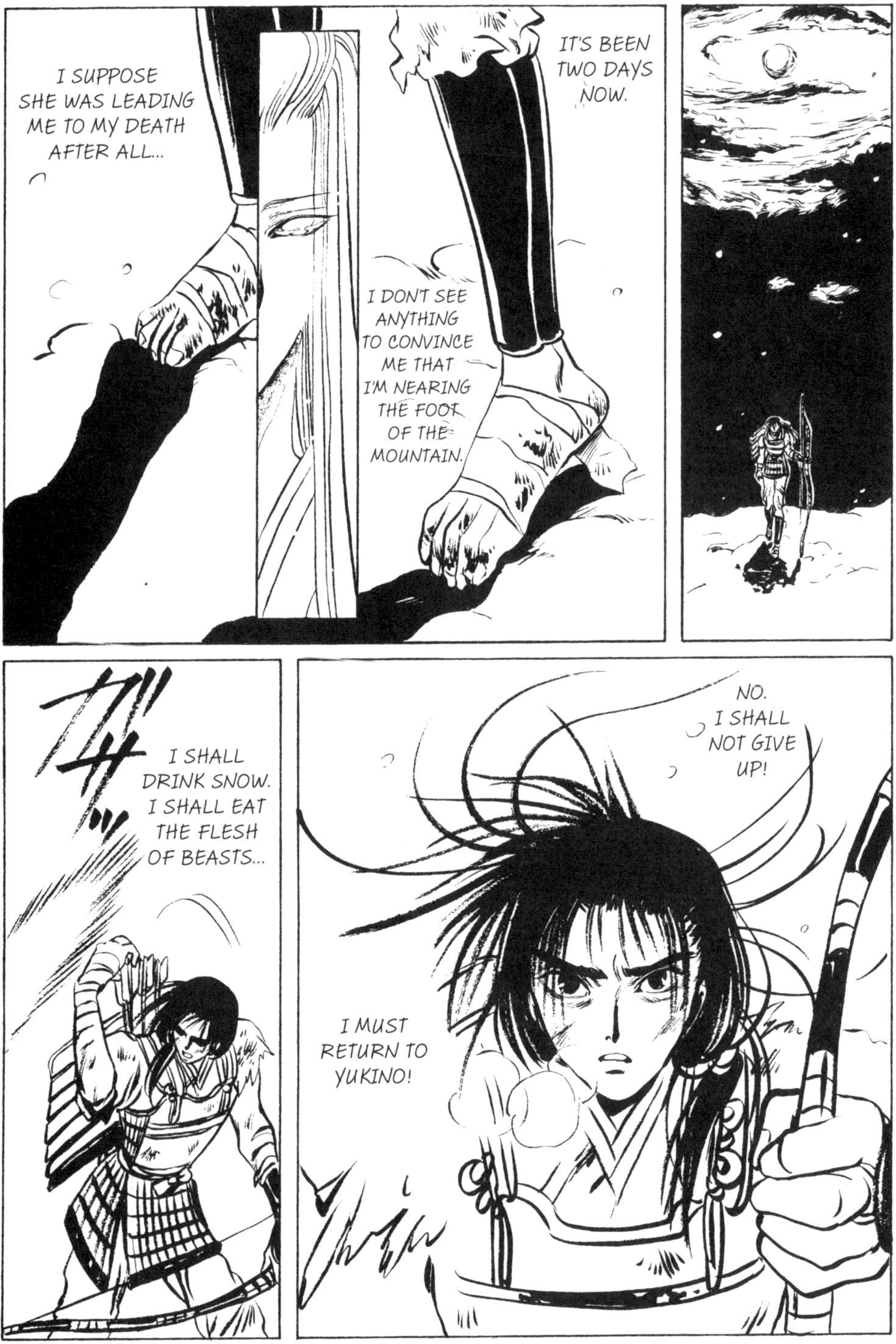
IT'S BEEN TWO DAYS NOW.
I DON'T SEE ANYTHING TO CONVINCE ME THAT I'M NEARING THE FOOT OF THE MOUNTAIN.
I SUPPOSE SHE WAS LEADING ME TO MY DEATH AFTER ALL...
NO. I SHALL NOT GIVE UP!
I MUST RETURN TO YUKINO!
I SHALL DRINK SNOW. I SHALL EAT THE FLESH OF BEASTS...

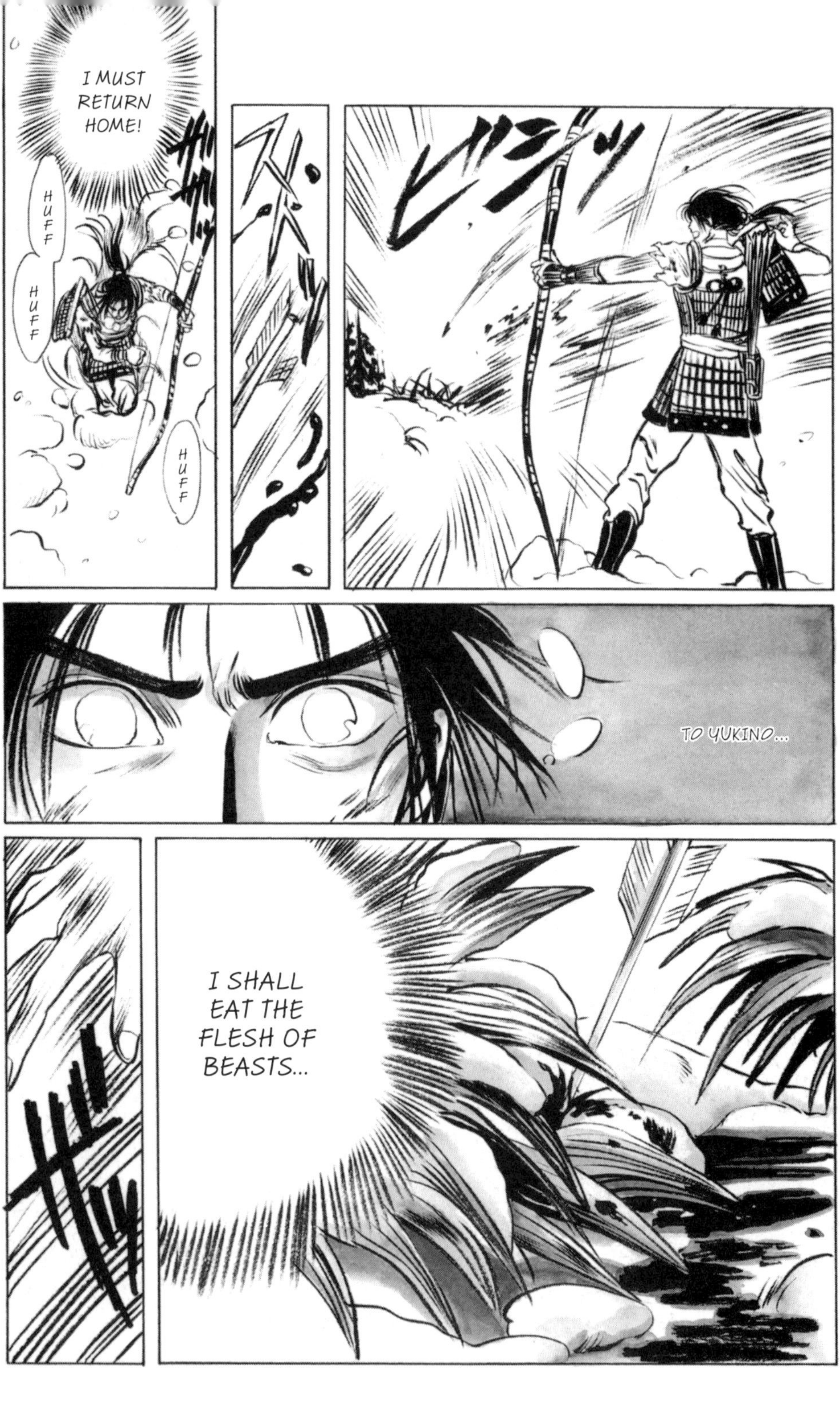
I MUST RETURN HOME!
HUFF
HUFF
HUFF
TO YUKINO...
I SHALL EAT THE FLESH OF BEASTS...

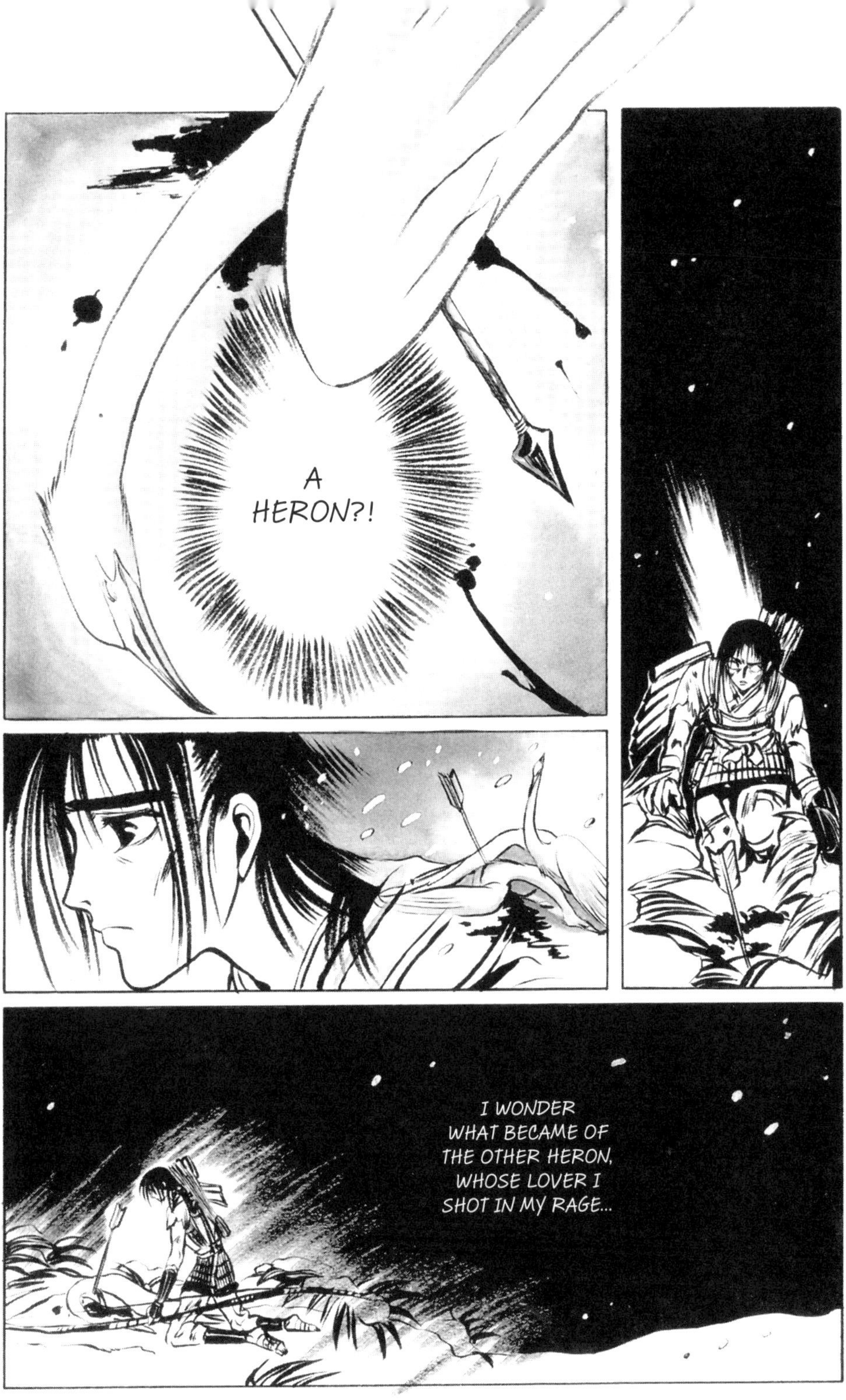
A HERON?!
I WONDER WHAT BECAME OF THE OTHER HERON, WHOSE LOVER I SHOT IN MY RAGE...

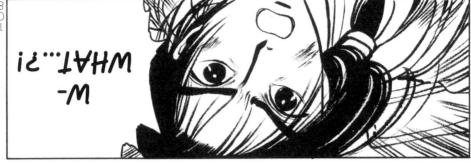

THIS HERON IS CARRYING SOMETHING...
SOMETHING INSIDE ITS WING?
W- WHAT...?!

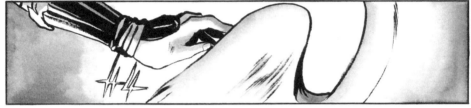

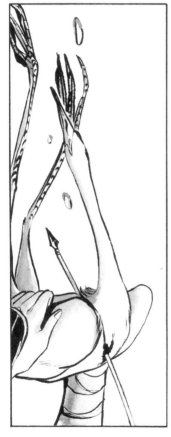

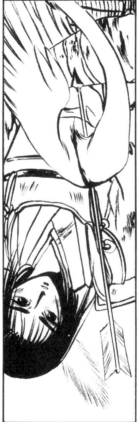

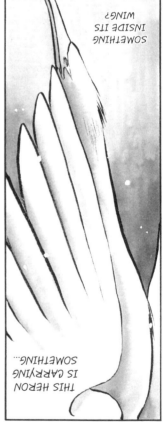

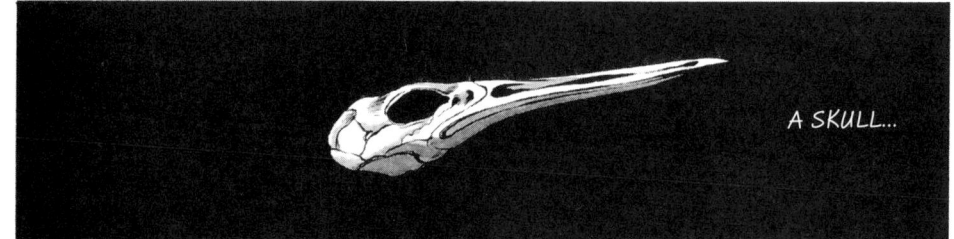

A SKULL...

IT
COULDNT
BE...

IT WAS CARRYING THE BONES OF ITS LOVED ONE ALL THIS TIME...

FORGIVE ME...

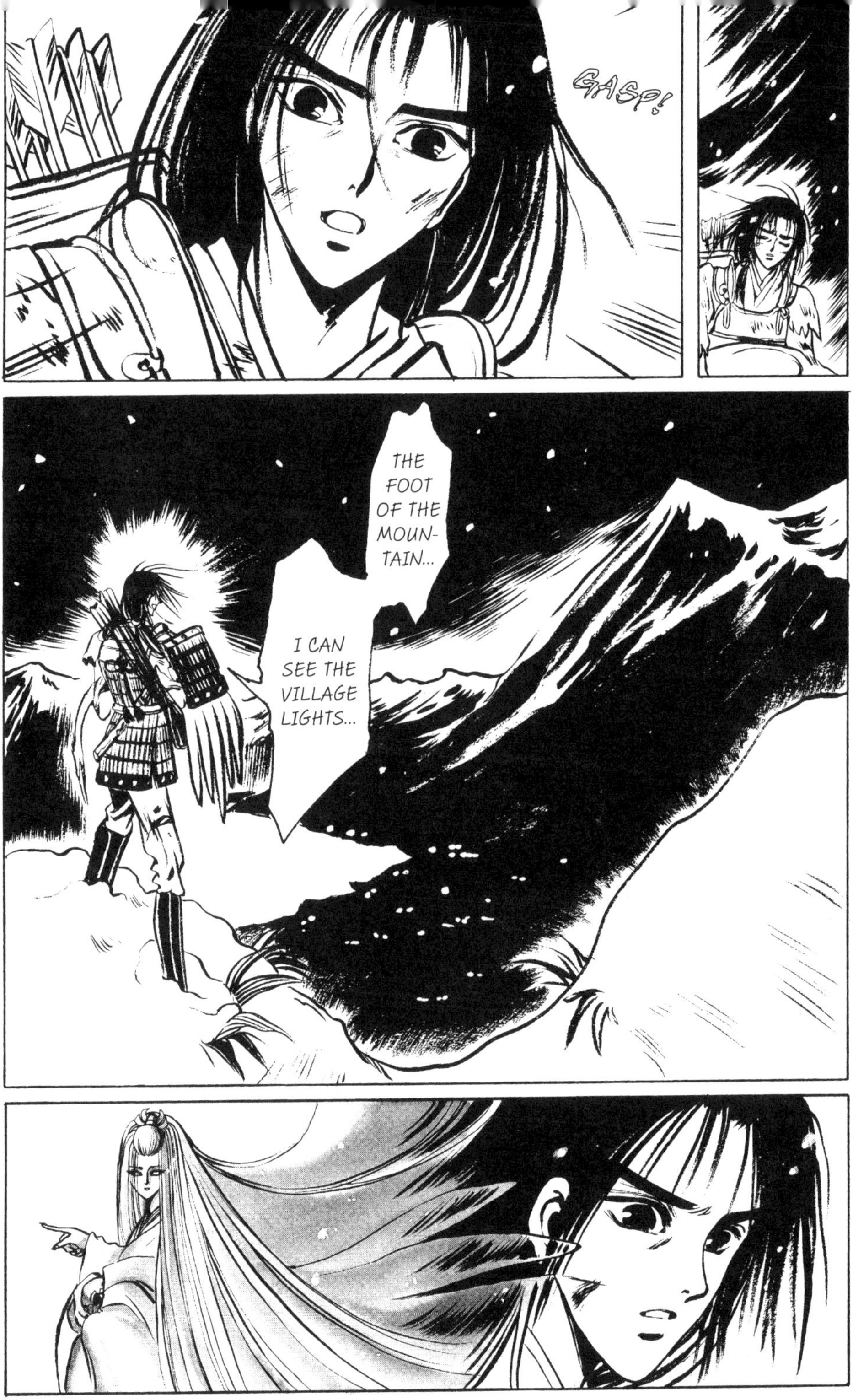
GASP!
THE FOOT OF THE MOUN-TAIN...
I CAN SEE THE VILLAGE LIGHTS...

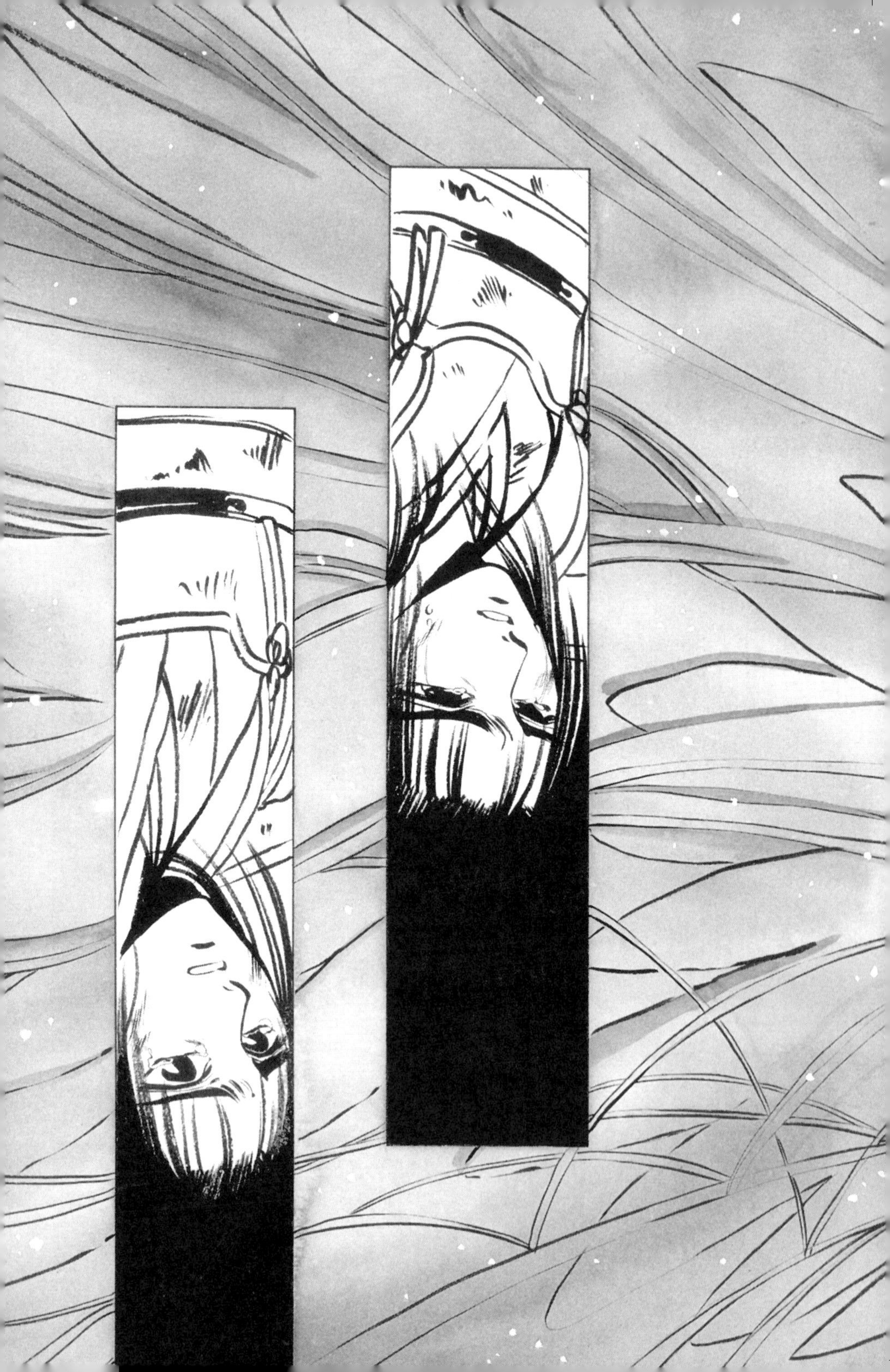

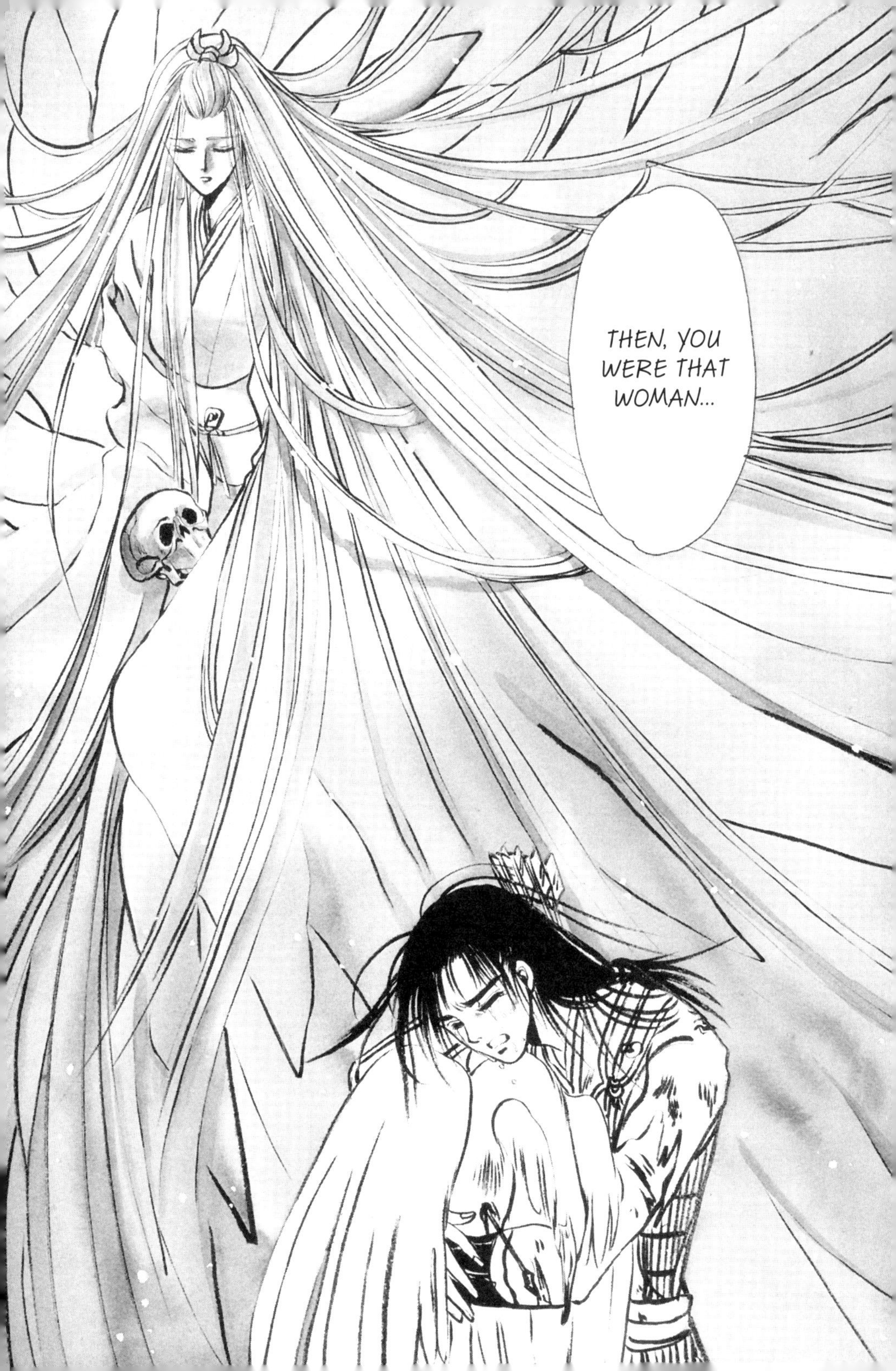
THEN, YOU WERE THAT WOMAN...

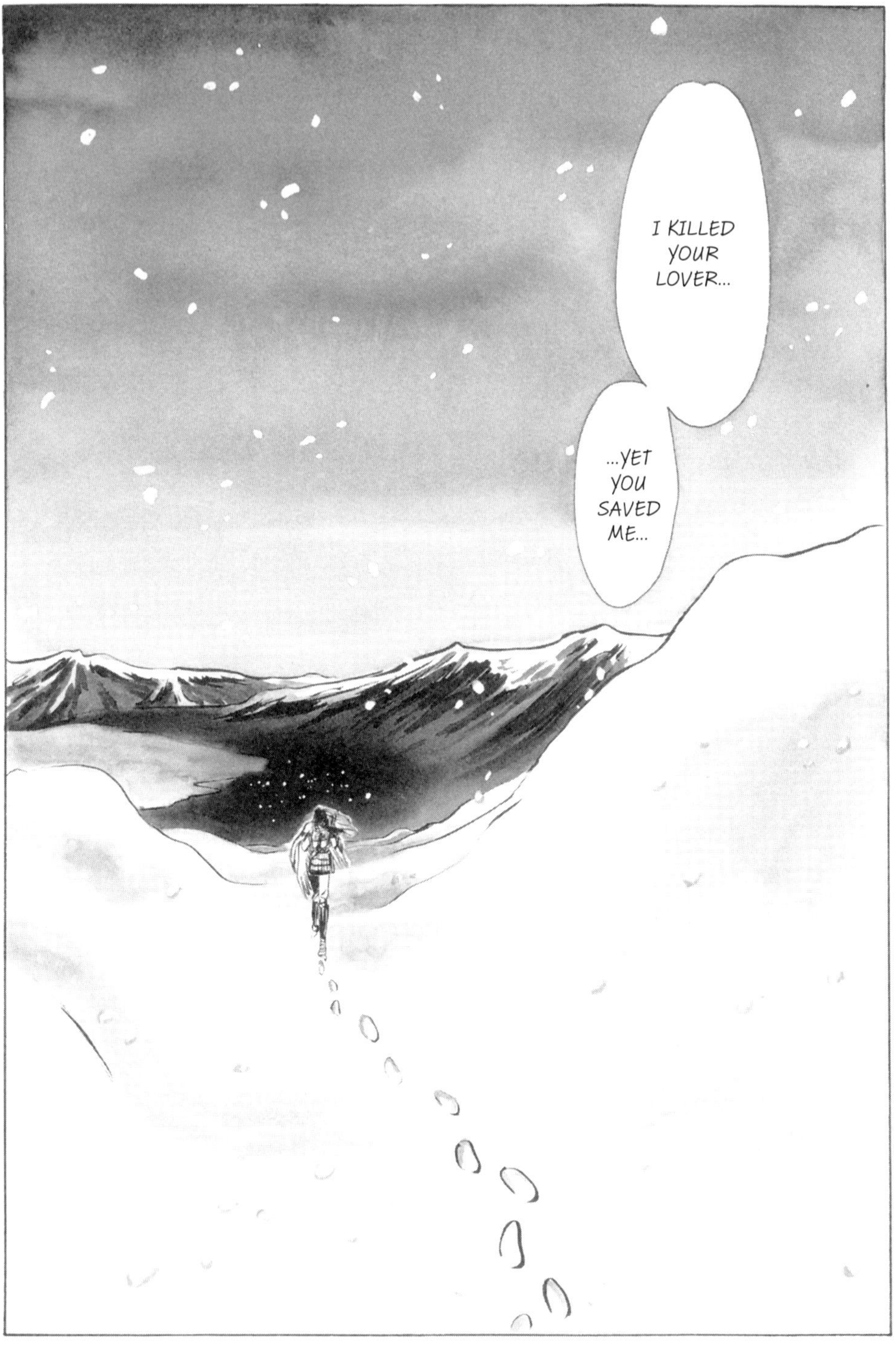
I KILLED YOUR LOVER...
...YET YOU SAVED ME...

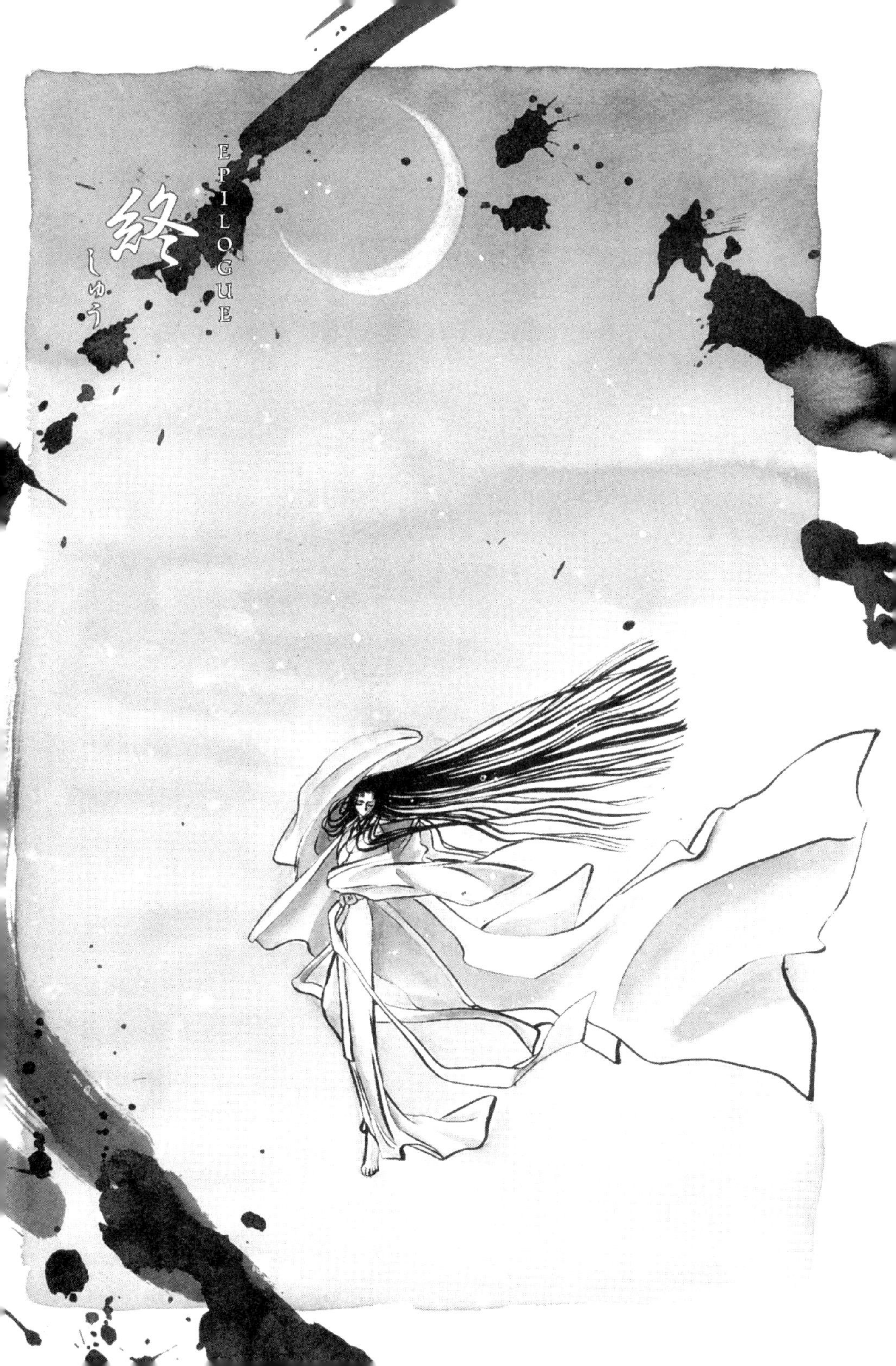
EPILOGUE
終
しゅう

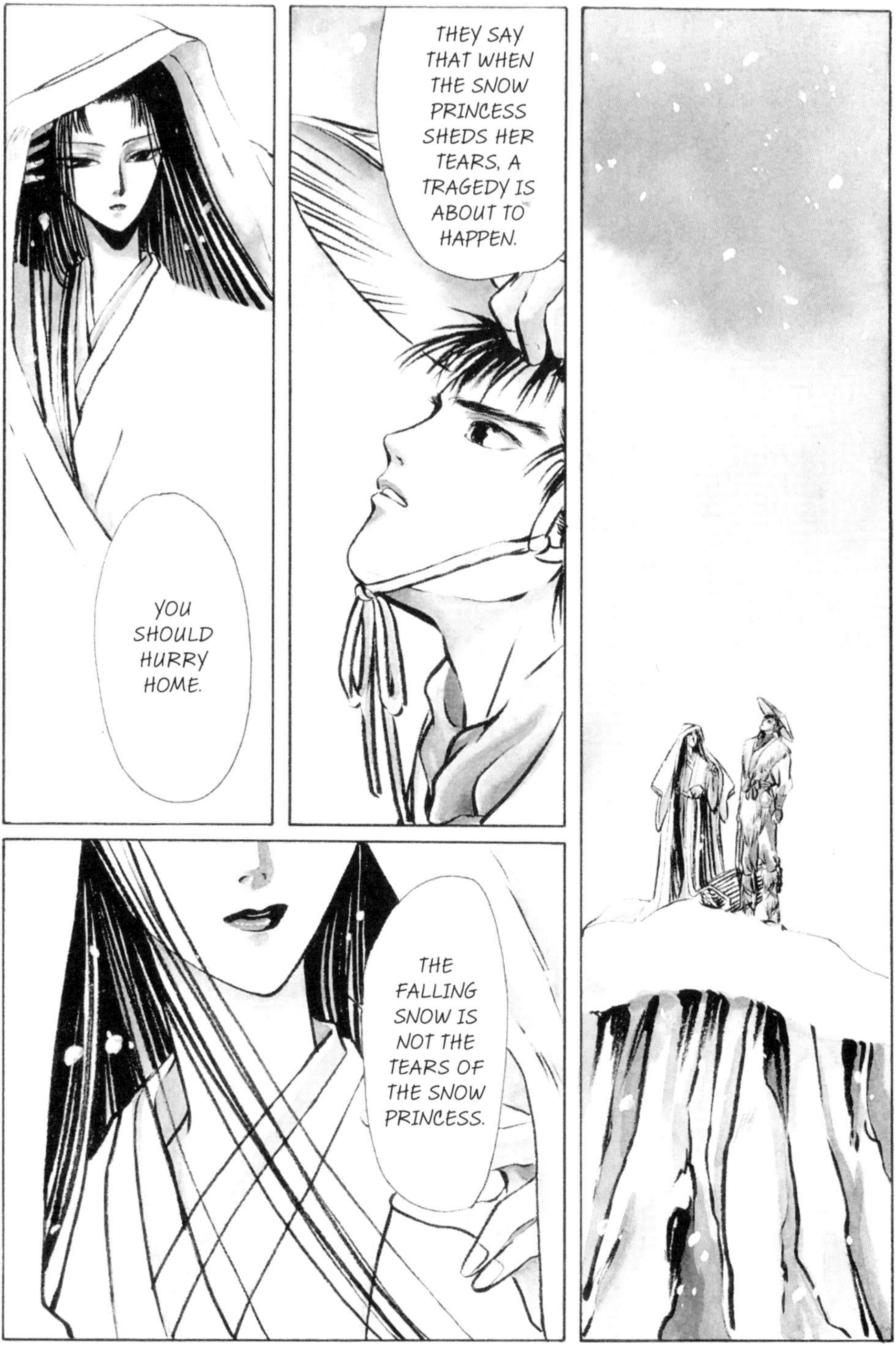
THEY SAY THAT WHEN THE SNOW PRINCESS SHEDS HER TEARS, A TRAGEDY IS ABOUT TO HAPPEN.
YOU SHOULD HURRY HOME.
THE FALLING SNOW IS NOT THE TEARS OF THE SNOW PRINCESS.

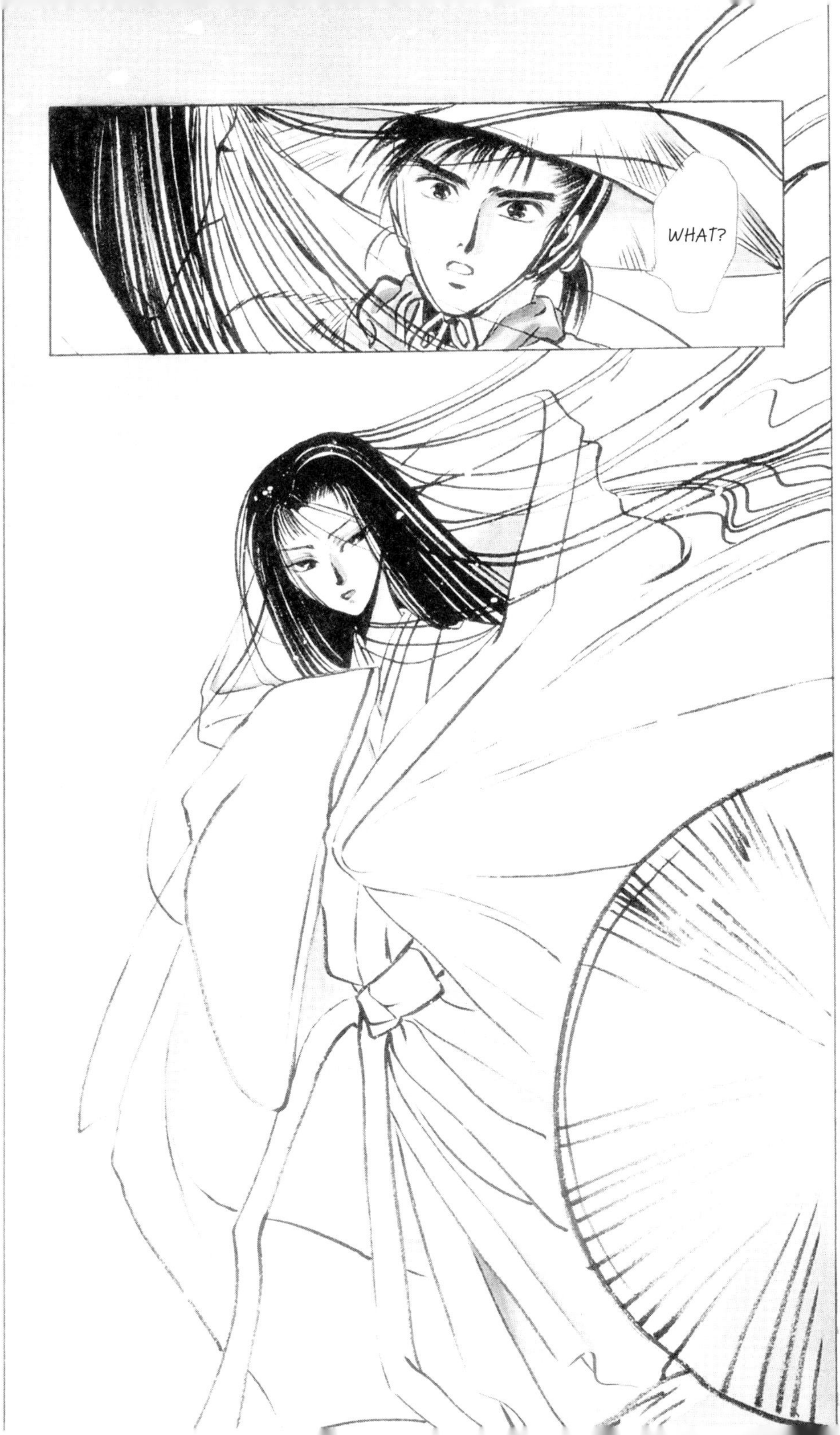
WHAT?

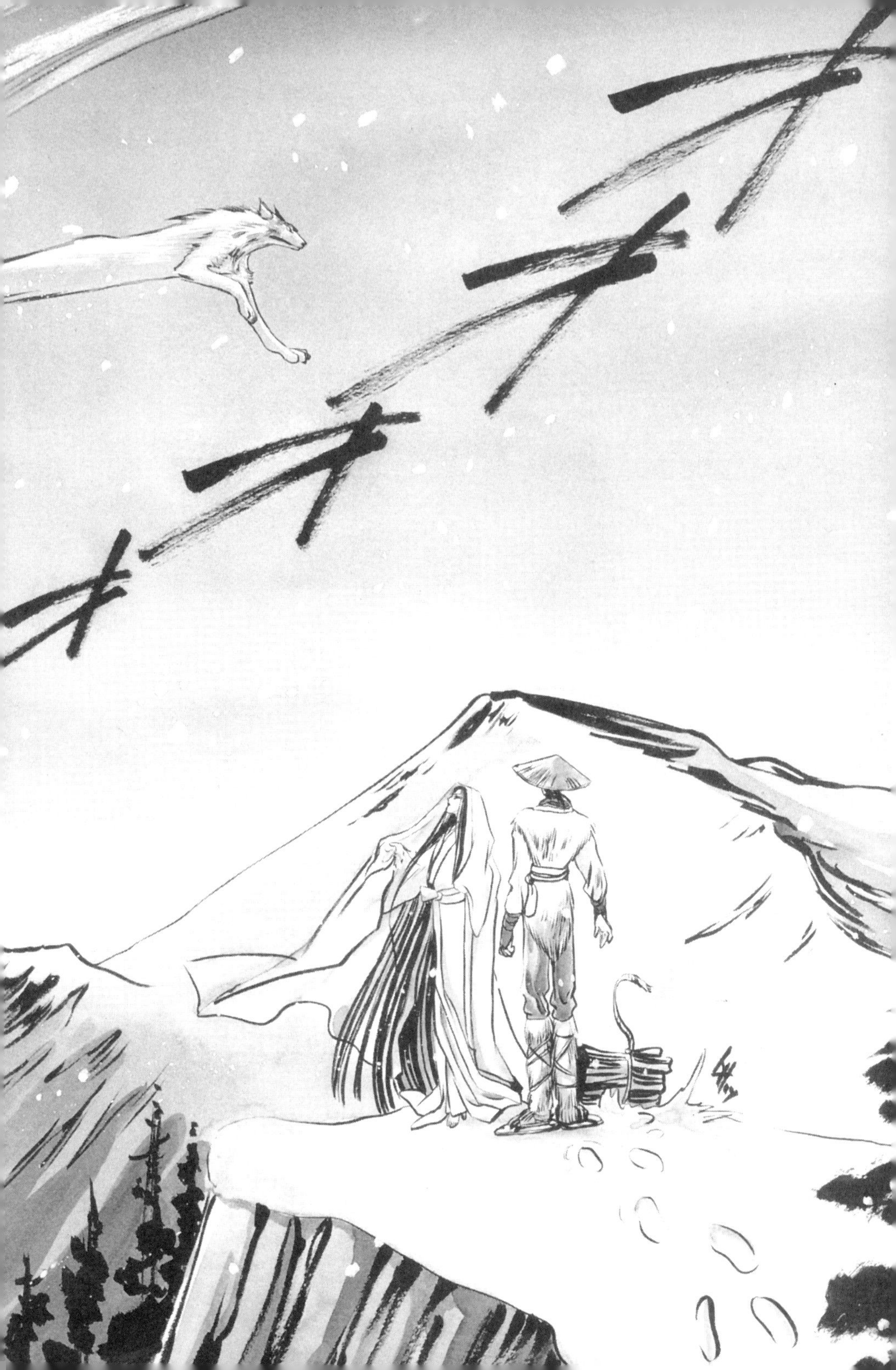
オオオオ

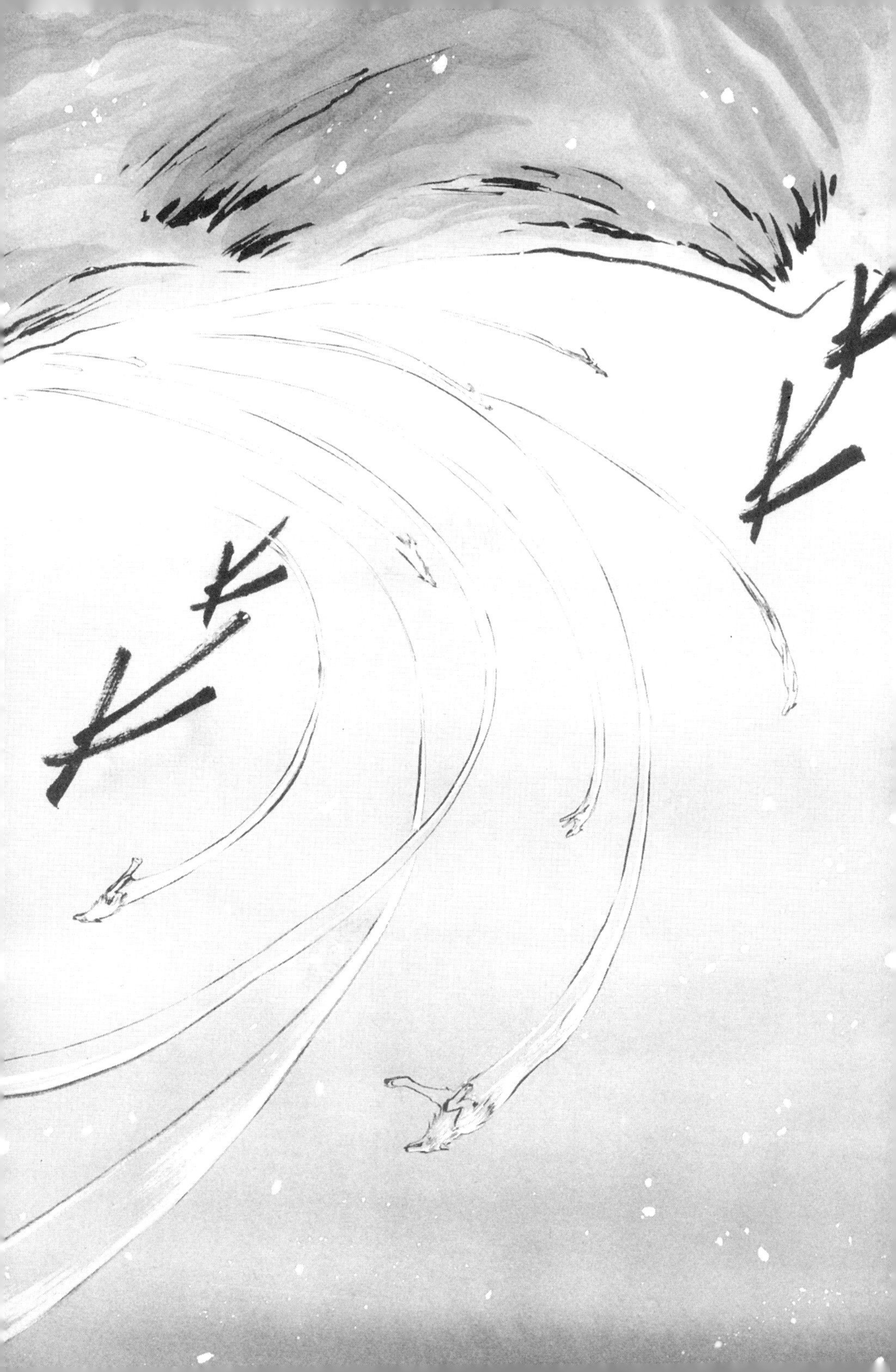

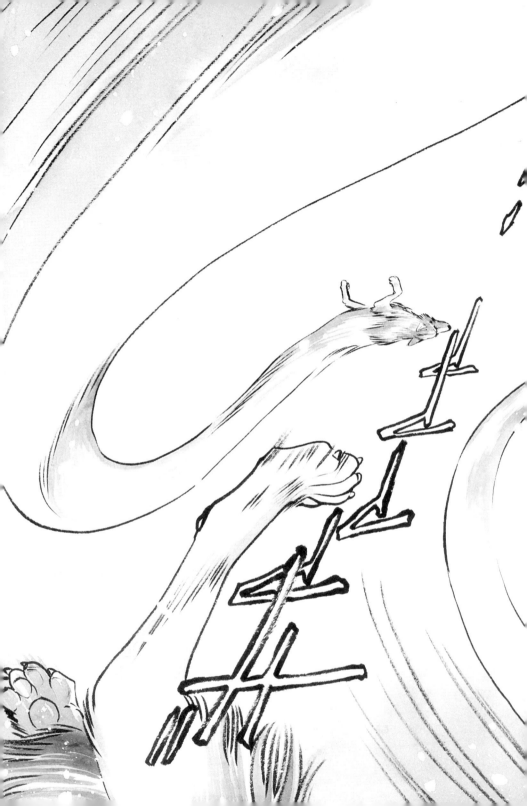

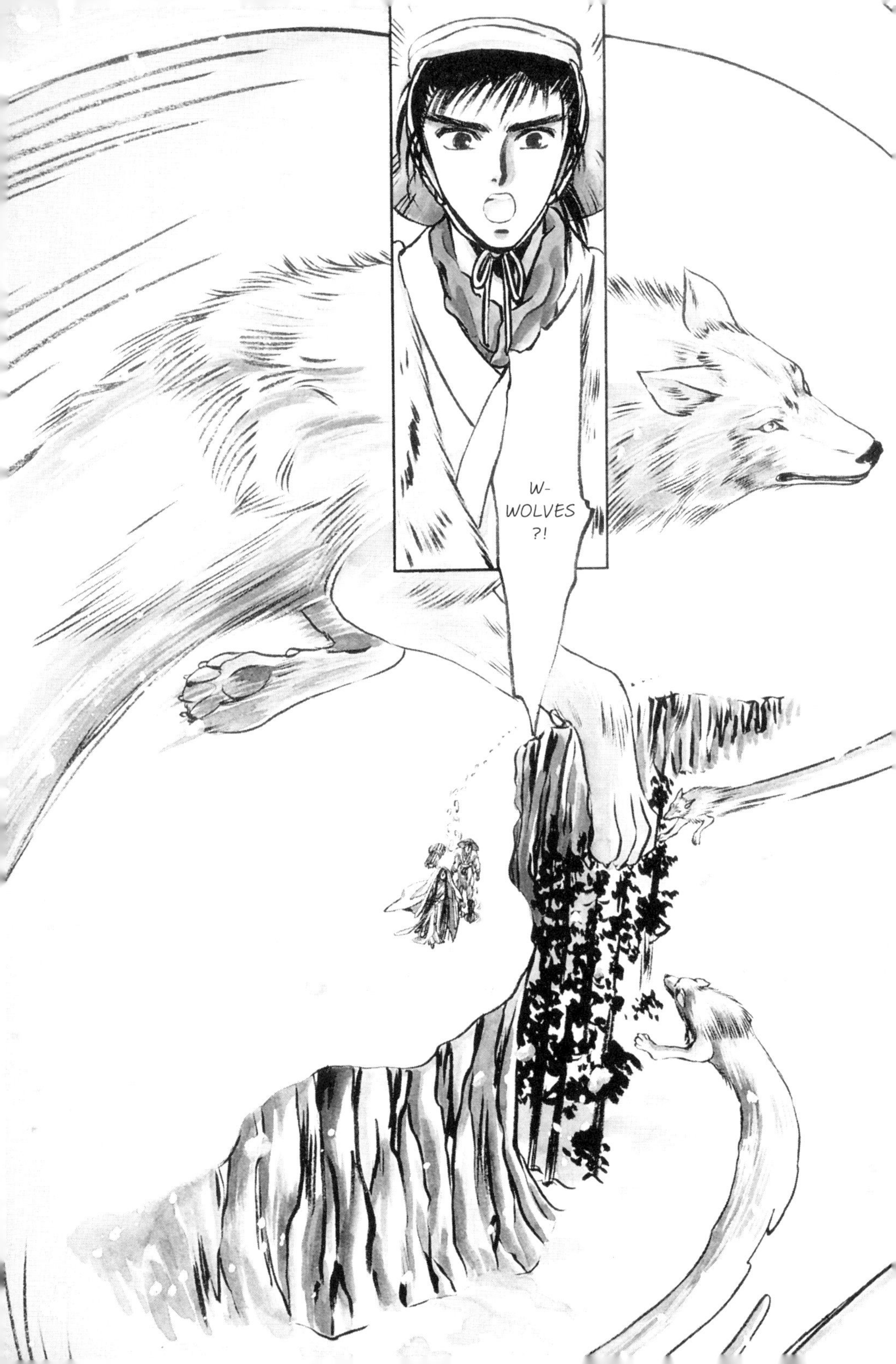
W-
WOLVES
?!

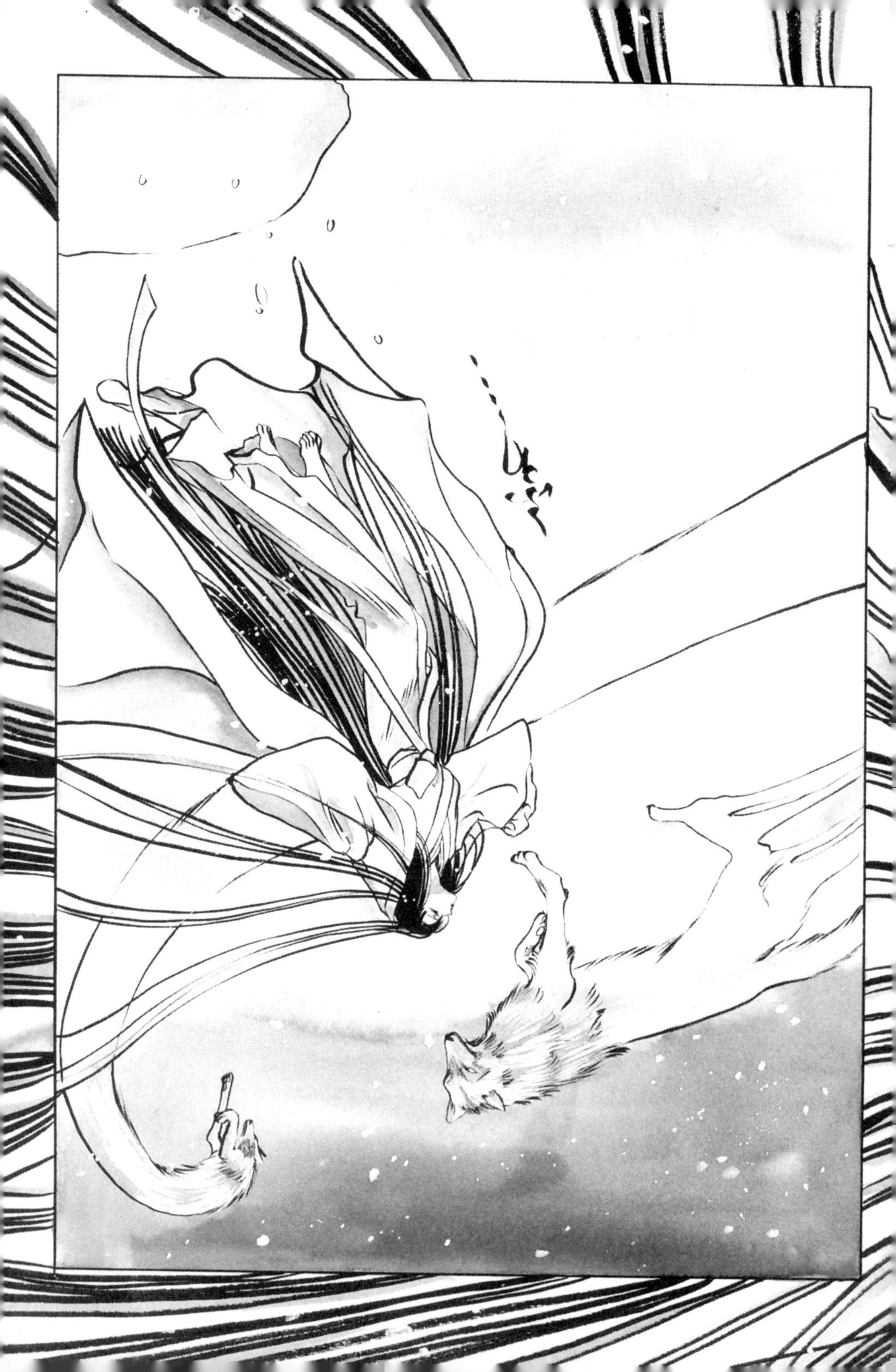

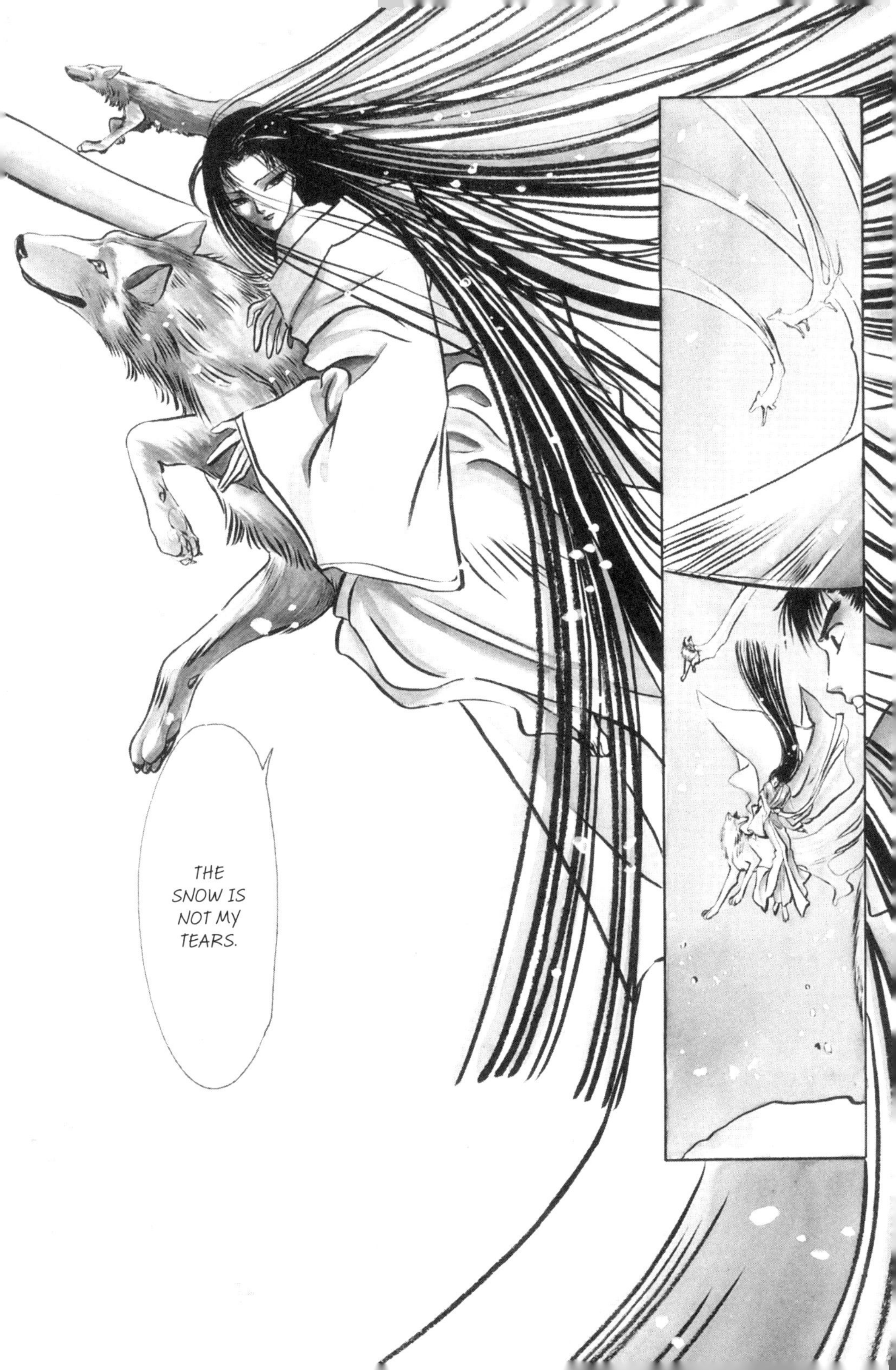
THE SNOW IS NOT MY TEARS.

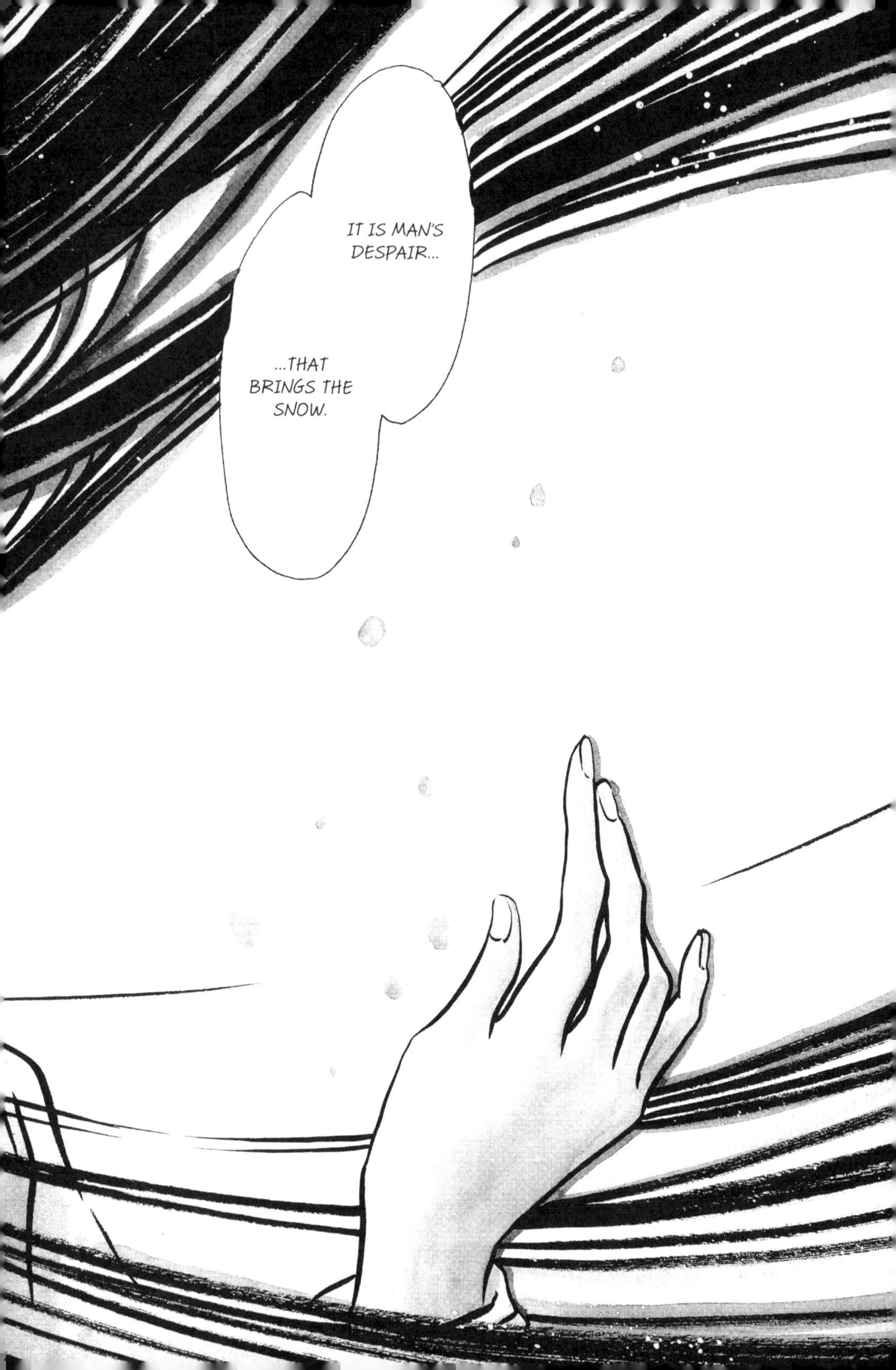
IT IS MAN'S DESPAIR...
...THAT BRINGS THE SNOW.

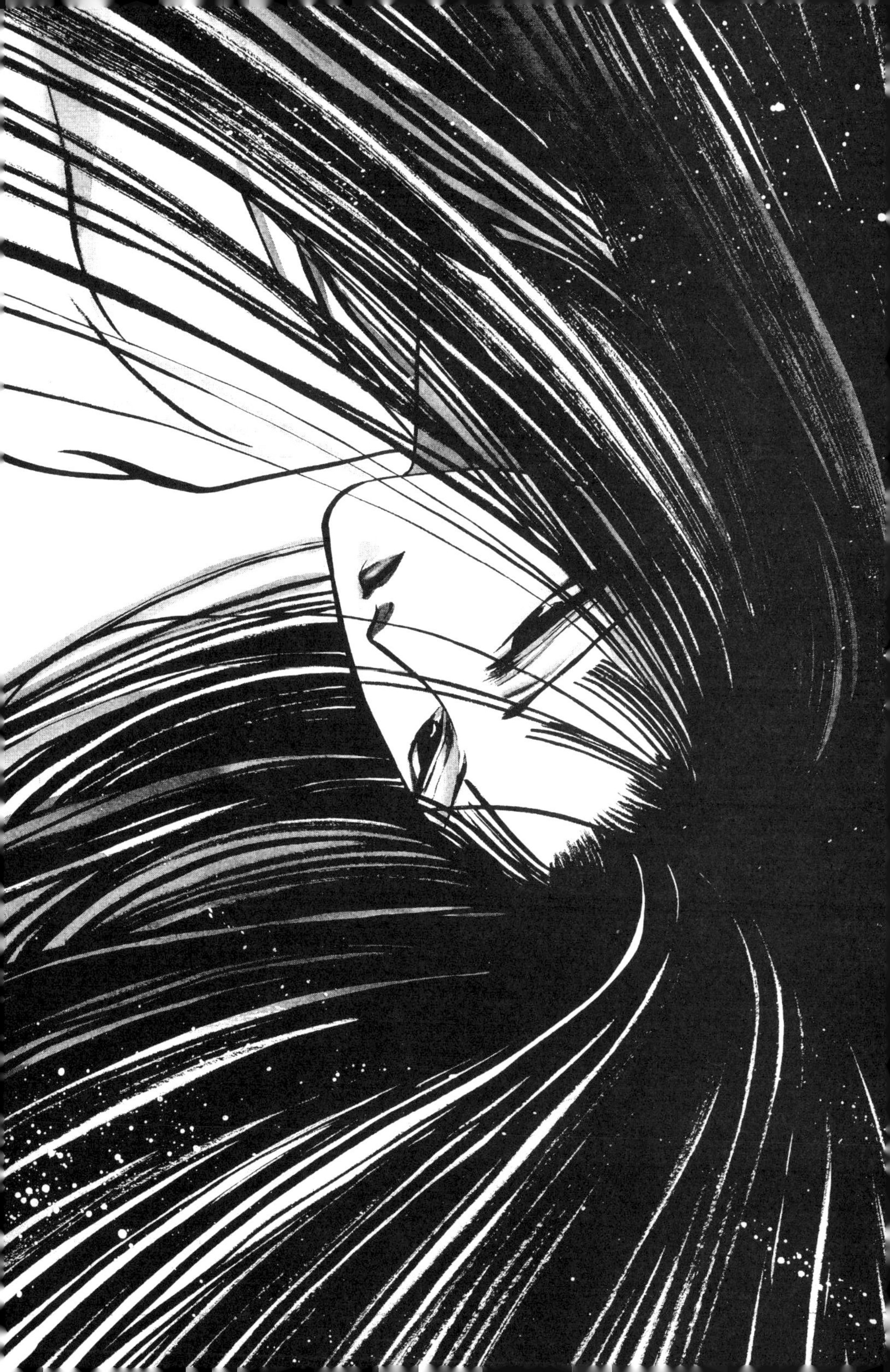

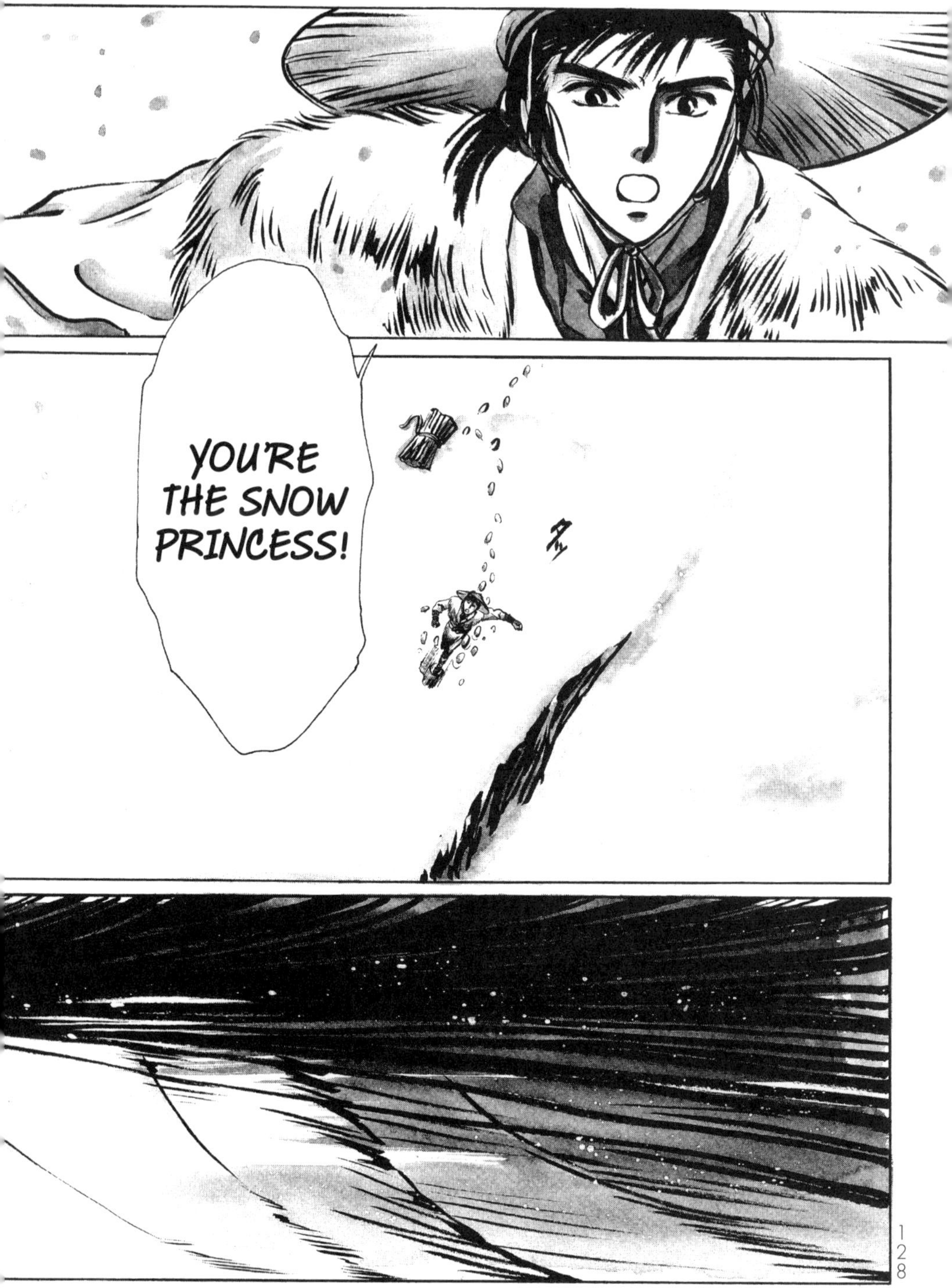
YOU'RE THE SNOW PRINCESS!

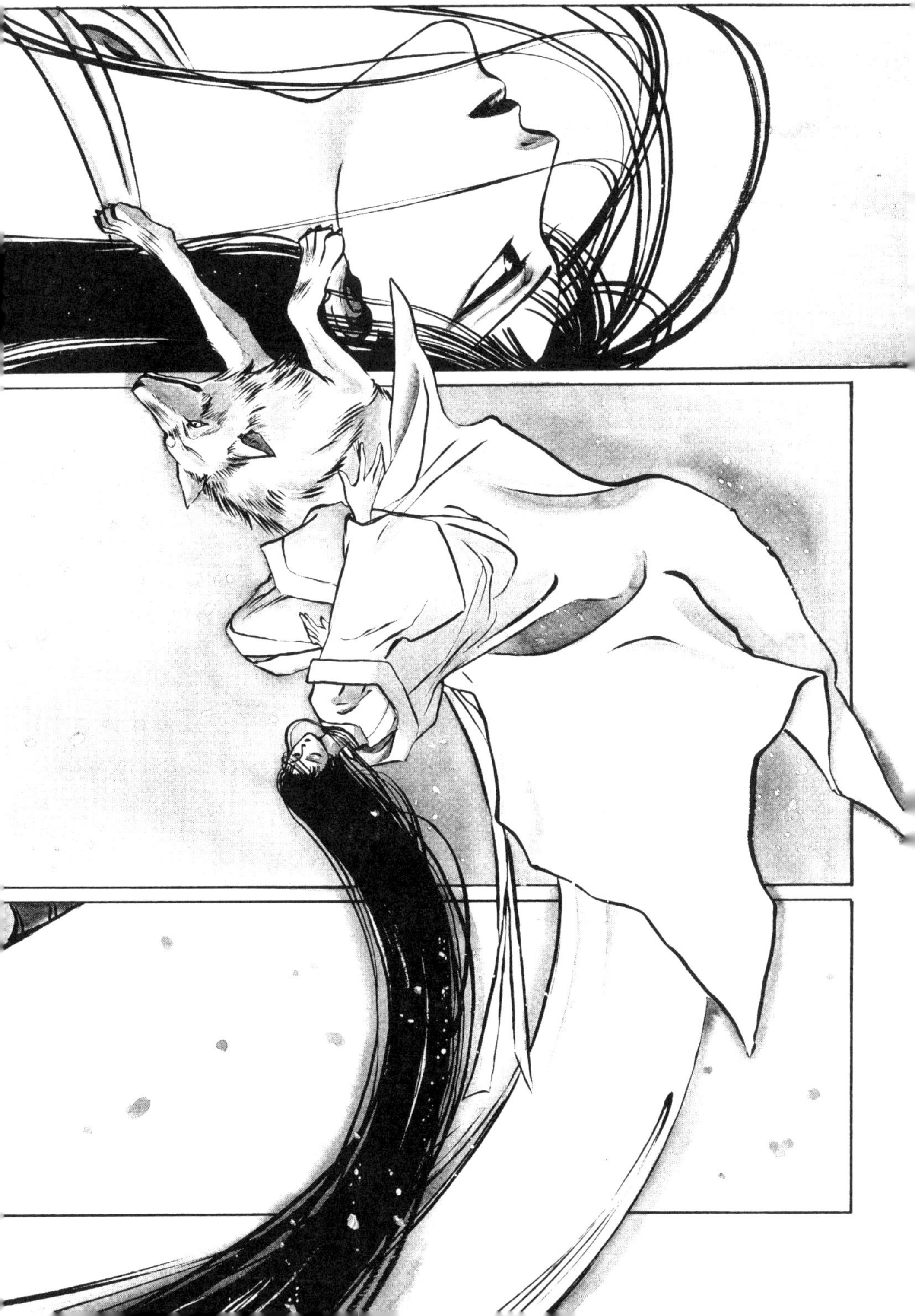

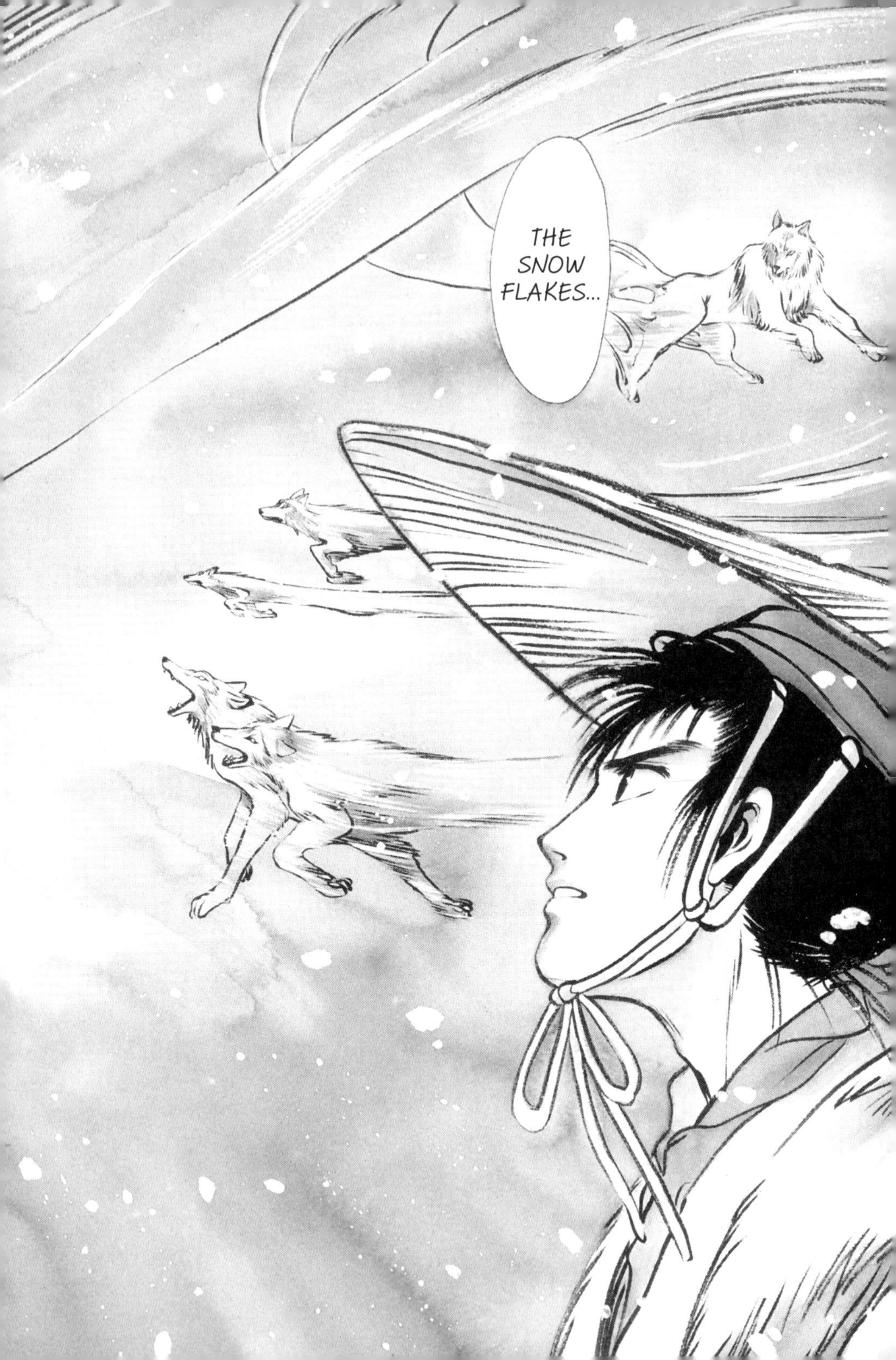
THE SNOW FLAKES...

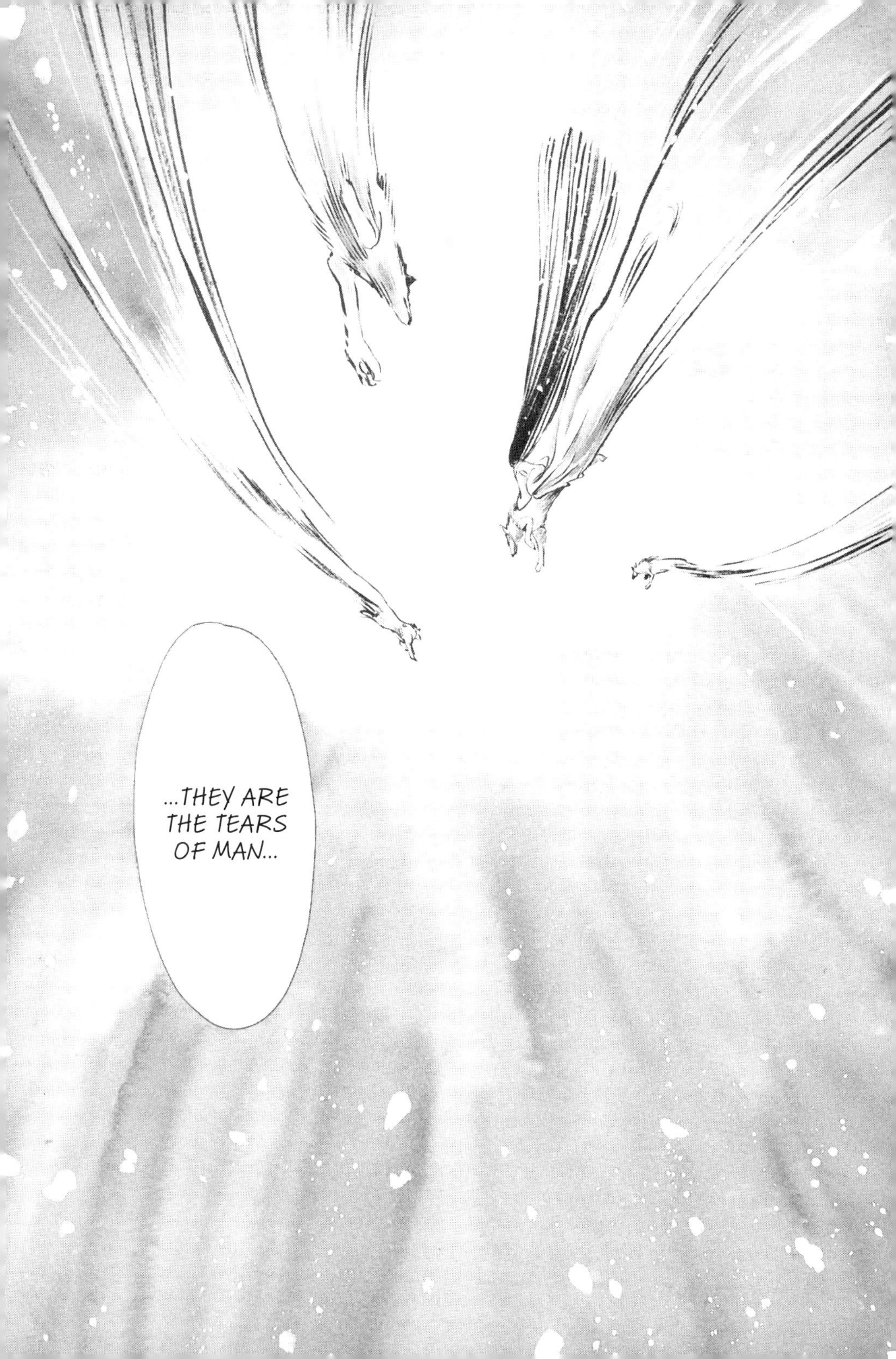
...THEY ARE THE TEARS OF MAN...

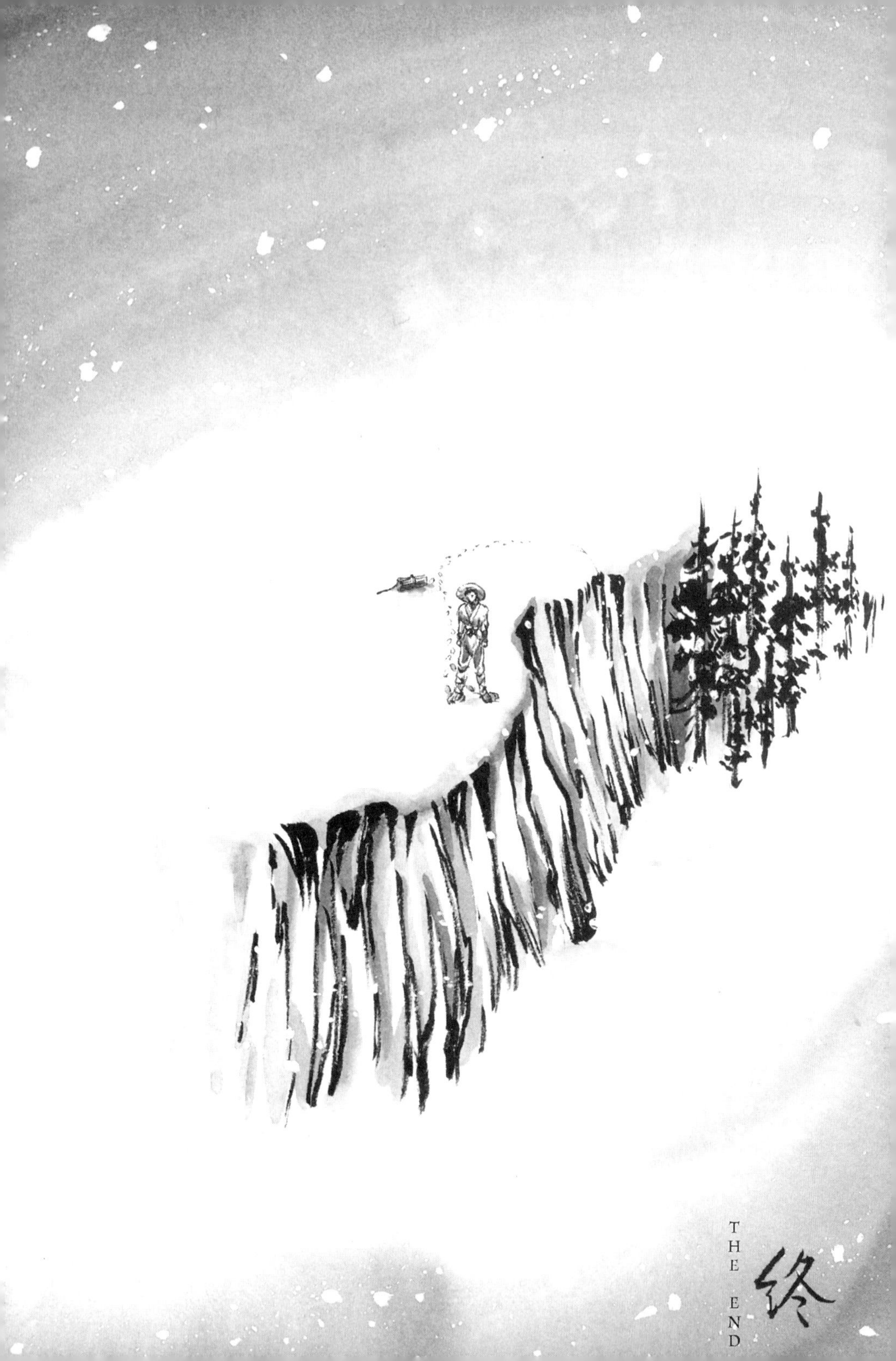

終
THE END

白姫抄

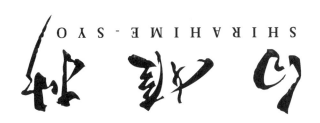

SHIRAHIME-SYO

ALSO AVAILABLE FROM TOKYOPOP®

For more information visit www.TOKYOPOP.com

ALSO AVAILABLE FROM 🔱TOKYOPOP®

MANGA

.HACK//LEGEND OF THE TWILIGHT
@LARGE
A.I. LOVE YOU February 2004
AI YORI AOSHI January 2004
ANGELIC LAYER
BABY BIRTH
BATTLE ROYALE
BATTLE VIXENS April 2004
BIRTH May 2004
BRAIN POWERED
BRIGADOON
B'TX January 2004
CARDCAPTOR SAKURA
CARDCAPTOR SAKURA - MASTER OF THE CLOW
CARDCAPTOR SAKURA: BOXED SET COLLECTION 1
CARDCAPTOR SAKURA: BOXED SET COLLECTION 2
   March 2004
CHOBITS
CHRONICLES OF THE CURSED SWORD
CLAMP SCHOOL DETECTIVES
CLOVER
COMIC PARTY June 2004
CONFIDENTIAL CONFESSIONS
CORRECTOR YUI
COWBOY BEBOP: BOXED SET THE COMPLETE
   COLLECTION
CRESCENT MOON May 2004
CREST OF THE STARS June 2004
CYBORG 009
DEMON DIARY
DIGIMON
DIGIMON SERIES 3 April 2004
DIGIMON ZERO TWO February 2004
DNANGEL April 2004
DOLL May 2004
DRAGON HUNTER
DRAGON KNIGHTS
DUKLYON: CLAMP SCHOOL DEFENDERS:
DV June 2004
ERICA SAKURAZAWA
FAERIES' LANDING January 2004
FAKE
FLCL
FORBIDDEN DANCE
FRUITS BASKET February 2004
G GUNDAM
GATEKEEPERS
GETBACKERS February 2004
GHOST! March 2004
GIRL GOT GAME January 2004
GRAVITATION
GTO

GUNDAM WING
GUNDAM WING: BATTLEFIELD OF PACIFISTS
GUNDAM WING: ENDLESS WALTZ
GUNDAM WING: THE LAST OUTPOST
HAPPY MANIA
HARLEM BEAT
I.N.V.U.
INITIAL D
ISLAND
JING: KING OF BANDITS
JULINE
JUROR 13 March 2004
KARE KANO
KILL ME, KISS ME February 2004
KINDAICHI CASE FILES, THE
KING OF HELL
KODOCHA: SANA'S STAGE
LAMENT OF THE LAMB May 2004
LES BIJOUX February 2004
LIZZIE MCGUIRE
LOVE HINA
LUPIN III
LUPIN III SERIES 2
MAGIC KNIGHT RAYEARTH I
MAGIC KNIGHT RAYEARTH II February 2004
MAHOROMATIC: AUTOMATIC MAIDEN May 2004
MAN OF MANY FACES
MARMALADE BOY
MARS
METEOR METHUSELA June 2004
METROID June 2004
MINK April 2004
MIRACLE GIRLS
MIYUKI-CHAN IN WONDERLAND
MODEL May 2004
NELLY MUSIC MANGA April 2004
ONE April 2004
PARADISE KISS
PARASYTE
PEACH GIRL
PEACH GIRL CHANGE OF HEART
PEACH GIRL RELAUNCH BOX SET
PET SHOP OF HORRORS
PITA-TEN January 2004
PLANET LADDER February 2004
PLANETES
PRIEST
PRINCESS AI April 2004
PSYCHIC ACADEMY March 2004
RAGNAROK
RAGNAROK: BOXED SET COLLECTION 1
RAVE MASTER
RAVE MASTER: BOXED SET March 2004

Translator - Ray Yoshimoto
Copy Editor - Bryce P. Coleman
Retouch and Lettering - James Lee
Graphic Designer - Gary Shum

Editor - Jake Forbes
Managing Editor - Jill Freshney
Production Coordinator - Antonio DePietro
Production Manager - Jennifer Miller
Art Director - Matt Alford
Editorial Director - Jeremy Ross
VP of Production - Ron Klamert
President & C.O.O. - John Parker
Publisher & C.E.O. - Stuart Levy

Email: editor@TOKYOPOP.com
Come visit us online at www.TOKYOPOP.com

A  Manga

TOKYOPOP Inc.
5900 Wilshire Blvd. Suite 2000
Los Angeles, CA 90036

Shirahime-Syo

SHIRAHIME-SYO © 2001 by CLAMP
First published in Japan in 2001 by KADOKAWA SHOTEN PUBLSHING CO., LTD., Tokyo.
English translation rights arranged with KADOKAWA SHOTEN PUBLISHING CO., LTD., Tokyo
through TUTTLE-MORI AGENCY, INC., Tokyo.

English text copyright ©2003 TOKYOPOP Inc.

ISBN: 1-59182-304-8

First TOKYOPOP printing: December 2003

10 9 8 7 6 5 4 3 2 1
Printed in the USA